From
MAJESTIC FJORDS
to the
MIGHTY MISSISSIPPI

A FARM BOY FROM WISCONSIN
FINDS HIS ROOTS IN NORWAY

✜ THE HELGESEN STORY ✜
1370–2010

RUSSELL B. HELGESEN

Copyright © 2010 by Russell B. Helgesen
All rights reserved.

2nd edition, January 2011

For permission to copy or share this work, please write

Russell B. Helgesen
7500 York Avenue South – Apt. 208
Edina, MN 55435
Tel: 952.835.5578
Email: russ@thehelgesenstory.com
www.thehelgesenstory.com

Ordering Information at www.thehelgesenstory.com

ISBN-13: 978-1456423513
ISBN-10: 1456423517

This book was lovingly designed by Russ Helgesen's daughter
Mary Helgesen Gabel, Gabel Graphics. www.gabelgraphics.com
Heading font is Brioso Pro, text font is Sabon.
Cover font is ITC Garamond Handtooled Bold
Cover symbols are Exocet Light

Cover photo from Google Maps of Lake Nisser, Heimdal, Norway

*To my parents, Paul and Helga Helgesen,
for the values they passed on to me*

To my wife, Lorraine, my love and encouragement

*To my daughter, Mary, proprietor of
Gabel Graphics, who exceeded all my
expectations in producing this book*

*To my parents, Paul and Helga Helgesen,
for the values they passed on to me*

To my wife, Lorraine, my love and encouragement

*To my daughter, Mary, proprietor of
Gabel Graphics, who exceeded all my
expectations in producing this book*

Contents

The Story Behind the Story............................vii

Book I — The Helgesens' Norwegian Roots 1
   Chapter 1   Telemark, Norway 3
   Chapter 2   Life in the Old and New Worlds............ 9
   Chapter 3   John Helgesen and the Civil War........... 13
   Chapter 4   The Years Following the War 19
   Chapter 5   The Helgesen Farm...................... 22
   Chapter 6   Myths Regarding the Old World........... 33

Book II — The Family of Ten 39
   Chapter 7   Doctor Elias, the First Born............... 41
   Chapter 8   Doctor Peter, Next in Line 45
   Chapter 9   Doctor John and the Incredible Story of Earl . 55
   Chapter 10   Thomas and Henry, a Bundle of Tragedy 65
   Chapter 11   Sever, Farmer and Entrepreneur 71
   Chapter 12   A Model Farmer and Two Sisters 81
   Chapter 13   The Life Story of Paul Tenny, the Tenth and Last . 87

Book III — Russ Tells His Story 113
   Chapter 14   "Good Old Russell B" 115
   Chapter 15   My Years of Growing Up 125
   Chapter 16   Russ's Personal Ten Commandments 135
   Chapter 17   My College Years 141
   Chapter 18   When God Needs Help 155
   Chapter 19   Russ as Entrepreneur 165
   Chapter 20   Secrets of the Heart................... 173

Book IV — A Career and a Family 189
   Chapter 21   Years of Committed Service 191
   Chapter 22   Time to Meet Our Family 229
   Chapter 23   A Family that Loved Camping 237
   Chapter 24   Just a Bit of This and That 243

Prologue.. 249

Personal Addendum.................................. 252

Book V — Genealogy 255

The Story Behind the Story

The author of *The Helgesen Story* is Russell B. Helgesen, the grandson of John and Ingeborg Helgesen whose roots were in Norway. For him, learning the details of this story really began in childhood, but the writing of the story came much later.

Russell's curiosity about his ancestors began at an early age. There were three "facts" about his ancestors that were commonly accepted by the family. The first was that his great-grandfather's name was Helge Moen; the second, that they had no living relatives in Norway; and finally that his ancestors came to America from Nissedal, Norway. Extensive research finally revealed that none of these were totally accurate.

He began his research for the story following his retirement in 1985 when he and his wife, Lorraine, began spending their winters in Arizona. One of the Mormon Genealogy Research Centers was located in Mesa and he made extensive use of their facilities and information. His research continued for several years and during that time he studied US census reports as far back as 1880 and began making contact with relatives who were very helpful in supplying information. The research and writing of the story has been an ongoing process for the last 25 years and today he has names and information on nearly 1,000

Helgesen family members in his computer.

In 1990 he engaged the services of Blaine Hedberg of the Vesterheim Genealogical Center in Madison, Wisconsin, who was very helpful in finding information on his relatives who had emigrated from Norway. In that year he and Lorraine took a trip to Norway in search of the Moen farm in Nissedal which, they believed, was the place from which their ancestors had come. While there, they made contact with many of the local Norwegian people who were most helpful in their search and it was then that they "struck pay dirt!" By chance, they met the pastor of the Nissedal church who knew all about the local farms and people who lived on them. He informed them that the Moen farm was then owned by Halvor Brekke, who still lived there. The pastor then took them to the Moen farm which was in Treungen, about 12 miles from Nissedal. It was a great thrill for Russell to stand on his grandfather's farm and sit in the bedroom where he had been born.

With this newly discovered information, he learned that his great-grandfather's name had been Hølje Päulsen Grovum (not Helge Moen), that he had come from Treungen (not Nissedal) and that he had hundreds of relatives now living in Norway.

A year later, Russ and Lorraine returned to Norway and met many of those relatives who were fourth or fifth cousins but treated them like brothers and sisters. They learned, however, that the Norwegian cousins who lived in that area all have the Tveit name and are highly regarded community leaders. Egil Tveit is a prominent businessman who owns and operates most of the businesses in Treungen. His brother, Sig is head of the music department at the University of Oslo and has earned an international reputation as a composer and Olav Jacob, the youngest brother, is pastor of a Lutheran Church which is near Treungen.

While genealogical research requires extensive effort, it also has rewards. Russell discovered that he has the "honor" of being one of the ninth cousins of Sonja Haroldsen, Queen of Norway. This relationship came about when in 1600 A.D. Tor Steinarson Fjagesund and Bergit Rolvsdotter Klevar married and had two sons, Steinar, from whom Queen Sonja descended and Aslaug, from whom the Helgesens came; thus resulting in the "ninth cousin" relationship.

Perhaps most satisfying of all was the happenstance of bringing together lost relatives who had never met one another. As you now read this story, don't skip the dramatic and tragic tale of one of the grandsons of Dr. Peter. The telling of this story begins, "One night a young man called Russell and identified himself as Paul Nelson. Somehow after a long search, he had found out that he was a Helgesen." Indeed it turned out that he was the grandson of Russell, son of Dr. Peter. However, no one living was aware of his existence and he knew nothing about his blood relatives. At the time, he was a flight attendant for American Airlines. Then on Dec. 20, 2003, the story came to a tragic conclusion when he was murdered in his apartment in Philadelphia. On January 10, 2004, his biological and adoptive families, who had never met, gathered at First Lutheran Church in Little Falls, Minnesota, for his memorial service.

Then don't miss "The Incredible Story of Earl Helgeson," son of Dr. John, who, never having seen his father from age four, saw him for the first time in his casket thirty years later.

You should note that Helgesen/Helgeson are not spelling errors. Earlier records are not conclusive but the ten children grew up with the "o" spelling. The story that seems to prevail is that the three doctors (Elias, Peter, and John) changed the spelling to "e" and Sever and Paul followed suit. The others kept the "o" spelling.

This is but a sampling of the strange, tragic, and loving tales of the Helgesen family. So, *The Helgesen Story* has finally been written but it is not finished. People are still being born and die, they arrive on the scene and disappear. We trust that as you read this story, you will be even more proud of your heritage.

Book I

The Helgesens' Norwegian Roots

CHAPTER 1

Telemark, Norway

Three miles north of the little town of Treungen in the District of Nissedal, County of Telemark, is a little farming community called Heimdal. From this area came one Jon Høljesen Grovum, known to his family as John Helgesen.

View of Lake Nisser from Moen farm, Treungen, Norway.

The Heimdal Farm

Heimdal is an old farm which is one of the primary farms in Treungen. Cultivation of the farm may have actually begun in the fourth or fifth century. Graves from Viking days have been found in this area. Some objects which were found about 1920, indicating that the farmers and their families in this area lived for generations by hunting, fishing, and agriculture, were sent to Nordiska Museum in Stockholm, Sweden. In the 17th century a market for products from their forests was established. They sold timber, floating it down to market on streams and rivers. Most of the timber was exported to the Netherlands, England, and other Europe countries.

The King of Denmark/Norway gave some merchants rights to harvest, sell, and export timber. Much of the profits were left in the hands of those merchants. Many farmers in Treungen got involved in trade with these merchants, some of whom, especially in Arendal, were highly mistrusted. Their ethics and business practices caused many a tragedy. The farmers sold their products to them and the merchants often paid with articles that the farmers did not need. To make matters worse some farmers borrowed money from those merchants.

In the centuries that followed, the Heimdal farm was divided into two parts and then gradually into several farms. During the latter part of the eighteenth century Jon Sigurdson Heimdal (b.1727) and his wife, Margit Tarjeisdåtter Sonderland (b.1729), lived on the farm. They had eight children and experienced some very difficult times. Only two of their children lived to adulthood (Sigrud, age 66, and Rasmus, age 49). Their son, Torov, died in 1763 well before his first birthday. During a period of six years (1769–1775), four of their children died at ages 2, 8, 11, and 16.

At the end of that difficult period, in 1775, Hølje and Margit were so deeply in debt that they had to mortgage their farm. The mortgage in the amount of "487 rd, 1 mark, and 23 shillings was held by businessman Anders Dedekam from Arendal." When the mortgage came due, they would have lost the farm except for the fact that Anders Dedekam could not find the mortgage papers. So an arbitrator was chosen who ordered Dedekam to give a receipt that showed that the farm was paid for.

The Moen farm, Heimdal, Norway, where Hølje Pålson Grovum and his son, Jon Høljesen Grovum, lived before leaving for America in 1861.

When their son, Sigurd Jonson Heimdal (1760–1826) and Tørbjorg Halvorsdåtter (b.1765) were married in 1785, they "took over Heimdal." By their twenty-fifth wedding anniversary they had ten children. One of the children died in infancy; the others lived to adulthood. In 1818, eight years after the birth of their youngest son, Olav, three of their children, including our great-grandmother, Margit, were married at the ages of 30, 28 and 23.

To continue to keep the farm through difficult times, Sigurd Jonson Heimdal borrowed money from the local sheriff, Rasmus Bakka. He was a hard creditor and, according to tradition, didn't always play fair. A number of farmers lost their land and property because of his greed. It is told that one of his victims trudged more or less on foot, together with his wife, to the King of Stockholm to complain about Rasmus. When Sigurd Jonson died (1826), he was indebted to Rasmus (an obligation of 500 rd).

A process went on for some years, ending up with Rasmus Bakka as the winner. The farm was sold out of the family at public auction, but some years later two of Sigurd's sons, Tarjei and Halvor (brothers of Margit), claimed the farm, based on the "old rights" (allodial possession). They each became owners of half of their father's farm: Halvor, on the part called "Bru"; and Tarjei, on the part called "Southern Heimdal." Today a two-mile long road forms a loop through the Heimdal area which consists of about a dozen farms, including the "Moen" farm.

The Moen Farm

The exact origin of the Moen farm is not known except that it was originally one of (or a part of) the Heimdal farms. Sometime before 1800, Tellev Tarjeison, from Kasa in Nissedal, purchased the Moen farm. In 1818, Margit (daughter of Sigurd Jonson Heimdal) married Hølje Pålson Grovum. Records state "in 1820, Hølje Pålson Grovum and his wife Margit Sigursdatter Heimdal came here." This also explains why some records refer to Hølje Pålson Grovum as Hølje Moen. While they lived on the farm they followed the Norwegian practice of taking the farm name, but when he came to America he dropped that name.

It is likely that they purchased the farm from its owner, Tellev Tarjeison. Because Margit's grandmother was Margit Tarjeisdatter, it is possible that Tellev Tarjeison, the owner of the Moen farm, was a near relative. It was on the Moen farm that Jon Høljesen Grovum was born in 1827. Today Halvor O. Brekke owns the Moen farm and the original house still stands and is in reasonably good repairs.

According to the Nissedal records of the Treungen Church, Jon was born October 6, 1827 and baptized in the Treungen Church on November 11, 1827. His tombstone in Perry Lutheran Church Cemetery at Daleyville, Wisconsin, incorrectly gives his birth date as September 29, 1827. Hølje Pålson Grovum and his wife, Margit Sigurdsdåtter Heimdal had four sons:

Sigrud (b.1819) moved to Holt, Norway, in 1841.
Pål (b.1821) moved to E. Rusoer, Norway, in 1840.
Tarjei (b.1825) moved to Kragero, Norway, in 1847.
Jon (b. 1827) immigrated to America in 1861.

Jon's mother, Margit, died in 1854 at the age of 64. That same year Jon was married. He and his wife, Jorund Gjermundsdåtter Jorundland, settled on the Moen farm where they lived with his father until they and his father, Hølje, left for America in 1861.

Jon was a remarkably versatile man, being a shoemaker, carpenter and stonemason in addition to his farming. According to the 1901 Commemorative Biographical Record of the counties of Rock, Green, Grant, Iowa, and Lafayette, Wisconsin "his brother Thomas later became a wealthy ship builder in Liverpool, England." However, records from Norway do not list a brother by that name.

The Treungen Church

At the time that Jon and Jorund lived on the Moen farm, the Treungen Church, which was started in 1395, was located on the Tveit farm, a short distance southwest of Treungen. By the early 1800s the church had fallen into a very sad state of repairs and serious rifts of long standing existed within the congregation.

The new Treungen Church.

To this day local residents speak of the history of the church in hushed tones. The one thing they seem to agree on is that alcohol had become a very serious problem. Special occasions, such as weddings and funerals, often turned into drunken brawls, which sometimes lasted for several days. In 1861 the tensions were finally resolved when the congregation made a decision to "start over." The church building was dismantled and a new building was erected on the Heimdal farm three miles northeast of Treungen where it still is in use today.

5/20/2000

CHAPTER 2

Life in the Old and New Worlds

For a fuller understanding of why our ancestors came to America, we will take a step back in time. At about 1000 A.D when the Vikings were ruling Norway, the Oneota Indians in America began pushing westward from what is today Green Bay, Wisconsin. By 1200 A.D. they had reached the western part of Wisconsin, later known as the Town of Moscow near Daleyville, and stayed there for almost 400 years. In the early 1500s this Indian community was struck by tragedy. Throughout the continent, diseases (such as smallpox, measles, and whooping cough) that were brought to America by European settlers, began to infest the Native Americans. Historians and archaeologists estimate that 80 to 90 percent of the Indians in that community died in the first wave of the epidemics.

Before they could repopulate their lands, European immigrants began filling the void. In many areas, including the village of Moscow just south of the Perry Norwegian Settlement, the immigrants actually began taking over deserted Indian village sites.

As we step back in time, again we note that when the Black Death Plague struck Norway about 1347 it's population of 300,000 was reduced by more that 50 percent. However, in the centuries that followed, the population grew so rapidly that by 1825 it had reached one million people. With that population explosion, the farmers could not produce enough food for the country. At that same time, the farms were being passed from fathers to sons, thus the farms were being divided and subdivided until they became so small that they could no longer support the people and animals living on them. The young men were faced with the choice of moving to the cities and pursuing a new, strange, and to them, frightful way of life or to go to America where they had the promise of productive farm land which would assure them of a familiar and comfortable way of life. Consequently, large numbers of families from Norway and other European countries who chose to leave their homeland and settle in this area of Wisconsin were called "Yankees." By 1860 most land in the historic Perry Norwegian Settlement had already been claimed and with the passage of the Homestead Act, many of these "Yankees" began moving further west. As they left, settlers, who were coming in large numbers from Norway, replaced them.

It was at this time and under these circumstances that Jon Helgesen and his family and father chose to leave for the new world. It is a reasonable conclusion that other families from their home community of Treungen left at the same time and settled in this same area. It is only conjecture as to why they came to the Perry Norwegian Settlement. Perhaps they had friends that were already there or maybe it was because southern Wisconsin was attractive to the Norwegians who came from the beautiful and rugged terrain of Norway. It was however, a place where they could acquire farmland at a reasonable price to continue a way of life that was familiar to them.

Life in the New World

In 1861 Jon and Jorånd left their farm home in Treungen, Nissedal in Telemark County, Norway, for America with their three little children together with Jon's father, Hølje.

>Margit (b.1855)
>Anne (b.1857)
>Halvor (b.1859)

At this point nothing is known about the journey of Jon and his young family to America. The majority of Norwegian immigrants in 1861 came by way of Quebec. Unfortunately the Canadian government did not begin retaining copies of the ship's passenger lists until 1867 so we have not been able to determine the name of or any information regarding the ship on which them came. Some facts however are worthy of note. During the Civil War, with few exceptions, emigration from Norway to America was illegal. Thus most Norwegians who wanted to come to America sailed to Hull, England, from which they took a train to Liverpool or to LaHavre, France. From there they sailed to Quebec, Canada, and then traveled to the United States. There are no records of the people who sailed from Liverpool. Their records were apparently destroyed in the normal course of business and very few records at all were kept in LaHavre. So this matter will have to be left to our imagination.

Little is presently known about the early years in the life of the Helgesens in America. They settled in the Town of Moscow, near Daleyville, Wisconsin, in an area known as the Perry Norwegian Settlement. From existing documents, it is evident that upon arriving in America, Jon changed the spelling of his first name from Jon to John. Later we will tell the story of the farm they later bought in 1870. It is only logical to conclude that, shortly after their arrival in America, before he left for the war, John made arrangements for housing in the community, but we have no information on what that might have been.

CHAPTER 3

John Helgesen and the Civil War

When John and family arrived in America, the Civil War had just begun. We can only speculate as to what motivated him to enlist in the Union Army. Many of the immigrants had little money and no means of supporting their families. Despite draft riots in New York, President Abraham Lincoln had just signed into law a bill permitting draftee's to pay someone $300 to take their place. It is unlikely that he chose that option. During that time there was a growing anti-slavery movement that appealed to many immigrants in Wisconsin and it is more likely that it was that issue that motivated him to enlist.

On September 15, 1861, several Norwegians gathered in Madison, Wisconsin, and resolved to attempt to organize a Norwegian (or Scandinavian) regiment. For many immigrants the war was more of a moral than a political issue. Because so many of the newcomers, who felt keenly about the slavery issue, had incomplete knowledge of the English language, a Norwegian Regiment would satisfy their needs. A Norwegian named Hans Christian Heg was chosen by the Governor of Wisconsin to organize the regiment and was given the title of Colonel. He was a very proud and loyal Norwegian who lived and died in the belief that the Norwegians were a breed without equal anywhere on the globe. As an officer, he proved to be exacting, correct, conscientious, and of unblemished behavior.

John responded to Colonial Heg's appeal and enlisted in the United States Service at Moscow, Wisconsin, November 26, 1861, as a private in Company "H" 15th REGIMENT WISCONSIN VOLUNTEER INFANTRY under Captain John Ingmundson and Colonel Hans C. Heg to serve three years or during the War. The commitment that he and other company members were given was to be paid "a bounty of $100" for enlisting plus a salary of $13 a month, as well as free clothes and food.

Their basic training was at Camp Randall near Madison. At the camp the sleeping quarters and dining hall were built of plain boards and were drafty and cold. There were no chairs so they had to stand while they ate and the food was not the best, but they either ate what was dished out or they starved!

Their training was completed and at 8 o'clock in the morning of March 2, 1862, they left Camp Randall in a blinding snow storm for active duty. When their locomotive got stuck in the snow, an extra engine was brought up to help pull them out. After four days of travel by train and boat, they arrived at Bird's Point, Missouri, (opposite Cairo, Illinois) and were immediately thrust into battle to secure the Mississippi River and keep it open to boat traffic at a point that was known as "Island no. 10." When the siege ended on April 8, 1862, with the surrender of the Confederate forces, they were transferred to Tennessee and spent the rest of the war in middle Kentucky, Middle Tennessee, and Northern Georgia.

The "Norwegian Regiment" as it was called, gained a reputation of being one of the finest and toughest fighting units in the Union army. In almost every battle the 15th Regiment was put in a place where they took the first hard push. As a result, they suffered very heavy casualties; the fourth highest losses of any unit during the entire war. Of the 905 soldiers that enlisted in the 15th Regiment, 299 or 33 percent were lost.

In late 1862, Major General William S. Rosecrans was named commander of the Union Army of the Ohio. He redesignated it the Army of the Cumberland and went on the offensive in Tennessee. The 15th Wisconsin, under Col. William P. Carlin fought in these battles.

The most costly battle of the entire war was the Battle of Chickamauga. Of the Union Army 16,971 soldiers were lost including Col. Heg. While leading the battle, mounted on his horse, Col. Heg, took a bullet through his abdomen. Though wounded, he continued to command the operation until he fell from his horse. He was taken to the hospital and died at 10:00 the next morning. John Helgesen fought in this battle and fortunately survived the heavy fighting. After Chickamauga, George Henry Thomas replaced Rosecrans. The Army of the Cumberland joined two other armies under Sherman in capturing Atlanta. So when Scarlet O'Hara said, "The Yankees are coming! The Yankees are coming!" she was talking about John Helgesen. However, after Atlanta, the 4th Corps was sent north to contain General John B. Hood, who was trying to draw the Yankees away from Georgia and back into Tennessee, so the 15th Wisconsin was not part of Sherman's March to the Sea.

Company H and other companies of the 15th Regiment was assigned to the 1st Brigade, 3rd Division, 4th Corps Army of the Cumberland, and participated in the following engagements:

> New Madrid, Missouri, March 3–16, 1862
> Island No. Terr. Tennessee, April 8, 1862
> Perryville, Kentucky, October 8, 1862
> Stone River or Murfreesboro, Tenn., Dec. 31, 1862–Jan. 1, 1863
> Chickamauga, Georgia, September 19–20, 1863
> Brizzard Roost, Georgia, May 5–9, 1864
> Kennesaw Mountain, Georgia, June 10–30, 1864
> Peach Tree, Georgia, July 12, 1864
> Atlanta, Georgia, July 20, 1864
> Jonesboro, Georgia, August 31, 1864
> John helped to lay pontoon August 20, 1864, and was the first to cross the Tom's River Mission Ridge, November 23, 1864

In 1862 John was wounded (apparently seriously) in action (maybe in the Battle of Stone River) and was hospitalized at the Regimental Hospital in Nashville, Tennessee, for about eight months. He was wounded again in 1864 and hospitalized at Madison for two months.

He "veteranized" in November 1864, and was discharged February 13, 1865. The Company Muster Out Roll from Chattanooga, Tennessee, States that John "was last paid August 31, 1864; his clothing account was last settled October 31, 1863, and was owing him $67.40 and his Bounty due was $100." The story of John's experience leads one to conclude that the Civil War was very costly (600,000 Union soldiers and a similar number of the Confederate army were lost), the soldiers suffered great hardships from lack of food, clothing, and adequate shelter, and probably did not receive a good deal of the money that they were promised. But John fought for a cause in which he deeply believed.

After John Helgesen's death December 29, 1894, a picture of the easel-shaped monument bearing his army record was dedicated to his memory by his widow, Ingeborg. The monument was presented to the family, April 12, 1895. It is now in the possession of great-grandson, John Helgesen, in Olatha, Kansas. It erroneously lists his company as "E" instead of "H." In the book *No Better Place to Die: The Battle of Stones River* by Peter Cozzens, it tells how on the first day of the battle, the Confederate Army of Tennessee, under Braxton Bragg, routed the Union soldiers: "The withdrawal of the Thirty-eighth Illinois, minutes later, left only Hans Heg and his 15th Wisconsin to cover the brigade's retreat." (p. 99)

The regiment that Heg recruited was largely from communities of German and Scandinavian immigrants in Wisconsin, Illinois, Iowa, and Minnesota. Heg's spirit was the moving force behind the organization of the unit in the fall of 1861 and reflected the independence and hardihood that was typical of its members.

Leaving his native Norway to cross the Atlantic with his parents at the age of eleven, Heg was in California panning for gold with the Forty-niners. On receiving word of his father's death in 1851, Heg returned home to Wisconsin. The two years spent in the gold fields had apparently satisfied his wanderlust. As a young Norwegian, he settled down to farming, became active in state politics, and won election as the Wisconsin prison Commissioner on the Republican ticket in 1859. He was the first Norwegian to be elected to a state office in the United States.

His appearance and manners were typically Scandinavian: Tall and straight, heavily bearded, strong and vigorous. Heg was of a quiet demeanor, taciturn manner, and sternness. His war record points out that "drawing on these qualities at Stones River, Heg kept his regiment intact long enough for the brigade to retire without the loss of a single artillery piece."

Life was not easy for John Helgesen and his young family in America. During his time of service in the Civil War, his father died. (According to the biographical record "he died at the advanced age of 92." However, according to official Norwegian records he was 77.) Also during the War, a daughter, Johanna was born in 1863 to his wife, Jorund who died in or soon after childbirth. Nothing is known about her death, as no records of the time or place of her death or burial have been located.

Easel with Civil War record of John Helgesen.

CHAPTER 4

John and Ingeborg Helgesen

The Years Following the War

According to the record book of Pastor John N. Field (an early traveling minister in the Mount Horeb area), he performed the marriage of John Helgesen and Ingeborg Eriksdåtter Dokken on May 10, 1865 in Adams, Iowa County, Wisconsin. Ingeborg was the daughter of Erik Olsen and Marit Olsdåtter. She was born in Norway (probably in the Valdres area) on August 14, 1847. In 1859 she came to America with her parents and settled in Moscow Township where her father died in 1867 at the age of 55. When Ingeborg and John were married she was 18 and he was 38.

Following the war, they farmed in the Town of Moscow where they managed to support their growing family. They loved their new land and became very loyal citizens. Their attitude was that "we live in America, we are Americans, and we will use the American language" and consequently they nearly discontinued the use of their mother tongue. Their progressive attitude was in turn passed on to their children. Though education was limited at that time, three of their sons (Elias, Peter, and John) completed medical school and became doctors and one (Sever) was educated as a pharmacist.

During the 25 years following their marriage, eleven children were born:

Elias	born Feb. 2, 1866, died at age 71
Peter	born Aug. 29, 1868, died at age 74
John	born Jan. 9, 1871, died at age 63
Thomas	born Nov. 1873, died at age 47
Henry	born May 19, 1876, died at age 51
Alfred	born April 19, 1877, died an infant
Mary	born Feb. 1879, died at age 81
Sever	born March 5, 1882, died at age 51
Clara	born Nov. 1, 1884, died at age 65
Albert	born April 19, 1887, died at age 72
Paul	born March 27, 1890, died at age 72

When they arrived in America, they settled in temporary quarters near Daleyville, Wisconsin. On May 23, 1870 they bought a farm that they owned for the rest of their lives. The farm "containing 80 acres, more or less" was purchased from John Nelson Lee and his wife, Gertrude, for the sum of $1,000 and was "free and clear except for a certain mortgage of $140." The farm title was in the name of "John Helgesen." In that deed his name was spelled with "e" instead of the usual "o." According to an affidavit given by Halvor Helgeson on December 16, 1926, for the purpose of clarifying the records, "On March 14, 1871, John and Ingeborg Helgesen conveyed title to the farm to Halvor Anderson and, on the same day, Halvor Anderson conveyed title to said premises to Ingeborg Helgesen, wife of John Helgesen." She held title to this farm until her death in 1901. See

In 1894 when their youngest son, Paul, was only four years old, John died a tragic death at the age of 67 years. During the Christmas holidays, neighbors were invited to a party at the Helgesen home. During the evening, John, who loved children, played games with them. He entertained them by putting a rug under a door with him on one side and the children on the other. The children would then attempt to stand on the rug while he would pull the rug out from under them. After a very happy evening, the party ended and the guests returned home. Shortly thereafter on December 29, 1894, John died of an apparent heart attack.

Seven years later, their youngest sons, Albert (13) and Paul (11), were left orphans when Ingeborg died a tragic death at the age of 54. On November 16, 1901, she was at a party at the home of one of their neighbors, the Homme family. While there, she accidentally tripped and fell down the stairs to her death.

When Ingeborg died in 1901, the farm was still in her name. Following her death, title was held by the following of her named heirs: S. E. (Sever) Helgeson, Mary Johnson Helgeson, Clara Kittleson Helgeson, H. C. (Henry) Helgeson, P. A. (Peter) Helgeson and Thomas H. Helgeson. On April 24, 1906, these heirs conveyed title to the farm to Halvor Helgeson who, 39 days later on June 2, 1906, deeded it to Vraal Peterson.

Following her death, Albert and Paul both went to New Glares; Albert lived with the Nick Zwiffle family on their farm and Paul lived with his older brother, Sever, and worked in his brother, Dr. Elias' drug store.

CHAPTER 5

The Helgesen Farm

In the Town of Moscow, Wisconsin

This portion of *the Helgesen Story* is a combination of fact and assumptions based on known conditions in the area at that time. The facts are that John and family came to Town of Moscow, Wisconsin, in 1861, that he enlisted in the Civil War on Nov. 26, 1861, and that he spent three years and three months away from home engaged in many battles. Those battles in which he fought are a matter of record as are the facts that he spent eight months in the hospital in Nashville, Tennessee, in 1862 and was hospitalized for two months in Madison, Wisconsin, in 1864. On June 30, 2003, I spent time at the Register of Deeds' office in the Iowa County Court House in Dodgeville, Wisconsin, and found the records relative to the farm that John and Ingeborg Helgesen bought and lived on until their deaths. In our story telling we generally focus on the "hero" that goes off to war and forget about their families that are left at home. Our attempt now is to "speculate" (based on some known facts) on what was happening to the family at home while John was off to war.

Life on the Farm While John Was at War

In the middle of the nineteenth century while living on the Moen farm in Treungen, Norway, John Helgesen had a dream. He wanted to leave his native land and go to America in pursuit of the "good life." To him part of that good life would be to enlist in the Union Army of the Civil War which had just begun and help in the cause of uniting the country and ending what he believed to be the evil of slavery.

At this time Norway was slowly emerging from the long and difficult period of economic hardship. Many believed that their country was finally on the verge of a "brighter day" but still John wanted to leave in pursuit of a better life. And so John left for America with his wife, Jorand, three small children [Margit (6), Anne (4), and Halvor (2)], and his widowed father Hølje along with an unknown number of other families from the Treungen community.

The first decade in America must have been very difficult for John and his family. As we now tell the story of those first ten years, keep in mind that some of the things that we say will be fact and other things will be assumptions based on known conditions at that time.

Other families from Treungen that settled in the same community gave John, Jorand, and family the support system that was needed to survive. The Perry Norwegian Settlement, to which they came, was not a Homestead area and, because there was no longer any land to be homesteaded, those who came had to buy their farms. John for sure came with only pocket money and was in no position to buy a farm. Before going off to war, he made arrangements for his family to settle in temporary housing where they would be able to survive with the help of his aging father. Because John's 76-year-old father was not in the best of health, they likely found housing where they could at least have a garden without the burden of operating a farm.

The first winter was very difficult. John left for the war in November. Dark and cloudy days followed. The wind blew and snow drifts piled high that winter. For the family it was a lonely time but, with the help and fellowship of friends and neighbors from Treungen, they managed to survive. The spring of 1862 finally came and it was time to plant their garden to provide much needed food for their table.

With the coming of spring, their spirits were lifted and they were now looking forward to a good year in their newly adopted land. News from John was slow in coming and when it came it was depressing. The Wisconsin Regiment of which he was a part had engaged in many hard fought battles. While fighting the Confederate army in Tennessee, John was seriously wounded and spent eight months in the military hospital in Nashville. That was only the beginning of bad news. Later in the year, Hølje developed a nagging cough, caused by congestion in his lungs, and fever that finally turned into pneumonia. With no adequate medical help available in the area, the fever worsened and within days he was dead. These were indeed dark days for Jorand, with her husband off to war and she alone with her three little children, but her neighbors and friends were very helpful.

Surely next year would be better. But as the year progressed it proved to be tragedy upon tragedy. John was again wounded in battle and spent two months in the hospital in Madison. Before the end of the year, Jorand gave birth to a baby girl, Johanna, and then died at the age of 33, either in childbirth or soon thereafter. With John away at war and no mother in the home to care for the four little children, what did they do?

We don't know the answer to that question but we do know that somehow they did survive and at this point we can only venture a guess. Not far away lived a family by the name of Docken. They had come from the Valdrus area of Norway in 1859 and settled in the community. Because of the friendship which developed with the Helgesens, they agreed that their daughter, Ingeborg Eriksdätter who was only 16 at the time but very mature and capable, should come and live with the children or perhaps they were even taken into their home. With the help of other neighbors and friends, she soon became like a mother to them and continued to care for the children for a year and a half until the war ended and their father returned home.

Then came the happy ending! John was discharged and returned home February 13, 1865 (Valentine's Day). He fell in love with their "baby sitter" and he and Ingeborg were married three months later (May 10, 1865). She indeed must have been an unusually fine, strong, and brave soul to become the step-mother of these four little children when she, at age 18, married John, who was 38.

Finally John had a partner with whom he could dream about their new life. Their goal was to work hard and save money so that they could buy a farm. Five years later the goal was accomplished. On May 24, 1870, they purchased a farm "containing 80 acres, more or less" from John Nelson Lee and his wife, Gertrude, for the sum of $1,000 and was "free and clear except for a certain mortgage of $140" which they were obligated to pay off. It is interesting to note that the deed in 1870 was made out to John only. Then for some unexplainable reason, on March 14, 1871, John and Ingeborg conveyed title to Halvor Anderson and on the same day Halvor Anderson conveyed title to Ingeborg, wife of John. Ingeborg held title to the farm until her death in 1901.

From 1870 until John's death in 1894 he and Ingeborg and their family lived on and worked this same farm. During those years, they added ten children to the four that he brought into the marriage. For them, education and religion were high priorities. Less than a half mile away was the Sandy Rock country school. Their children attended as faithfully as possible depending, somewhat, on their involvement in the necessary farm work. Some distance away was Perry Lutheran Church in Daleyville. The church had recently been started and had built its first stone church the year before John and family came to America. The whole family faithfully attended worship which was conducted in the Norwegian language. It was there that all of their children were confirmed.

One by one the children grew up and left home—three became doctors. But then, at the age of 67, John suddenly died and once again Ingeborg was left in charge. What happened during the next seven years until her untimely death? When John died, Paul, the youngest was only 4, Albert was 6, Clara was 10, Sever was 12, Mary was 15, and the five others ranged in age from 18 to 28. The four from his first family had all left home by that time. Being a very strong character, Ingeborg undoubtedly got along quite well with the help of the younger children and perhaps the neighbors from time to time.

The Story of the Farm

In 1901, Ingeborg suddenly died at the age of 54 as a result of a fall down the stairs at her neighbor's home. At that time the farm was still in her name. We have not discovered any deed of record indicating transfer of ownership, but on December 16, 1926, Harvor filed an affidavit stating that following her death, "title was held in the name of the children who were her named heirs: S. E. (Sever) Helgeson, Mary Johnson Helgeson, Clara Kittleson Helgeson, H. C. (Henry) Helgeson, P. A. (r) Helgeson and Thomas H. Helgeson." Five years later, on April 24, 1906, these heirs conveyed title to the farm to Halvor Helgeson who, 39 days later on June 2, 1906, deeded it to Vraal Peterson. At that time Halvor was 42 and farmed nearby. Though it is not a matter of written record, we know that he was involved in different ways in the operation of his deceased stepmother's farm during this period of time following her death. In fact it is reasonable to believe that for the five years following her death, he actually took over the operation of the farm until it was sold.

For those who wish to pursue the question of the ownership of the farm further, we are setting forth some of the legal and technical details that have been recorded with the Iowa County Registrar of Deeds. I personally visited the Register of Deeds Office, at Dodgeville Monday morning, June 30, 2003. For some reason that I cannot explain, the deeds and affidavits were filed with the Iowa County Register of Deeds and indicate that the property was in Iowa County but the Notary Public who executed the documents was in Dane County.

The search first took me to Vol. 9, page 389, where I discovered that Charles H. Rogers had deeded a farm to John Helgeson. On more careful examination, I discovered that the legal description did not fit the farm in question and that the date of October 27, 1859, when the deed was executed, was two years before our John Helgesen arrived in America. I concluded that this was another John Helgeson and it was a different farm.

Finally the search paid off and in Vol. 123, page 105 we found recorded the warranty deed whereby the farm was deeded by John

Nelson Lee and Gertrude Lee to John Helgesen.

Two things about the deed were interesting: (1) Helgesen was spelled with an "e" and both of the Lees signed their name with an (X). Following is the deed:

> This Indenture, Made the twenty fourth day of May in the year of our Lord One Thousand Eight Hundred and Seventy between John Nelson Lee and Gertrude his wife of the County of Iowa and State of Wisconsin parties of the first part and John Helgesen of said place of the second part Witnesseth, that the said parties of the first part, for and in consideration of the sum of $1,000 (one thousand dollars) to them in hand paid by the said party of the second part, the receipt whereof is hereby confessed and acknowledged, have given, granted, bargained, sold, remised, released, aliened, conveyed and confirmed, and by these presents do give, grant, bargain, sell, remise, release, alien, convey and confirm unto the said party of the second part his heirs and assigns forever the following described track of land situated in the County of Iowa & State of Wisconsin to wit: The North East quarter of the South East quarter & the South West quarter of the North East quarter of Section No (23) twenty three in Township No (5) five North Range No (5) five East containing (80) eighty acres being the same more or less.
>
> Together with all and singular the hereditaments and appurtenances thereunto belonging or in anywise appertaining; and all the estate, right, title, interest, claim or demand whatsoever, of the said party of the first part, either in law or equity, either in possession or expectancy of, in and to the above bargained premises, and their hereditaments and appurtenances.
>
> To Have and to Hold the said premises as above described, with the hereditaments and appurtenances, unto the said party of the second part, and to his heirs and assigns Forever. And the said John Nelson Lee for himself, his heirs, executors and administrators, do covenant, grant, bargain and agree, to and with the said party of the second part his heirs and assigns, that at the time of the ensealing and delivery of these presents, he is well seized of the premises above described, as of a good,

sure, perfect, absolute and indefeasible estate of inheritance in the law, in fee simple and that the same are free and clear from all encumbrances whatever, except a certain mortgage of one hundred and forty dollars which shall be paid by the said party of the second part and that the above bargained premises, in the quiet and peaceable possession of the said party of the second part his heirs and assigns, against all and every person or person lawfully claiming the whole or any part thereof, he will forever Warrant and Defend.

In Witness Whereof The said parties of the first part have hereunto set their hands and seals the day and year first above written. Signed with Xs by John Nelson Lee and Gertrude Lee May 24, 1870 and recorded at 1:30 P.M., July 19, 1870.

I did not discover any other records relative to the ownership of the farm until I came to affidavits that had been filed by Harvor Helgeson on December 16, 1926, at 10:00 A.M. It is apparent that at that time there arose a problem with the deed that was held by the present owner. The problem(s) could only be resolved by Harvor, who was still alive and had been involved personally in the various legal transactions over the years and had personally known all parties involved.

His first affidavit in 1926 was as follows:

> Halvor Helgesen, being first duly sworn on oath, says that he is a resident of Iowa County, State of Wisconsin, and is the same identical person who is described as grantee in deed recorded in the office of register of deeds of said Iowa County, April 24, 1906, in volume 76 of Deeds, on page 227, and that he is a step son of Ingeborg Helgeson, deceased, described in final judgment recorded in Book 68, page 484, and a son of John Helgeson, deceased; that S. E. Helgeson, one of the grantors in said last mentioned deed, is his brother and the same identical person, named in said final judgment, as Sever Helgesen; that Mary Johnson Helgeson, grantor in said deed, is his sister and the same person as Mary J. Helgeson, named as heir in said final judgment; that Clara Kittleson Helgeson, grantor in said

deed, is the same identical person as Clara Helgeson in said final Judgment and is affiants sister; that H. C. Helgeson, grantor in said deed, is also his brother and the same identical person as Henry Helgeson in said final Judgment; that P. A. Helgeson, grantor in said deed, is his brother and the same identical person as Peter A. Helgeson, one of the heirs in said final judgment; that Thomas H. Helgeson, one of the grantors in said deed, is his brother and the same identical person as Thomas Helgeson, one of the heirs in said final Judgment.

This affidavit is made for the purpose of correcting the title to the following described premises: The North East quarter of the South East quarter & the South West quarter of the North East quarter of Section No (23) twenty three in Township No (5) five North Range No (5) five East, Iowa County, Wisconsin.

(SS) Halvor Helgeson

The second affidavit that he filed on December 16, 1926 at 10:00 A.M. was as follows:

Halvor Helgeson, being first duly sworn on oath, says that he is a resident of Iowa County, Wisconsin; that affiant is 67 years of age and the son of John Helgeson, deceased, grantee in deed from John Nelson Lee and wife, dated May 24, 1870, and recorded July 19, 1970, in the office of register of deeds of said Iowa County, in Volume 23, page 105, and which said deed conveyed to his said father the North East quarter of the South East quarter & the South West quarter of the North East quarter of Section No (23) twenty three in Township No (5) five North Range No (5) five East, Iowa County, Wisconsin; that his said father and wife Ingeborg conveyed said premises to one Halvor Anderson March 14, 1871, by deed recorded in said office March 15, 1871, in Volume 23 of Deeds, page 387, and on the same day, the said Halvor Anderson conveyed said premises to the said Ingeborg Helgeson, wife of said John Helgeson and this affiant's step mother by deed recorded in said office March 15, 1871, in Volume 23, page 388; that said Ingeborg Helgeson died in 1903 [actually she died 11/16/1901] seized of the above described premises, and that said premises were conveyed by the heirs of said deceased, to this affiant by deeds, recorded April 24, 1906, in said office of register of deeds, in Volume 70 of Deeds, page 96, and in Volume 76 of Deeds, page 227; that this affiant conveyed said premises to Vraal Peterson by deed recorded in said office June 2, 1906, in volume 72 of Deeds page 528; that the name of said grantee was through an advertence and mistake erroneously written or copied on the records as Vraal Pederson;

That during all of the times mentioned above, since the acquiring of the title to said lands by his said father and until this affiant sold the same to the said Vraal Peterson, the said premises were in the actual, open, exclusive and continuous, peaceful and uninterrupted possession of said John Helgeson and Ingeborg Helgeson, and their heirs and later, for a short time, in this affiant, as aforesaid and that no person whatsoever, whether mentioned in connection with said title or otherwise, ever made any claim or demand against said premises in any manner antagonistic to the rights, title and interest of this affiant or his said father mother and their heirs.

Affiant further says that the above mentioned John Nelson Lee, grantor in deed to his said father, is the same identical person as John Nelson, grantee in deed recorded in said office in volume 11, page 396.

(SS) Halvor Helgeson

Subscribed and sworn to and acknowledged before me this 22nd day of November, 1926. Signed, executed and acknowledged by A. T. Torge, Notary Public, Dane County, Wisconsin.

So ends the story of the Helgesen Farm, Town of Moscow, Wisconsin.

Rev. Russell B. Helgesen, May 17, 2004

Helgesen tombstone in Perry Lutheran Cemetery, Daleyville, Wisconsin.

CHAPTER 6

Myths Regarding the Old World

From my childhood and until I began working on the family genealogy in 1990, there were three "myths" that were readily accepted by our family.

The first was that our grandfather came from Nissedal, Norway. Actually he came from the Moen farm, which was located a few miles from Treungen, which is a little town 12 miles south of Nissedal. It is located near the southeast shore of Lake Nisser, which is the largest and one of the most beautiful lakes in Norway. I had heard the story that Treungen got its name following the Great Plague in the 1300s. It was told that all the residents of the area died, except for "three young ones." Thus the name: "Tre–ungen" was given to the area. Cousin Egil from Treungen agrees that the story is likely correct.

The second "myth" was that our great-grandfather's name was Helge Moen. Most Norwegian records list him as Hølje Pålson Grovum. His name meant that he was Hølje, son of Pål, and was born and raised on the Grovum farm which was located half way between Nissedal and Treungen in the area (County) of Telemark. He did, however, live on the Moen farm for a number of years before coming to America and thus was known locally as Hølje Moen.

The third "myth" was that we have no living relatives in Norway. All of Hølje's four sons left the Telemark area. We have not been successful in locating their families so we do not know whether or not any of them are living in Norway at this time. However, in 1992 we discovered that Jacob Tveit, our third cousin, was living with his

Jakob E. Tviet in 1993

family in Treungen. In 1993 we visited them. Jacob was quite old and feeble and has since died. His son, Egil, operates the businesses with his brother. A third son Olav Jacob is now pastor of a parish near Treungen. Egil has done a great job in developing the family tree and now has over 44,000 names of ancestors and descendants of the Tveit and Helgesen families in his computer.

Helgesen-Tveit Genealogical Link

Egil Tveit has traced our common ancestry back to Tarjei Tarjeison Hatveit (1692–1730) as follows:

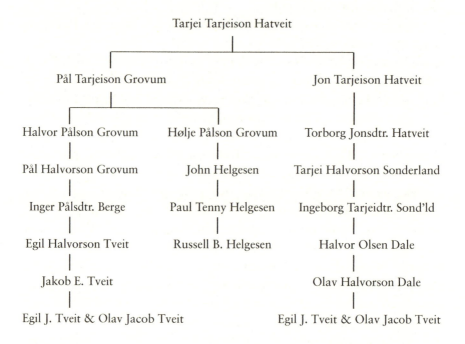

During a visit to Treungen, Norway, in 1993, Egil J. Tveit (right) shows Russ Helgesen some of the 1,100 names, dating back to 1370, in their common genealogy. As of this writing, Egil's genealogical work has yielded nearly 80,000 relatives. Russ's son-in-law, Thomas von Fischer, is in the background.

Today, the tiny town of Treungen and the Tveits are nearly synonymous. There is a large Jakob Tveit supermarket and general store; they have a fleet of JBT tanker trucks that deliver fuel oil to the entire region; they have a large mink farm and supply mink food to the other farmers in the area.

Visiting them in 1991 and again in 1993 was an exciting experience. We met a number of family members and explored the area. We stood on the site of the home (now gone) which once stood on the Grovum farm where great-grandfather, Hølje, was born. We walked the Moen farm and visited the house, which was still in good repairs. We stood in the room where grandfather Jon Helgesen was born. There we offered up a prayer to God for all the blessings that have come to us through the myriad of ancestors that have gone to their eternal rest.

Egil's ancestral search has taken our family tree from Hølje Pålsen Grovum back to 1370 A.D. and includes over 1,100 individuals. He explained that the search ended at that point because it was the time of the Great Plague when most of the people died and most of the records were lost.

Those of us who pride ourselves in being "pure Norwegians" should be advised that, in the lineage of more than a thousand names, there is one Dane and one German!

The Search Goes On

I have been working on our genealogy for nearly 25 years and have on file a great volume of information on our American cousins. The collection and editing of inform which I have in my computer is an ongoing process. It is my hope that someone in our family will carry on the project. Having made the recent discovery that the Tveits of Treungen and the Helgesens and Tveits in America are cousins, has really enlarged the scope. In 2002 an "immigration homecoming" (family reunion) was held in Treungen. Over 100 cousins from America attended the reunion. Kevin Tveit who has and is doing the American side of the genealogy has over 25,000 names of "cousins" originating in Treungen who are living or have lived in America. I now have nearly 1,000 names in the American Helgesen/son genealogy and cousin Egil in Norway has a figure that is nearing 80,000. The search goes on!

7/20/01 Revised 5/8/2004 and 1/27/2010

Helgesens and Tveits, all decendents of Tarjei Tarjeison Hatveit, grandfater of Russ's great-grandfather, Hølje Pålson Grovum. Truengen, Norway, 1993.

Egil Tveit and Russell Helgesen inside the home on the Moen farm, 1993.

Russ Helgesen's daughter, Mary, demonstrates the length of the bed from her great-great-grandfather's day in the very room on the Moen farm where her great-grandfather Jon Høljesen Grovum (John Helgesen) was born.

Russell Helgesen stands with his wife Lorraine née Sampson, on the site of the home (now gone) which once stood on the Grovum farm where Great-Grandfather Hølje was born.

Book II

The Family of Ten

CHAPTER 7

Doctor Elias, the First Born

Elias was the first-born son of John and Ingeborg (Docken) Helgesen, born February 2, 1866, in Moscow Township, Iowa County, Wisconsin. His education was all acquired in the district schools and he remained at home until he was twenty-one years of age. On January 26, 1886, he married Josephine Weiss, daughter of John and Susan (Winner) Weiss.

They had four children:

John Selmer	
Walter J. E.	b. 1891
Reuben L.	b. Jan. 5, 1893
William J.	b. Oct. 7, 1895

At that time, he matriculated at the College of Physicians and Surgeons at Keokuk, Iowa, and was graduated in medicine in 1893. While he was a student at the medical college, he studied under a preceptor and for two years before receiving his diploma, he had practiced in Badger, Iowa. After completing his professional training in Keokuk, Iowa, he practiced for two years in Forest City, Iowa. In 1895 he located in New Glarus where he opened a drug store in connection with his practice. Three years later he went into business with A. Godfrey, a pharmacist graduate of the University of Chicago. The Commemorative Biographical Record of 1901 states "His practice has been constantly on the increase until, at the present time, he has all that he can possibly attend to. Nature endowed him with a kindly, sympathetic nature that inspires his patients with confidence and makes his presence in the sick room most welcome.

The 1901 Record further reports:

> Both the Doctor and his wife are Lutherans in their religious faith but as the only English speaking church in New Glarus is the Methodist Church, they attend that and are active in its work. Dr. Helgesen belongs to the A. O. U. W. and the M. W. A. Through his Alma Mater, he is a member of the Alumni Medical Association of Keokuk, Iowa. Politically the Doctor is a staunch Republican and was a delegate to the State convention that nominated Gov. Bob La Follette. At present he is serving as justice of the peace and this attests to high esteem in which he is held, as he is the first person to hold office in New Glarus outside of the Swiss people. He is progressive and public spirited and has endeared himself to classy people.

Early in their marriage, Feen's sister Kate (Kathryn Weiss) came to live with them and help with their three little children. In 1895 a daughter, Lillian, was born to her and she and her daughter continued to live with them as part of their family until Lillian was old enough to leave home.

After the death of Elias's widowed mother, Ingeborg, in 1901, his youngest brother, Paul who was 11 years old at the time, came to live with them in New Glarus. At an early age Paul began to help out in the drug store and continued to make his home with them until he reached adulthood.

In 1917, Elias sold his drug store and medical practice in New Glarus and moved with his family to Evansville, Wisconsin, where he establish a very successful practice and continued throughout his life. In the 1920's he bought a farm near Magnolia as an investment. He never farmed it himself but rented it out to tenant farmers.

While in Evansville he earned a very fine reputation as a doctor and was often called on by neighboring doctors to assist them in very difficult cases. When his brother, Paul, and wife, Helga, were expecting their second child, their family doctor (Thompson) determined that the baby was hydrocephalic. In the midst of the birth process when Dr. Thompson was unable to deliver the child, he called on Elias who succeeded in delivering the still born child and was credited with saving the mother's life.

In 1937 Elias died at the age of 71. His family and friends from his church and city paid high tribute to one of their highly respected departed loved ones.

CHAPTER 8

Doctor Peter, Next in Line

Peter Andrew was the second son born to John and Ingeborg (Docken) Helgesen. He was born August 29, 1868, in Moscow Township, Iowa County, Wisconsin. He grew to manhood on the home farm and received his early education in the district schools. Later he took a course at the Northwestern Business College and Academy in Madison and in 1887 he entered Rush Medical College of Chicago, Ill. Subsequently he became a student in the College of Physicians and Surgeons in Keokuk, Iowa, from which he was graduated in March, 1891. In 1889 while in medical school he married Anna Dakken. Following graduation, he opened an office in Lake Mills, Iowa, where he continued to practice medicine throughout his entire life. The Mayo brothers were members of his graduating class and, at the time of graduation, invited him to join them in a medical practice which they were planning to establish. Later in life he sometimes said, "I wonder what my life would be like if I had joined the Mayo brothers?"

He and his wife, Anna had four children, two of whom died in infancy:

Walter Andrew	b. 1891
Lillian E.	b. Feb. 10, 1893 – d. July 20, 1896
Lillian J.	b. April 15, 1897 – d. June 25, 1897
Russell John	b. July 23, 1898

Anna died on June 14, 1911, after 15 years of illness with Bright's disease. A year and a half later, on November 12, 1912, Peter married Maude E. Thomas who had been a life long resident of Lake Mills. Two years later one son, Harold, was born to them.

Maude was born on October 20, 1879, the daughter of George Thomas who was the son of Joshua Thomas, the first white man to settle in what is now the Lake Mills area. Joshua settled on an 80 acre timber claim near Rice Lake which he had purchased from the U.S. government for $12 an acre.

One late fall day, Joshua needed to go to McGregor, Iowa, on foot to buy household staples for winter. He told his son, George, to take good care of the dwindling food supply in the log cabin and also good care of his sisters. His wife was not living. Winter set in early and Joshua was gone about three weeks. One day some Indians came to the door of the cabin, walked in and spied a bag of corn meal hanging up under the rafters. One young Indian jumped up on a chair and was about to grab the bag when young George gave him a blow to his jaw. This shocked the Indian, but he was also so impressed with George's bravery that he patted him on the back and shook his hand. Thereafter, the Indians brought food to the family every day until Joshua returned.

Times were hard for Joshua and it was difficult for him to eke out a living for his family. Inspired by the tales of the "gold rush of the '49ers," he loaded his wagon with his seven children and his worldly goods and started for California. The journey was very difficult. One of his oxen died on the trip and their milk cow had to pull the wagon. The milk that was not used for drinking was hung in a pail under the covered wagon. As the wagon rolled along, it was churned into butter. After two years and no "pot of gold," he returned with his family to Lake Mills. His farming career was now successful and eventually he owned as much as 360 acres.

Maude's father died when she was seven years old and left her mother with one married son, Charles, and three daughters. Maude and her twin-sister, Myrtle, and sister Mayme, were members of the first graduating class of the Lake Mills high school in 1896. After graduation, Maude attended Iowa State Teachers College, Cedar Falls, received her bachelor degree in didactics in 1898 and her master's degree in didactics in 1911. She came to the Lake Mills schools as assistant principal and soon was promoted to high school principal, which position she held for four years. Along with her position as principal, she taught advanced algebra and English. Later she taught Latin and English in the Waterloo High School and was principal of the Waukon, Iowa, public schools. From the age of seven she was a faithful member of Asbury Methodist church.

Dr. P. A. Helgesen, as he was known, established his practice in Lake Mills in 1891 following his graduation from medical school. In addition to his medical practice, he went into partnership with Albert Stensrud in the local drug store. He had his medical degree and now became a registered pharmacist. The drug store filled prescriptions and sold toiletries, gift items, school supplies, and Sunday School books. However, before long his medical practice grew to the extent that he didn't have time to be involved in the pharmacy, so he gave up that interest. For a short time his brother John (Dr. J. M. Helgesen) associated with him. Dr. P. A. was widely known throughout northern Iowa and was held in high esteem by members of his profession. His entire life was one of devoted service to his fellowmen. His practice in Lake Mills continued until his death in 1945.

He was highly respected and dearly loved. On May 11, 1941, Lake Mills paid tribute to him for the fifty years of faithful service to the community. The school auditorium was filled to capacity and tributes were given by various members of the community. The Lake Mills high

Dr. Peter shown in 1941 with Irving A. Nelson, the doctor's "first baby," and Arnold Burnell Grunhovd, the doctor's "last boy baby."

school band led a procession of people ranging in age from eight months to fifty years each wearing a banner, "I am a Helgesen baby." During his fifty year medical career, he had delivered about 2,000 babies. Dr. P. A. and Maude rode in a convertible in the parade as crowds of people watched along the street. A photographer from *Iowa News Flashes* was present to cover the Helgesen anniversary. The motion pictures of the event were shown widely throughout Iowa. During the celebration, he was portrayed as "a man of diverse talents, who met his patients on common ground, always ministering to them faithfully and with meticulous care and concern for their welfare. Many are the stories that could be told of his efforts through the years, starting with the horse and buggy days, the bobsled rides through drifted snow to deliver a baby, the midnight races for nearby hospital when emergency operations were necessary and many, many other pathos when the doctor was a valued friend." Many stories of his Lake Mills years were told. He became ill and in February 1901 was hospitalized. From his hospital bed he placed an ad in the paper reminding his patients to pay their accounts, as he was in need of the money they owed him.

When David Price, a local resident was born slightly ahead of schedule, Dr. P. A. rushed to the farm to find Mrs. Shirley Price alone and making a last minute attempt to get her bread ready for baking. He ordered her to bed, rolled up his sleeves, built a fire, put the bread in pans and placed them in the oven. Before he left, little David was in his crib, and the bread was out of the oven!

During his practice in Lake Mills, he was often in his office at 8:00 A.M. treating people and skipped dinner and worked until 8:00 o'clock in the evening. He commented that his long hours were worthwhile, however, because he had been able to cure many patients. After many years, his hands became badly scared from administrating X-ray treatments.

In addition to his medical practice he was also a very dedicated and prominent community leader. Beginning in 1898 he served as mayor for many years and was one of the founders and president and director of the local bank. He was one of the leaders in local republican circles, was from 1912 to 1914 chairman of the county republican central committee and was many times called to public office.

In his religious belief, he was a Lutheran and fraternally belonged to the Masons, the Independent Order of Odd Fellows, the Ancient Order of United Workmen, and the Modern Woodmen of America. In addition to his large private practice, he was a surgeon for the Chicago & Northwestern Railroad.

One of my memories as a youth on our farm near Mount Horeb, Wisconsin, was that every summer Uncle Pete came to visit us with Aunt Maude and Harold and stayed for several days. When Harold was little (maybe 6 to 8 years old), we were amazed at how spoiled he was. At that "advanced age" his mother would tuck a napkin under his chin and feed him his orange with a spoon! When he got older and was permitted to drive, he liked (and we loved it) to drive us boys to Mount Horeb in their "BIG" car. We were very loyal about never telling his dad how fast (and I do mean fast) he drove. It made him feel grown up and we enjoyed him and the ride.

Two things I remember especially about Uncle Pete: He smoked a pipe and loved to hold the bowl of the pipe in his hand and press it against our checks. It was really hot and he apparently enjoyed it much more than we did. At that time, when I was about 5 years old, I had given up drinking milk. It came about one day when my dad who liked to drink sour milk played a trick on me, switched his glass of sour milk with my glass of sweet milk. Never again, after that, would I touch any milk. Uncle Pete was concerned about my lack of milk intake and offered me a nickel a glass for drinking it. In those days that was big money but I still couldn't manage it. Those, however, were very memorable days!

One of the favorite stories, told within our family, was that of his helping to finance his nephew Francis' college education. Francis was the son of his brother, Dr. John. It was during the Great Depression and Francis, like most people, had no money but he very much wanted a college education. Being something of an entrepreneur and a very determined young man, he solicited his relatives for funds but no one had any money except Uncle Pete. Pete agreed to give him tuition for one semester and sent him a check but the check bounced! Uncle Pete explained that the bank had just gone broke, so he sent him a check on another bank. That check also bounced and again came the explanation that that bank, too, had gone under. So a third check was sent with the explanation that that check would not bounce because it was written on a new bank that he and several other businessmen had just started and there was money there to cover the check.

After 54 years of medical practice, Dr. Pete died of a massive heart attack on January 19, 1945, at the age of 76. He and Maude were visiting their son, Harold, in Phoenix, Arizona. He had been feeling very bad that day. It was on a weekend and a doctor who lived in the other half of their duplex was home. When Harold rushed to get his help, the doctor refused to come because "it was his day off and Pete was not his patient!" With no help from the doctor, Pete died. This really hurt Harold as he remembered all the times that his father had gone and helped anyone, anytime.

The Family Tree

Walter Andrew, son of Peter and Anna Helgesen was born in Lake Mills, Iowa, in 1891. He was baptized and confirmed in Salem Lutheran Church, Lake Mills, and graduated from the Lake Mills schools. He married Cora Sybilrud who was born Nov. 11, 1892, and died May 21, 1975. They had one son, Dale. After completing his education in 1925, Walter set up practice as an optometrist in Lake Mills. His office was over the Stensrud Drug store.

The one thing that everyone remembers about Walter was that he was always seen with a cigar in his mouth. In October 1943, which was during World War II, Stensrud Drug was out of cigars for the first time so Walter bought himself a pipe. In 2002, while attending a family reunion in Norway, I met a cousin who now lives in Lake Mills. He knew Walter very well as did everyone in Lake Mills. He said that because of his cigar smoking, everyone called him "Stuffy Helgesen." He also said that he fitted everyone with glasses who came to his office. The reason, he said, was that while Walter was examining their eyes, he always lit up a cigar and the smoke he blew obscured the patients' vision so they all believed that they needed glasses!

Russell John, son of Peter and Anna Helgesen was born July 23, 1898, in Lake Mills, Iowa. He, too was baptized and confirmed in Salem Lutheran Church and graduated from the Lake Mills schools. He married Fern Erica Flatland who was born June 23, 1901, in Slater, Iowa, and died in Lake Mills Dec. 21, 1941. Because they did not have funds with which to buy a cemetery plot, she was buried in the P. A. Helgesen family plot in Salem North Cemetery.

They had two children:

Gloria Jeanne   b. May 11, 1925 – d. Jan. 6, 1986
Marilyn Faye   b. April 25, 1931

During his lifetime, Russell struggled with many health problems and business reverses. He operated his own dry cleaning establishments in Lake Mills and other small Iowa towns as well as in Minneapolis, Minnesota. In 1939 his wife, Fern, suffered a stroke and when she died two years later, their daughters were 16 and 10 years of age. Later Gloria became one of the five original stewardesses of Northwest Airlines which flew out of Minneapolis. Several years after Fern's death, Russell married Hilda Walkup who had come from Panama. She had one son, John Walkup, and on September 9, 1946, a daughter Susan was born to them.

Russell died April 4, 1982, and donated his body to the University of Minnesota for medical research. His ashes, and those of hundreds of others from the U of M medical program, were buried in unmarked graves in Lakewood Cemetery, 3600 Hennepin Avenue, Minneapolis. Many years later, a woman by the name of Kerry Adelmann did an extensive search for the grave of her baby son who had died and had been cremated by the University of Minnesota 27 years earlier. As a result of her efforts, a large red granite monument with the inscription "University of Minnesota, dedicated to the memory of those whose generosity extended beyond life" was erected and dedicated May 8, 1999, in Lakewood Cemetery to those whose bodies (including Russell's) were cremated and their ashes were buried by the University of Minnesota. Hilda died in 1992.

In 2001 a very dramatic family event occurred which was made possible by all the genealogical information that family members had been supplying me. One night a young man called and identified himself as Paul Nelson. Somehow after a long search he had found out that he was a Helgesen and had located my phone number. He had learned that he was born to Susan on Jan. 13, 1964, and was the grandson of Russell and Hilda, however no one living was aware of his existence. During the first week of his life he had been placed for adoption by his mother to Paul and Marcia Nelson of Little Falls, Minn. I was able to put him in touch with his sister, Eva Rose, his uncle, Johnny Walkup, and his aunt Marilyn. What a shock in hearing from him after not knowing anything of his existence.

As a result, they were then able to get acquainted and catch up on family history including medical history which was important to Paul. At the time he was an attendant flying with American Airlines over seas out of New York. On Dec. 20, 2003 the story came to a tragic conclusion when he was murdered in his home in Philadelphia. On January 10, 2004, his two families gathered at First Lutheran Church, Little Falls for his memorial service.

Harold (Doc) Irving, son of Peter and Maude Helgesen was born in Lake Mills on Jan. 7, 1914. He also was baptized and confirmed in Salem Lutheran Church and graduated from the Lake Mills High School in 1931. He graduated with an associate in arts degree from Waldorf College, Forest City, Iowa, in 1933 and received his

Paul Nelson, second from right, visiting the Gabel family outside of Philadelphia. Russell and Lorraine Helgesen are far right and left with their daughter Mary Gabel and grandchildren Zoe and Tobias Gabel.

bachelor of arts degree from the University of Iowa in 1935. In 1937, he received a doctor of law degree from the University of Iowa Law School and was a member of Sigma Chi raternity and the Delta Theta Phi Law Fraternity. On June 12, 1938, he married Evelyn Mabel Arneson who was born in Joice, Iowa, on July 12, 1913. Following graduation, he was an attorney at law with a firm in Sioux City, Iowa, for six years. In 1943 he joined the FBI and retired as a senior resident special agent in 1965.

In 1965 he and his family moved to Florida where he sold real estate for a few years. On Sept. 18, 1977, his life came to a tragic end in Singer Island, when he died of choking while dining at a local restaurant. Evelyn died 24 years later on Feb. 5, 2001, in Jupiter, Fla.

They had two children:

John	b. Jan. 8, 1954
Mary Evelyn	b. May 5, 1955

August 27, 2004

CHAPTER 9

Doctor John and the Incredible Story of Earl

John Martin Helgesen, was born January 9, 1871, on a small farm in the Town of Moscow, Green County, Wisconsin. He was the third son of Norwegian immigrants, John and Ingeborg Helgesen who had come to America only ten years before. Following John's early education, he enrolled at the Lutheran Seminary in St. Paul, Minnesota. During his first year there he decided to follow in the footsteps of his two older brothers and become a medical doctor.

He attended the Upper Mississippi Medical School in Keokuk, Iowa. He interned at the Cook County Hospital in Chicago and did his post-graduate work at Rush Medical College. During that time he was part of a medical fraternity which met on the top floor of the old Sheraton Hotel in Chicago (because it was the cheapest room) to perform autopsies. At that time he was quite studious and was interested in criminal psychology. He spent a lot of time doing physical examinations of prisoners.

About 1895 (date unknown) he married Teresa Bakke whose family lived in the state of Oregon. On November 23, 1897, a son, Earl was born to them. When Earl was about 3 or 4 years old, John and Teresa were separated. She remarried and John lost touch with Earl. She and her husband, Stephen Temple, lived with Earl for a time in Michigan and then moved to Oregon where they had a daughter, Ruth. Earl's mother finally died in a hospital in Salem, Oregon, on

Christmas 1914 when Earl was 17. John never again saw his son but on July 25, 1934, Earl saw his father for the first time in his casket (see Earl Helgeson Story). About the turn of the century John married Margaret Burns who was born in Albany, Wisconsin, near New Glarus and was much younger than he. It was about this time that John followed the example of his two older brothers who were doctors and changed the spelling of his name from "son" to "sen." Earl, however used the "son" spelling throughout his life. Margaret was baptized at St. Patrick's Catholic Church in Albany. John was Lutheran and retained that faith throughout his life.

Around 1905 Margaret was a school teacher at St. Rose's Catholic School in Broadhead, Wisconsin. Her mother was the daughter of Richard Doyle. Margaret Burns Helgesen's father was a Union soldier in the Civil War. There is information about him in the State Capitol at Madison. Both the Doyles and Burnses came from Ireland in 1849 or 1850. They came first to Boston and then to Southern Wisconsin. John and Margaret had five children:

John Kermit	b. Ladysmith, Wis., Aug. 8, 1907
Francis Marion	b. Rice Lake, Wis., Nov.29, 1909
Paul Arnold	b. Menaqua, Wis., Aug. 30, 1914
Charles	b. Stevens Point, Wis., Jan. 5, 1919
Mona Mae	b. June 9, 1923

Doctor John's first private practice was established in Albany in 1905. His location there must have had something to do with Margaret's teaching school at nearby Broadhead at that time. This fact and the date of their marriage is not known at this time. When John Martin was born two years later they were in Ladysmith, Wisconsin, and two years after that when Francis was born, they lived in Rice Lake, Wisconsin. Five years later when Arnold was born, they were living in Menaqua, Wisconsin.

I do not have information on his medical practice for the next ten years but in the late 1920's he attempted to establish a practice in Mount Horeb. When the family moved to Mount Horeb, they were close to John's two younger brothers, Albert and Paul (my father). John was a very competent medical doctor but had difficulty establishing a practice because of alcohol problems.

In about 1928 when my youngest brother, Phil, was about two years old he became gravely ill with pneumonia. "Uncle Johnny" offered to come to our home on the farm and stay with us and treat Phil as best he could. At that time there were no drugs with which to treat pneumonia. I remember his telling us that the "crisis" would come on the tenth day and the pneumonia would break and he would get well or, if this did not occur , he would die! We prayerfully waited for the crisis and were so grateful to the Lord and Uncle Johnny when Phil recovered.

One morning during the time when he was with us, he told us about having a "vision" during the night: a large and bright star appeared in his bedroom. It was obviously a traumatic experience for him but we do not recall ever getting an explanation or interpretation. It was obvious, however, that for him this was a very profound spiritual experience.

During the several years that the family lived in Mount Horeb, Charles and Mona Mae used to visit us on the farm. They loved the farm life with all it's activities but we had difficulty comprehending how "dumb" these "city slickers" could be. Charles even called the cows "he!" As farm kids, we were amazed at their stupidity! But we had a lot of fun trying to mesh city and rural culture. During that same time cousin John (Dr. John's son) worked as a salesman for Wrigley Gum Company. He would stop and visit us when he was in the area. At that time my father, Paul, had quit smoking and had switched to chewing gum as a substitute. Each time John stopped by he would leave a 100-stick sample box of Wrigley's gum. Dad and we loved it!

Sometime around 1930 Dr. John and family moved to Madison and he attempted to establish a medical practice in Cassville, Wisconsin. Unbeknownst to anyone at that time they had moved to within a few blocks of his son, Earl, whom he had lost track of when he was 3 or 4 and had not seen in over 30 years. In July 1934 Earl found out about his father (see Earl Helgeson story) and he and Margaret planned a reunion. Several days before the proposed reunion John suddenly died on July 25, 1934, of a massive stroke while walking down the street of Cassville. He never saw his son but

Earl first saw his father in his casket at the funeral at Perry Lutheran Church, Dalyville which is about 20 miles southwest of Madison. He was buried in the cemetery next to the Perry Church for which he had carried stones when it was built when he was a young man. His tombstone reads, "John Helgesen, Served Mankind." Margaret Burns Helgesen died in Minneapolis in 19?? and is buried in St. Mary's Roman Catholic Cemetery at 46th and Chicago Avenue South in Minneapolis, Minnesota.

The family Tree

John Kermit, son of John and Margaret, was born in Ladysmith, Wisconsin, on August 8, 1907. As a child and young man he was known as Kermit but later began using the name John. He married Evelyn Bronson (b. 1916) in Fort Dodge, Iowa, in 1945. Evelyn had a son, Gregg Stuart by a previous marriage to a man named Erickson. Until their marriage Gregg was ostensibly raised by two great-aunts and uncles until he was six. When Gregg was about ten, John adopted him and gave him the name Helgesen.

When Gregg (b.1939) was 20 years old, John and Evelyn had a daughter, Lisa Burns, who graduated from Gustavus Adolphus College, St. Peter, Minnesota, and has a daughter, Amy Wolf (b.1985). John died in 1977 and Evelyn spent a number of years in a nursing care facility in Gibson City, Illinois, and died December 23, 2000. Gregg is now a practicing clinical Psychologist in Champagne, Illinois, and his wife, Marne George Helgesen, is a member of the faculty at the University of Illinois at Urbana-Champaign.

The family describes John and Evelyn this way: "Evelyn was a truly beautiful woman. She was a model when she was young. My uncle John was a very funny man, and called her Pete, which she was known as all her life."

They had two children:

    Gregg Erickson   b. June 8, 1939
    Lisa Burns   b. April 1960

Francis Xavier second son of John and Margaret, was born Francis Marion in Rice Lake, Wisconsin, November 29, 1909. He went to the University of Wisconsin in the class of 1933. It was during the Great Depression and he, like most people had no money. Being an entrepreneur and a determined young man, he solicited his relatives but no one had any money except his Uncle Pete (Doctor in Lake Mills, Iowa). Pete agreed to give him tuition for one semester and sent him a check but the check bounced! Uncle Pete explained that the bank had just gone broke so he sent him a check on another bank. That check also bounced and again came the explanation that that bank, too, had gone under. So another replacement check was sent with the explanation that that check would not bounce because it was written on a new bank that he and several other businessmen had just started. Francis's aunt owned a house at 543 Campbell in Madison which he managed while an undergraduate student. Around this time he changed his name to Francis Xavier, reportedly because he wanted to go into politics and he thought it was a more impressive name. (His name Marion came from a teacher whom his father had admired.) Cecilia Stella Kowalewska was a social worker and she and several friends rented an apartment at the house that Francis managed. They were married May 6, 1933, in Chicago, Illinois. She was born November 20, 1903, in Winona, Minnesota. She graduated from Winona State Teacher's College. They moved to Minneapolis in 1934. Francis worked for a while at the Ford plant in St. Paul, and later as an instructor for the Civil Conservation Corps (CCC) in Bemidji, Minnesota, and as a sales rep for Wrigley Chewing Gum Company.

He went to St. Paul Law School (now the William Mitchell College of Law), and passed the bar in 1941. He then worked for the National Labor Relations Board (NLRB). In 1945, he became head of the New York Region of the NLRB, in Rochester, New York. He returned to private practice in 1947. A newspaper article reports, "Francis X. Helgesen Quits NLRB in Protest of the Taft-Hartly Law." He practiced labor law until he died of a stroke on July 16, 1983. Francis and Cecilia had three children:

Barbara Lynn	b. Mpls., Minn., June 9, 1938
Stephanie Margaret	b. Mpls., Minn., Oct. 12, 1943
Timothy John	b. Buffalo, NY. May 25, 1946

Paul Arnold, third son of John and Margaret, was born in Menaqua, Wisconsin, August 30, 1914. He was always called Arnie. He contracted polio when he was eleven. Francis always said that Arnie would have been the tallest of all the boys, but his spine was severely affected by the polio so he was very hunched, wore a leg brace, and walked with a severe limp. He married Hermoine Kolstad (b. Aug. 13, 1923) on June 23, 1943. They had three children:

Michael Paul	b. Mpls., Minn., May 15, 1944
John Thomas	b. Mpls., Minn., April 29, 1945
Mary Margaret	b. Mpls., Minn., Oct. 1, 1946

Arnold died on August 10, 1989.

Charles Richard, the fourth son of John and Margaret, was born in 1919. In 1958 he earned a Doctor of Rhetoric degree from the University of Denver and then returned to Western Michigan University in Kalamazoo where he taught for 30 years. He married Anne Marie LaFollette June 22, 1947. She died Nov. 11, 1976. They had five children:

Sally	b. St. Cloud, Minn., July 1, 1948
Rebecca	b. Denver, CO, May 21, 1951
Martha	b. Burlington, VT, Feb. 13, 1955
Charles, Jr.	b. Kalamazoo, MI, Nov. 10, 1958
CeCe	b. Kalamazoo, MI, Dec. 10, 1961

Charles married Luanne Morey in January 1983. He died April 26, 1997.

Mona Mae, the last child and only daughter of John and Margaret was born June 9, 1923. She married William Elsham in 1945. He sold insurance for Prudential Insurance Company. They had four children:

Nancy	b. Mpls, Minn., Aug. 8, 1946
Susan	b. Mpls, Minn., July 25, 1949
William, Jr.	b. Mpls, Minn., Dec. 13, 1951
Robert Burns	b. Mpls, Minn., Dec. 4, 1953

Mona Mae and Bill were divorced and she then married Dr. Richard Zarling.

July 31, 2002; revised January 26, 2004

The Incredible Story of Earl Adrian Helgeson*

When Earl was perhaps three or four years old, his father, John, and mother, Teresa Bakke, separated. Later, his father married Margaret Burns who was not interested in keeping in touch with Earl and in time all contact ceased and his father lost touch with him completely. In the mean time Earl's mother married Stephen Temple and they lived for a period of time in Lansing, Michigan. From this time until 1914 when Earl was 17 years old information is sketchy and uncertain. After a short time they moved to "small acreage a couple of miles east of Silverton, Oregon" in a small wooden two-room house.

Note: Russell B. Helgesen, Earl's cousin, wrote this account based on the "legend" he heard as a child, on the written memoirs of Earl's half-sister, Ruth Temple [1996], and on a conversations with his widow, Marguerite, at Methodist Health Center in Madison, July 21, 1996. She was then 93 years old and was experiencing failing memory. She has since been deceased.

His half-sister, Ruth was born when Earl was about 11 years old. It was apparent, however that his mother was not in good health, they were very poor, and Earl lived a very difficult life. His schooling was very limited. For a while he attended Evans Valley School with Hilda Nerison as teacher and he managed to complete the grades by age 16. During this time it seems that his stepfather exited from the scene and he and his stepsister and mother, who was in poor health, lived with their grandmother, Nicolina Bakke in Oregon. After a lingering illness, his mother died in a hospital in Salem, OR, on Christmas, 1914 when Earl was 17. He continued to live with his grandmother until she died of pneumonia in March of 1915.

Earl soon enlisted in the military and served in World War I. When he returned to Portland, OR, he met Marguerite Dutcher who lived with her parents in Portland. Her father was a Methodist minister. They were married in 1924. Following their marriage, Marguerite finished school and then worked while Earl got his education. He was granted scholarships from Oregon State and the University of Washington where he earned his Bachelor's degree. He then enrolled at the University of Wisconsin, Madison, and earned his Ph.D. While studying for his Ph.D., he did some teaching at the UW. In one of his classes he had a student by the name of Helgesen (supposedly one of Sever's granddaughters, but I have not been able to identify the person). The time was about 1932–34. At the time neither Earl nor his father knew that they were living only a few blocks apart in Madison. Because of Earl's difficult life and with no memory of his father, he expressed no desire to locate his father. Dr. John, however, as well as our entire family always wondered, "where his lost son was."

After class one day, this "Helgesen" student mustered the courage to ask him if per chance he was the "lost son." After receiving his father's address and phone number, he called and talked to Margaret. At the time Dr. John was in Cassville attempting to establish a medical practice. Earl and Margaret agreed that they would have their long awaited reunion during Dr. John's next scheduled weekend return to Madison. Margaret then wrote to Dr. John and told him that she had "a big surprise waiting for him when he returned home." He wrote back, "Could this be the answer to my prayers?" While walking down the street in Cassville the next day, Dr. John suffered a fatal stoke! The first time that Earl saw his father after all those years was in his casket. The funeral was held at Perry Lutheran Church, Daleyville and he was buried in that cemetery on January 25, 1934.

After receiving his Ph.D., Earl joined the faculty of North Dakota State University, Fargo, North Dakota, became head of the Botany Department and taught there for 35 years. After retirement, he and Marguerite moved to Tucson, Arizona, where they lived until his tragic drowning in their family swimming pool in 1979.

CHAPTER 10

Thomas and Henry, a Bundle of Tragedy

My knowledge of Thomas is very limited and few written records exist. He was the fourth son of John and Ingeborg Helgesen's family of ten children. At an unknown date he married a widow, Mary Brats, who had one daughter by a previous marriage. To Thomas and Mary was born one son:

Benjamin J.   b. Town of Moscow, Wis., Nov. 2, 1910

In November of 1920 Thomas died at the early age of 47 years. Because this was just a month after I was born, I do not have any personal knowledge of him. However, I have some remembrance of his son Benjamin who was ten years older than I, and I also remember his mother, Mary. She was a very religious person and loved to drive a Model A Ford. She and Benjamin would usually come once a year to visit us on our farm near Mount Horeb. We always talked about how much fun it was to see them driving along the highway and singing Gospel Hymns. Like his father, Benjamin died at the early age of 53 years. Thus ends the saga of Thomas Olaus who left this earth without any descendents.

The story of Uncle Henry is a story of untold tragedies! Henry was the fifth son to be born to John and Ingeborg Helgesen on their farm in the Township of Moscow, Iowa County, Wisconsin. His life span was

Henry and Hannah Helgeson

short. Born on May 19, 1876 he died just 51 years later on Oct. 28, 1927. He was really an itinerant farmer and never owned any land. He rented at least five different farms and moved often.

Henry's tragedies began with the death of his first wife Anna Amundson less than two years after their marriage. They were married on Nov. 16, 1897, and without children, she died on Aug. 27, 1899. Two years later on the 21st of September, 1901, Henry married Hannah Catherine Wilkens who was the daughter of immigrant parents who had come from Ireland and lived in Arena, Iowa County,

Wisconsin. To their union were born eleven children including one set of twins. Only eight of the children lived to adulthood. Hazel Colletta died when she was 4½ years old; Lemon Vivian died at the age of nine months; and Violet Thelma lived only one day.

Beulah T.	Blue Mounds, Wis., March 16, 1904
Lemon Vivian	Blue Mounds, Wis., Jan 16, 1906
Leon Vivian	Mazomanie, Wis., Dec 15, 1908
Irvin Stanley	Mazomanie, Wis., July 16, 1910
Glen Joyce	Blue Mounds, Wis., Sept 15, 1912
Lela Maxine	Vermont Twp, Wis., March 12, 1915
Lynette Eldred	Vermont Twp, Wis., March 12, 1915
Hazel Colletta	Vermont Twp, Wis., Jan 13, 1917
Mabel Twila	Vermont Twp, Wis., July 26, 1918
Violet Thelma	Arena, Wis., March 29, 1921
Delbert	Arena, Wis., May 25, 1922

The decade of the 20s was a time of unspeakable tragedy for the family. On the 29th of March Henry's wife, Hannah, gave birth to a baby son, Lemon Vivian, who died the next day. Just four months later on July 29, their daughter, Hazel Collette died at the tender age of 4½. Less than one year after that tragedy, Delbert was born on May 25, 1922, and his mother, Hannah, died just two weeks later. With the help of their older children, Henry carried on as best he could under those very difficult circumstances. His oldest daughter, Beulah, was married in 1924 and shortly after that, because of Henry's failing health, came to live with him to do the house work and care for the younger children.

Henry did not regain his health and died on Oct. 28, 1927. To add to that tragedy, Beulah died just two month later, on Dec. 28 at the age of 23. When Henry died, I (Russell B. Helgesen), was only seven years old but still remember his funeral. According to the custom at that time, the service was held in his home. Blocks of ice were placed beneath the casket to cool and preserve the body. The open casket was placed between the living room and the parlor. Rev. E. R. Anderson, pastor of Mount Horeb Lutheran Church, conducted the service. I can still see him standing behind the open casket, reading scripture and singing the old familiar hymn, "I am but a stranger here, heaven is my home. Earth is a desert drear, heaven is my home. What'er my earthly task, I shall reach home at last. Heaven is my fatherland, heaven is my home."

The only contact that I had with Henry's family since my childhood was nearly 50 years latter when Delbert's daughter, Rose Ann, made contact with me in 1991. Having received information from one of her relatives on our family tree that I had compiled, she began correspondence with me.

In her letters that followed, she shared a good deal of personal information about her family. On April 12, 1992, she wrote,

> Delbert's mother, Hannah Catherine Wilkinson, died when Delbert was about two weeks old and then just five years later, his oldest sister, Beulah, and his father died. Aunts and uncles wanted to take care of the younger children but the older ones refused to have the family split up so they raised each other and always remained close to one another, even in later years. All Delbert's brothers and sisters are now dead except for Mabel and Lynette.
>
> Delbert married my mother, Marjorie Cliff, when she was only 18 years old. Just three months later he was drafted into the army and was shipped overseas where he was stationed in Italy as a half-track driver. At the end of the war when he was discharged, he and his wife, Marjorie, lived together for only a few weeks and then split up. I was the only child of that marriage and I had little contact with my father until I was over 30 years of age. My relationship with my father 'was poor.'
>
> Delbert later married Ada Hale who had two children, Ann and Tom, by a previous marriage. During their marriage, Delbert and Ada had two daughters, Dell Mae, on Jan. 3, 1957, and Suzan Lea, on March 2, 1962. Della lives in St. Peter, Minn., and Suzan in Mobile, Alabama.
>
> My father was always in poor health and was not really able to work very much. They lived on his VA pension and took care of children for additional income. He would also do carpentry work when he could find odd jobs. Delbert and Ada were very

active in church and helped build their church in Mobile. They were very kind and loving people. I wish I had known them better but I value the few years we did share. I don't think Delbert ever knew how much he had to be proud of in his grandfather and especially his grandfather's Civil War record. Delbert probably knew less about our family than I do.

So ends the story of Henry Edward Helgeson and his family. With the help of Rose Ann Phelps and Maurene England, a cousin by marriage, I have identified nearly 100 of Henry's descendents. All family members would have their own stories to tell, each would speak of joys and sorrows, challenges and blessings, but all would unfold their common tale of tragedy.

CHAPTER 11

Sever Helgesen and his wife, Mary

Sever, Farmer and Entrepreneur

Sever was the sixth child born to John and Ingeborg (Docken) Helgesen. He was born on March 5, 1882, while they were living on their farm in the Town of Moscow, Dane County, Wisconsin. Sever died an unfortunate death at the early age of 52 as a result of what his doctor brother thought was a 'botched" surgery for ulcers. He left behind his widow, Mary (pictured above with Sever), and eleven children ranging from twenty-eight to four years of age.

When Sever was only twelve, his father died suddenly of a heart attack. At that time three of his older brothers had left for medical school and the seven children who were still at home ranged from nineteen to four years of age. Little is known about the life of Ingeborg and her family during the next seven years, at which time tragedy struck again when Ingeborg died as a result of a fall down the stairs during a party at the home of one of their neighbors, the Homme family.

In due time, Sever became weary of farming and decided to follow his three brothers in the medical profession. At about twenty years of age, he enrolled in the Marquette Medical College in Milwaukee, Wisconsin, to become a pharmacist. While there he played in the John Philip Sousa band. After a year, he and Mary Kunnard were married and when their first child, Edna, was born he quit medical school and became a farmer. To him and Mary were born eleven children:

Edna Alvina	March 26, 1906
Marvin Fredlein	September 30, 1907
Hilda	September 12, 1908
Lillian	October 21, 1912
Elmer	September 12, 1914
Lester A.	September 2, 1917
Merwood	September 16, 1919
Alvin	May 23, 1924
Robert	1926
Donald	March 8, 1928
Richard	1930

His first farm was in Pine Bluff, Wisconsin. He was not satisfied with farming and after a short time decided that he wanted to try the International Harvester business. To make this possible, the boys took over the farm. Sever was a very friendly person but was not a good business man. Things did not go well for him and in due time Marvin and Elmer took over the business. Edna's husband, Carl Beyers, and Sever's wife, Mary, went around collecting accounts that were due but that did not go well as they were running a losing operation. When World War II began and the rest of Sever's sons went off to war, Elmer kept the business running until the boys came home.

Marvin and Elmer were under 18 years but the implement company trusted them and the business kept going. When Elmer took over, he worked under the supervision of Bill Cain who was the Regional Manager for International Harvester Company. For several months, Kenneth Helgesen (Paul's son) worked for them for $5 a week plus room and board but shortly left to work for his uncle Albert on the farm for $10 a week.

What now follows is a personal account of those years which was written by Sever's son, Elmer, who was very much involved in the story he now tells.

> For many years I have been hoping to sit down and write some history of our family, and now that I am 82 years of age and semi-retired, I am going to take some time to do that. Our family is getting smaller by the passing of five of our members. Our family was about average size for farm families, as most members were needed on the farm for there was always work for everyone. We were all born on a farm except Edna, who was born when our father was in medical school in Milwaukee. When Richard, who was the last to be born because of mother's age, it was decided to take her to the hospital for the delivery. Those of us born on the farm were delivered by our uncle Elias, as our father had 3 brothers that were doctors. Elias lived closest and in those days doctors made house calls, very few people went to a doctor's office. The cost for the delivery of a child in those days was $50 but I doubt if our uncle ever collected, as people in those days weren't so money conscious. As we were all born between 1906 to 1930, we enjoyed a life that will never be enjoyed by generations to follow. That was a chapter in history that will never be repeated. Those were the years of a really free country.
>
> We didn't need a license to fish or hunt or drive a car. There was no age limit for those things. We did not need a permit to build a home or any other structure. We paid no income tax, no sales tax, no gas tax, or any other tax other than real estate tax which was small as there were no snowplows needed for the roads as auto mobiles were not used in the winter. The roads were graded by horse power and about the only gasoline needed

was to operate a small gas engine to pump water when there wasn't enough wind to operate the windmill.

We had eight horses to do the field work and pull the wagons in the summer and the sleighs in the winter. Mother had her own special driving horse and buggy to go to town shopping. The farm grew all the feed for the horses so there was no need to buy gasoline for operating the farm.

The farm provided us with nearly all our food. We raised wheat that was taken to a flour mill once a year to supply all the flour needed. A large garden provided all the vegetables for winter and summer.

We had an orchard to provide us with apples, cherries and grapes which were stored or canned and kept in the basement for winter use. The woods were full of wild berries that Mother would gather and can for a year's supply. We raised our own meat and milk. The only things we had to purchase were salt, sugar and spices and as we had more eggs then were needed, the surplus was taken to a grocery store and traded for those items. There was always some cash left over. Living on a farm during the years of the depression of the 30s was a great advantage over city people.

In 1930 our father went to Janesville to enter into the farm equipment business and it was up to the boys to run the farm. Edna was married by then and Hilda and Lillian worked at the Parker Pen plant in Janesville and were able to ride there with our father each day. Everything was going along well until one day in March of 1934 when our father, who had suffered many years with stomach illness, became very ill and went to Madison to a clinic to secure some relief from it. On the way home his stomach burst and he was rushed to the hospital but it was too late and a few days later he passed away at the age of 52. He didn't realize that his passing was to change the lives of all of us.

He left us a farm equipment business that was to start the brothers on the road to a way of life that would never have been possible without our father's efforts to keep the business operating with great difficulties during the depression years.

Marvin, Lester, and I (Elmer) were operating a 320 acre farm north of Janesville. It was decided that I was to leave the farm and go to Janesville to manage the business and our mother was to be my partner. My salary was to be $5 a week. We had one employee who was a mechanic and would receive $10 a week.

The business was heavily in debt as most businesses were as the result of the great depression of the 30s and money was almost impossible to borrow.

The first year was very difficult but we were very fortunate that our father had made many farm friends in the area and as he had lots of farming experience to help farmers and sell them the farm equipment they needed. That was our best asset.

Because of Hilda and Lillian's employment at the Parker Pen Plant they were able to provide the family with groceries and other things needed. They paid the $30 a month rent on the home that the family was living in and as six brothers were in school it took most of their salaries to keep the bills paid, as the business had not yet shown a profit. But we were fortunate that the International Harvester Company sent a territory representative to work with us four days a week. Without his assistance it would have been very difficult to keep the business operating successfully.

We had very little cash to work with and pay the $30 a month rent on the building we were occupying, but one day a farmer and his son came in and told us he would like to help us get started. His name was Chas Deitrich and was a good friend of our father. He purchased a new 10-20 tractor and plow for $650 which was to be the only tractor we where to sell that year. We made a profit of $120 on the deal and that was the first real money we were to have to pay our rent and expenses for months to come.

We made it through 1934 and business then looked more promising for 1935. Marvin gave up farming and came to town to join us and replace the one employee who had decided to retire. The brothers that were in school were able to help on weekends and were to receive a little spending money for their help.

The year of 1936 was an improvement over 1935. Farmers were coming into more money and needed new machinery for their farms. Our first business venture was to be experienced.

Mr. Kane, the Harvester co-representative, asked me to go to Madison to the company branch office. We went to the office of the branch manager and Mr. Kane asked him how many new tractors were on hand. We were told there were 26 of different sizes. Mr. Kane told him we would take all of them.

This took the branch manager by surprise and could hardly believe what Mr. Kane was saying but he agreed to the deal if we could get them out of the warehouse in two days as the other dealers would be asking for them.

We took as many people as we could find to Madison to drive them back to Janesville, a distance of 40 miles. The top speed of those tractors was three miles an hour as they all had steel wheels. Tractors did not come with rubber tires in those days. It caused a lot of attention along the way. We lined them all in a row in our building and when our farmer customers came in, they could hardly believe what they were seeing but Mr. Kane's intuition proved to be right, as in six months they were all sold.

Our first big setback was to come in the spring of 1937. The building we were renting was sold and we would have to move. After searching all over town the only building available was a large abandoned church a block up the street. We were able to purchase it for $3,500. After three months of remodeling, we were ready to move in. The depression was finally ending and the business was starting to prosper and we were able to buy the home on Chatham Street that we were living in. The brothers were able to join in the business and each was given a job in the operation. We also had four other employees. This was to be the year that we were to begin our first business expansion as one day an older gentleman and his son came in and asked to see me in our office. He informed me that he was in the farm implement business in Footville and was selling Minneapolis Moline farm equipment but his son would like to buy a McCormick Deering F1 tractor from us. I assured him that would be OK and we closed the deal.

As we left the office, he looked around our main showroom floor and parts department and then turned to me and said, "It looks like you have too much help." He didn't know they were mostly all brothers doing their job. The next statement took me by surprise, "Why don't you come out to Footville and buy me out as I would like to retire."

When I went home that night, I told my mother of his offer. Lester had taken on a car agency, selling a small car and truck named Willys in his spare time. That would be a good chance for him to get started in his own business. The next morning Lester, Mother, and I went out and looked the place over. It looked like a good deal so we went to the Footville Bank and borrowed $2,500 which was what Mr. Wilke was asking for the building and business inventory and Lester was now in business. He had a good business that year and needed some extra help so Merwood went out to work for him. Merwood bought a motorcycle and became the town's police officer to increase his income.

The next year Mr. Kane, the Harvester Company representative, told me the Harvester dealer in Orfordville was complaining that we were taking most of his business. Mr. Kane's reply was, "why don't you sell out to them?" Mol Brunsell's reply was that he would if they would come over and ask him. The next day Merwood, Mother, and I went to see him and we made a deal for $3,500 which we borrowed from the Orfordville Bank. As the building was not in the deal, we located an abandoned small warehouse for $800 and with some remodeling, Merwood was now in business. After a few years of good management, he was to build a new modern building on the edge of town.

We now had three businesses that were all prospering until 1941 when the war started and International Harvester Company was required to stop manufacturing farm machinery and start production of motor trucks and tanks for the army.

I decided to go back to farming. I purchased a 320-acre farm five miles from Evansville. I sold my share of the Janesville business to Marvin who took on the Oliver franchise as that company had no war contracts. He was able to purchase farm equipment from them and had a very successful business.

A short time later, Merwood joined the army, Alvin joined the air force, and Robert enlisted in the marines. Merwood asked me to manage his implement business. It wasn't too difficult, as I had plenty of help to run my farm.

In 1944 Merwood came home from the army and took over his business again. In 1945 Alvin came home from the air force as the war had ended and he and Robert, who was wounded in the Battle of Iwo Jima and was released from the marines next, were to join the Evansville business. In the early 1950s Donald purchased Lester's business in Footville. Richard started a marina next to Marvin's implement business. Some years later he built a garage south of Janesville and sold automobiles. As years went by automobile and steel building businesses became the main business ventures and remain so today.

In 1949 we were to start a new enterprise. The eight brothers formed a new corporation and purchased a 425-acre farm near Albany, as we all had farming experience. This was to be a new and different experience. The farm has many acres that were covered with large oak trees. We hired two large bulldozers to dig them up and we salvaged hundreds of logs from them and in 60 days we had 400 acres of corn planted which was seed corn for the DeKalb Co. The return from this crop was enough to pay for the farm. When winter came, we set up a saw mill to turn the logs into lumber with which to build a new farm house and other buildings. We also purchased an AO Smith Harvestore silo which was later to become another business venture. The AO Smith Harvestore Co. asked Lester to sell and erect Harvestores. The next year, Merwood closed his implement business and joined Lester. They were soon to become the largest AO Smith Agency in the world."

So ends Elmer's family story. Some of us cousins watched this fascinating story unfold and will now relate some of the stories about Lester which became legend.

Following World War II the word was "scarcity." New cars had not been manufactured for several years. Farm machinery was hard to find and most other things were in short supply. About that time Lester came on the scene with a business that he established in Footville, Wisconsin. He called on farm machine dealers who had a very short supply of farm machinery. His question to them was "what are you going to do with the machines that you have?" Their answer was that they would distribute them to dealers on as fair a basis as possible. Lester's advice to them was that their plan would not work; nobody would believe that he was being fair and this would bring them only trouble. "Sell them all to me and I will do the distribution!" So word got around that if you want machines, go to Lester Helgesen. His business flourished.

As the story continues, Lester called on a certain dealer who had about a hundred pump jacks. When the dealer admitted that no one was buying pump jacks any more, Lester bought them for a song. At another dealer he found a hundred freezers which didn't sell because they had no motors and at that time motors were not available. Again he bought them for a song. Ingeniously he took the motors off the pump jacks, put them on the freezers and again made a sizable profit.

As the years went by and he prospered, he built a "mansion" of a home. At one point he was contacted by a tour company that had passengers who wanted to see his home and they asked him to arrange dinner for the group. Instead of referring them to a restaurant he enlisted his family to serve them in his home, again for a neat profit.

His interest at one point turned to collecting cars. His prize was several presidential limousines. On the edge of town in Janesville he built a building and started a car museum. Business did not go well and he was loosing considerable money. About that time the city concluded that his sign was in violation of building codes and closed him down. This was just what he wanted to stop his losing operation. In turn, he changed the museum into a private car show room where people were only admitted by appointment and he began to turn a profit.

A number more of such tales could be told but we will end the saga here. Lester had many ups and downs in various ventures but was most proud of his Harvestore Silo business and laid claim to owning and operating the largest Harvestore business in the world! In 1992 his story was cut short when he died at the early age of 75.

Sever was the seventh son in the John Helgesen family of eleven children. Left without a father at the age of 12, he struggled to get an education in the medical field and then spent most of his short life in farming and business. When he died at the early age of 52, he left behind eleven children and "countless" offspring whose stories you have just read. In many ways, his story is a colossal story of success which is held in high esteem as a significant piece of *The Helgesen Story*.

CHAPTER 12

A Model Farmer and Two Sisters

Of the 11 children that John and Ingeborg Helgesen had, only two of them were girls. Mary J. was number seven and Clara was number nine. Mary was born Feb 2, 1877, in the township of Moscow, Iowa Co., Wisconsin, and Clara Mathilde was born in the same county, on the same farm on November 1, 1884. Both Mary and Clara married farmers and lived in the Mount Horeb area. Because I have very little information on these families and had only limited personal contacts with them during my childhood, their stories will be brief.

Mary's Story

Mary was joined in marriage to John E. Johnson, a farmer in the Dane County, Wisconsin, area. To them were born ten children.

Earl	January 22, 1902
Irene	June 29, 1903
James M.	June 11, 1905
Aldro	July 24, 1907
Hazel	Sept 2, 1909
Alvin	December 2, 1912
Milford	March 21, 1914
Marvin	March 29, 1917
Russell V.	May 19, 1920
Janice Charleen	1922–1922

Most, if not all of their married lives were spent on a farm south of Mount Horeb, near Black Earth. This was in a very hilly area and the farm was not very productive. Their son, Russell, and I shared a common name and were the same age so it gave us a common bond. On occasions our family would visit them on a Sunday. We were always invited for dinner and spent the afternoon visiting.

Mary was very congenial but a bit naïve and my dad used to take advantage of that and was given to teasing her. This was back in the days when Oleomargarine was being produced in Wisconsin and was a sensitive issue for dairy farmers. My dad was a broad minded farmer who believed that if people wanted to eat Oleo instead of butter, the farmers should produce it. For one Sunday afternoon dinner Aunt Mary had chosen to serve Oleo. Dad was aware that at that time, Oleo was made from lard and colored artificially. To take advantage of her naivety, Dad very seriously asked, "Mary, do you know what Oleo is made of?" She had no idea, so Dad informed her that it was made from dead hogs! She didn't realize that lard couldn't come from live hogs and so in horror said, "Johnny, we're never going to eat Oleo again!"

Their marriage finally ended when, on the 17th of September, 1948, Johnnie died at the age of 71. Twelve years later on April 16, 1960, Mary completed her earthly journey at age 81. They left a family including 14 grandchildren.

Clara Mathilde's Story

Clara was married to Jacob Edmund Stolen who lived on a farm in the Mount Horeb, Wisconsin, area and was a member of the large Kittleson family. A number of the Kittleson boys, including Jake, changed their name to Stolen. The name came from their farm in Norway. To them were born these four children:

Roy Marvin	March 3, 1904
Ida Elmira	August 2, 1906
Torris Jerome	April 8, 1909
Cora Marie (AKA Betty)	October 1, 1912

Jake was a "gentleman farmer," a real entrepreneur. About all I know about him was that he started by buying one farm and cultivated it successfully. In fact so successfully that he bought a second farm and a third and finally a forth. In each case he financed the purchase by mortgaging the previous farms. In the end this type of financing caught up with him and he lost all the farms. His lifestyle of big cars and "high on the hog" living was finally a thing of the past and financially he never recovered from the losses even though he never gave up believing that, given a little more time, he would be rich. Clara died on Nov. 17, 1949, at the early age of 65 and Jake died four years later on Sept. 5, 1953, at the age of 71.

Albert, The Model Farmer

Of all the family of John and Ingeborg, Uncle Albert was the closest to our family. When he was 7 years old, he was left without a father and his mother died when he was 14. He and his younger brother, Paul, who was three years younger than he, had to face life without parents at this early age.

Both of these young boys lived with friends or relatives in New Glarus, Wisconsin, until they were old enough to go out on their own. Albert, by circumstances became a farmer while Paul spent most of his early years working in his brother Elias's drug store in New Glarus where he was a practicing country doctor. By circumstances of which I am not aware, they both married sisters (Alpha and Helga) from nearby Kittleson Valley. Albert and Alpha, who were married three days after Christmas in 1912, were the parents of three children who in turn were our double cousins.

Kennell Jordan	December 11, 1913
Agnes Ione	August 3, 1915
Crystal June	June 27, 1924

Following their marriage, Albert and Alpha bought their first and only farm from Kittle Kittleson, who was Alpha's father. It was the farm on which Alpha had been brought up. Though they farmed it

Brothers Albert and Paul Helgesen who married sisters Alpha and Helga Kittleson

successfully, the Depression during the 30s was too much for them and they were not able to make the payments according to the terms of the contract. Because most farmers were in the same predicament, Kittle agreed that they should pay only as much as they were able and that the amount would be applied toward the interest which was probably seven percent. When the depression ended, Kittle forgave all the arrears and they were able to keep the farm.

During their lives, Albert and Paul had a very close relationship but had very differing philosophies of life. Both were farmers. Albert was very conservative while Paul was more progressive. This showed itself especially when it came to their attitude toward formal education. Because of the death of his parents when he was a teenager, Albert had at most a seventh grade education. By the time Kennell had completed grade school, Albert saw no need for him to continue his formal education. His argument was that Kennell was his only son who would receive his farm from him and for that, he needed no further education. And as far as Agnes and June were concerned, they would marry and have families so further education for them would be a waste of time and money. By the time Kennell finished grade school, he had proven his creative and artistic abilities. His uncle Paul tried unsuccessfully to convince Albert that Kennell should go on to high school. On that subject they had very heated arguments but Albert prevailed and Kennell spent the rest of his life as a farmer with no further education.

As a farmer, Kennell was very successful but throughout life he struggled with the use of the special talents with which he had been gifted. With no formal education, he blossomed in many areas. He had a great deal of musical talent and taught himself to play the violin. In their living room they had a player piano and how we loved it when they put one of the playing roles into the piano and we could watch the keys move as it played a variety of beautiful music. Kennell also did very well as an artist, producing paintings of high quality.

During his years as a farmer, he was also an inventor in his own rights. His most notable invention was a devise to be used on the rubber tires of tractors in place of chains which were necessary during muddy conditions. He succeeded in patenting the invention but unfortunately was never successful in marketing it, so in the end it never was financially productive for him.

One of the fond memories I have from childhood was our Sunday visits with Uncle Albert and Auntie Alpha's family. We would often have dinner together, followed by an afternoon of conversation which often became boring for us kids, but the part of the afternoon ritual that we enjoyed was when we "men" would walk the fields. How we enjoyed hearing our dads' conversation as they inspected the crops, analyzing their progress, as we walked from one field to another.

Another fond memory was the annual blackberry picking on Uncle Albert's farm. All of us children, along with our mothers (but never our fathers), would head for the woods on the back forty of the farm. With milk buckets in hand along with gloves and long sleeve shirts to protect us from the vicious thorns of the blackberry bushes, we took of on our expedition. As one would expect from children, we began the ritual with glee which in time turned to groaning. We were aware, however, that we were a part of the ritual of gathering the berries for a winter's supply of jelly and sauce, which all of us looked forward to, and what a

Kittle Kittleson, father of Alpha and Helga, with his first wife Anne Marie. Kittle owned the farms bought by Albert and Paul before the Great Depression.

Brothers Paul and Albert Helgesen in buggy.

supply it was. By the end of the day, several 12 quart milk pails had been piled high with the luscious fruit.

In due time, Agnes and finally June married and left home and established their own families. Tragedy visited Agnes and her family when her husband, Joseph Slatten, died at age of 45 and left a family of four children. Six years latter, Agnes married Ivan Rhyner and lived to the age of 92.

Kennell remained on the farm throughout his working life. In 1938 he married Alma Roen. They had no children and Alma died at the age of 59. Two years later, Kennell married a widow, Edna Paulson Kellesvig, and they lived together until he died in 1998 at the age of 85.

CHAPTER 13

The Life Story of Paul Tenny, the Tenth and Last

John Helgesen and his first wife, Jorand, had four children. Following her death in 1863, John married Ingeborg Docken. They in turn were blessed with ten children. The stories of nine of those children have just been told. We are now about to tell the life story of the tenth and for that we dedicate a new chapter. Because he was their tenth and last child they named him Tenny. Born on March 27, 1890, Paul was indeed the last of their children, but in fact was their eleventh. Birth records show that on the 19th of April, 1877, a son, Alford, was born to them but died a short time later. In keeping with the practice of that day, when infants died shortly after birth, they were not included in the family records and so Paul was always considered their tenth child.

Paul was a very unusual person. His father died when he was only four and his mother when he was eleven. Being orphaned at that early age, he received only a fifth grade education.

The story of his life will be divided into the following categories:

1. Paul as husband and father
2. Paul as farmer
3. Paul as educator
4. Paul as musician
5. Paul as statesman and politician
6. Paul as "doctor"

Paul as Husband and Father

On August 27, 1913, Paul and Helga Kittleson were married. In the years to come had six (or in fact seven) children.

Kenneth Joel	August 10, 1915
Gilford Sylvan	April 23, 1918
Russell Burnell	October 6, 1920
Ila Arlene	July 28 1922
Paul Phillip	October 14, 1926
Dolores Marie	May 1, 1930

Some time after the birth of Kenneth, their first son, Paul and Helga experienced a very sad event. This story was never told in our home but we learned it from neighboring children and late in life it was affirmed by Mother. In those days people didn't often talk about personal matters, particularly those relating to birth and/or the death of infants. What was to be our parents' second son turned out to be a hydrocephalic, commonly known as a "water head." This fact was not known until the doctor discovered it when labor had begun. What followed nearly claimed Mother's life. Because of the unusual circumstances, the family physician was unable to deliver the child. To save Mother's life, they called for Paul's brother, Elias, who was a doctor of outstanding reputation in nearby Evansville, Wisconsin. With his expertise, he was able to save her life but not that of the child.

Paul Helgesen married Helga Kittleson on August 27, 1913.

Helga and Paul on the farm.

When the delivery was completed, Dad, with tender love, chose not to let Mother see this deformed child, so all alone he placed him in a shoe box and buried him just outside the fence of the graveyard of their church. Mother never spoke about this but, late in life, shared with daughter Laurie that she had always regretted not having been permitted to see the child. At some point before birth, this child was a living being and at his death, whenever that may have been, his soul was taken to our Lord in heaven. Because of this, we can look forward to meeting our "other brother" someday. During the years that followed, the Lord blessed this couple with five more healthy children.

As the story of my father is told, it should be noted that Mother had a significant part in everything. Without a kind, talented, supportive, and often aggressive wife, he could not have been the man he was. He and Mother worked as a team and she was always a strong supporter of the things he did. Because of the leader he was, it was he who most often was in the spotlight. But behind the scenes, Mother did so much for him, in addition to carrying the primary responsibilities for their six children. She was up early every morning, did her share of the milking and all the cleaning of the milk house and milking utensils and was always the last one to bed at night.

The following story will help understand the loyalty that this couple had for each other. A play was being given in our local school and Mother had a leading role. Though money was very scarce at that time, Dad looked on this as a very significant event and insisted that she buy a new dress.

At that time a literal interpretation of Proverbs 13:23 prevailed ("He that spares his rod hates his son but he that loves him chastens him at times.") In our home the dominant factor was love. When it came to discipline, the responsibility rested with Dad. This was a bit strange because he at times was more like a kid himself. Perhaps Mother believed that this role belonged to the father. To carry out this responsibility Dad chose the razor strop. I do not ever remember being the subject of that instrument and others of our siblings will testify that it really never hurt if and when they were subjected to it. Now we understand that he chose the razor strop because it made a lot of noise when the two pieces of leather struck each other, but really didn't hurt.

Brother Phil remembers the time when Dad announced to him that he needed a beating and sent him to the willow grove to cut a switch. Phil selected the smallest switch he could find so that it wouldn't hurt. Gil in turn remembers the one time that Mother disciplined him. His punishment was to sit on a stool in the corner of

Helga tending a Holstein calf on the farm.

the room. He relates that as time went on, he got so terribly tired that he could hardly sit there. Mother began to feel sorry for him and told him that he could get off but Gil refused! He insisted on sitting there until his time was up. He doesn't remember how it ended.

Only one time that we can remember, Dad lost his temper. It was during milking time when one of the cows got unruly. Upset by it, he went outside and found a broken piece of a steel axle and severely beat the cow. We couldn't intervene, though we considered calling the Humane Society. Afterward, we did go outside and gather up any scrap pieces of wood or metal and took them to the dump. Nothing like that ever happened again.

We remember Dad as being kind and loving but despite his warm feelings and affection for us, I never remember his saying the words "I love you." The conservative Norwegian culture of that day caused him to keep his emotions inside rather than express them in words. His love for us, however, was clearly demonstrated through the things he did and said. Dad was a great role model and for that I shall forever be grateful. The values he passed on to us children, especially during our formative years, shaped our lives forever.

He and Mother had a solid Christian faith. They believed strongly

Back row, left to right: Gilford, cousin Kennell, Kenneth,
Front row: Ila, Phillip, Russell

Paul and Helga Helgesen

in baptism and Christian education and in that way passed the faith on to their children. His faith was the undergirding in his life and in our home. We never asked whether we should go to church on Sunday; we just did. It was part of our value system. He didn't wear his religion on his sleeve but practiced it in the things he did. The religion in our home was shaped by the typical reserved Norwegian way of life. We always had prayer at meal time but never had family devotions, never read from the Bible in our home, nor prayed out loud except for the Lord's Prayer. Every night after Mother and Dad had gone to bed, we heard them ending the day by praying together the Lord's prayer. In our home we always knew that church was the center of our lives.

When there was work to be done around the church, Dad always did more than his share. His convictions led him to doing the things he believed were right even though they may at times have offended others. At one time, he undertook the rearranging of some of the grave stones in the cemetery of our church. The lack of order of the stones made it difficult to mow the grass and keep the cemetery looking neat. Most of the men believed it would be sacrilegious to

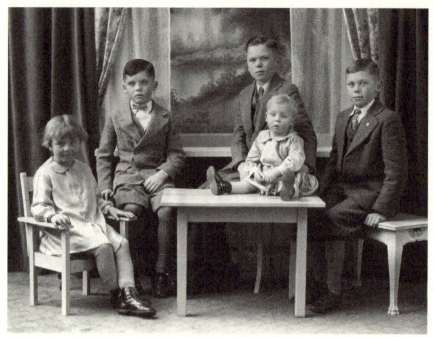

The Paul and Helga Helgesen family c. 1927. Left to right: Ila, Russ, Ken, Phil (baby), Gil.

move any markers. Dad, with no support from others, took it on himself on a cemetery workday to do some necessary realigning. In the process, he offended no few of the parishioners, but in due time most of them appreciated what he had done.

Dad was always concerned about the example he was setting for his boys by the things he did. At that time smoking by adult men was an accepted practice. He smoked with care and in moderation. A ritual of his smoking was to smoke just one cigar a week and that was in the house on Sunday afternoon. We enjoyed the mild aroma and for years, to me, cigar smoke always "smelled like Sunday." During the week he smoked a pipe. Being concerned about the possible fire hazard in the barn, he always used stick matches, lit them with care, put the burned matches in his pocket and returned them to the house at the end of the day. We can still see him striking a match on the raised leg of his farm overall as he walked from the house to the barn and doing it without missing a beat!

As we boys became teenagers, we some how became "anti-

The Paul and Helga Helgesen family c. 1948. Left to right: Ila, Phil, Paul, Russ, Gil, Helga, Ken, Laurie.

smokers" and tried to convince Dad to quit. At a time during one of his extended illnesses, when it was not possible for him to smoke, we boys took his pipe and tobacco, put them in one of our 4H trunks, and padlocked it. Dad did not have a key to the trunk so he could not open it but even if he had had a key, he was so moved by that experience that he never smoked again.

Beer was also an issue with him. When the doctor once recommended moderate use of it for his health, his deep concern was, "what if I do this and as a result, my boys decide to follow my example and one of them should become an alcoholic?" Dad could not get himself to go into the tavern to buy the beer so Ken bought it for him. Apparently the treatment was not successful, as he did not do it again.

From childhood, Christmas was a time of great celebration and spoke loudly of his values. To him it was a very important time from both a religious and secular point of view. For us Christmas really began at 3:00 P.M. on the day of Christmas Eve. At that time the shades in our living room were pulled to prepare for the arrival of

Santa Claus. Then at 4:00 P.M. our church janitor, Ole Jevne, made his way across our farm to the church where he rang the church bell. As the sound of the bell filled the air, all the neighbors who were within hearing distance knew that Christmas was arriving. About that time, we all headed for the barn to do the chores, including milking the cows. On that special evening the cows were fed the best and most tender second crop alfalfa hay that had been harvested for just that occasion. Because it was such a special night, we did the milking and chores before we had our supper.

The meal that night was simple, just oyster stew, which we all loved. The table had to be cleared and dishes done before Santa Claus could arrive. Yes, Dad believed in Santa Claus, and gift giving was an important part of it. Even during the Depression when money was scarce, he wanted to give his children the best gifts possible. Following the meal, he would peek through the keyhole into the living room, where the shades had been pulled earlier that afternoon. When he reported that Santa had come, it was time to celebrate around the tree by opening our gifts.

Because our church was part of a three- or at times four-point parish, we never had church on Christmas Eve nor maybe even on Christmas Day but sometime during the holiday there was always a church service and the children's Christmas program. The Christmas tree for the church was a large, freshly cut evergreen with real candles that were lit during the service. Because of Dad's concern for fire, he always provided a five gallon bucket of sand as his private fire department. Following Christmas, he took the tree down and, before disposing of it, cut the top off and made it into a Norwegian stir stick which Mother used in the making of mush or rumagrout. On the days following Christmas we did a lot of partying with the neighbors and really enjoyed the Norwegian ritual of ragamuffin. The name means "a ragged disreputable person." We would all dress up with foolish costumes including masks and would do silly things until the neighbors guessed who we were. When they guessed our name, we had to remove our mask. When all the masks were removed, they would treat us to homemade root beer and Christmas goodies.

In his relationship with his children and especially his three oldest boys, Dad was something of a "kid" himself. When Ken and Gil were

Paul Helgesen postponed the cutting of trees for firewood to help his sons build this log cabin in the woods to use as their hideout. The two-story playhouse stood for over 50 years.

very young, he bought them each a tricycle. In the winter time when they could not ride outside, he helped them set up a race track in the living room of our house. They loved racing but when the peddles of their trikes cut grooves in the wainscoting of the walls, Dad got himself in no little trouble with Mother, but for him it was important for the children to have fun.

His biggest projects for the two oldest boys were the 4H Club and the Dane County Fair in Madison and the Wisconsin State Fair in Milwaukee. Through those, he taught them how to raise and groom purebred Holstein calves and show them at the fairs. As a result, they got their share of blue ribbons. By the time his third son came on the scene, some of his initial enthusiasm had worn off, but as the third son, I benefited from his work with the two oldest boys and do recall winning a calf judging contest (with a bit of coaching from him) at the fair. The heavy responsibilities of farming and his constant poor health must have made it very difficult to continue his high level of activity especially in working with his children.

Despite all this, one of our greatest experiences with Dad was during Easter vacation in about 1930. He had planned that the big project would be the annual cutting of trees for firewood with which to heat our home for next winter. But his three sons, Ken, Gil and Russ had other plans. They were dreaming of building a log cabin in the woods which they could use as their hideout. When they presented the idea to Dad, he could have justifiably told them to put the plan on hold because the fire wood had to be cut, but not Dad! He not only approved the project but caught the spirit and entered into it wholeheartedly. The trees did not get cut during that vacation but somehow were done later. The log cabin did get built and what a beauty it was! Dad even got our neighbor, Ole Jevne, to "chink" the logs which made the walls more weatherproof. In size it was about six by eight feet, two stories high, and even had a tar paper roof.

After the excitement of building the cabin was over, we did use it from time to time and what a joy that was. Some years later, on a winter day, we hitched four horses to the cabin and pulled it on the snow out of the woods to the pine grove next to the farm house where it sat for many years. Finally, more than some 50 years after it was built and by then in deteriorating condition, the owners of the farm, with the permission of the boys who had built it, tore it down.

Paul As Farmer

Following their marriage in 1913, Dad and Mother bought their first farm from Kittle Kittleson, Mother's father. The farm seemed like an ideal place for them to settle down and raise a family. It was only ten miles from their home area and two miles south of the village of Mount Horeb. The farm was 156 acres with the East Blue Mounds Lutheran Church and cemetery occupying four acres on the corner of the farm. Only a half mile away was the Lukken Cheese Factory and next to it the Lukken School where the children would get their education. They signed a contract with Kittle for $20,000 for the farm and another $10,000 for livestock and machinery with an interest rate of seven percent. Kittle wanted to include the livestock and machinery in the farm mortgage but Dad insisted that it be a separate Chattel Mortgage

Paul Helgesen bought his first farm near Mount Horeb, Wisconsin, (pictured here) from this father-in-law, Kittle Kittleson.

which later proved to be a very wise decision for him.

Though they were very good farmers, the Depression of the 30s was too much for them and they were not able to make the payments according to the terms of the contract. Because most farmers were in the same predicament, Kittle agreed that they should pay only as much as they were able and that the amount they paid would be applied to the accruing interest. When the depression ended, Dad continued to make what payments he could on the interest of the farm mortgage and made regular payments on the Chattel Mortgage until it was paid in full.

Finally by 1945 he decided to give up the farm as trying to pay for it was a

Tor Kittleson and wife, Russell Helgesen's great-grandparents.

Paul Helgesen at the grain elevator with sons Rus and Gil up top.

hopeless situation. At that time the farm was worth only $2,500 but Kittle held the mortgage for $20,000 and refused to change the terms. Dad's brother, Albert was in the same predicament but Kittle forgave him all the arrears and let them keep the farm. For some reason which was never articulated, he was unwilling to give Dad the same deal. Fortunately, however, because the Chattel Mortgage had been paid off, Dad was able to retain the livestock and machinery. In the winter of 1945 he had an auction which was very successful and netted him nearly $10,000 which was enough money to buy a small farm near Cottage Grove, Wisconsin, and start over again at age 55.

As a farmer, Dad's basic philosophy was, "you always leave a farm in better condition than it was when you first acquired it." As a result he worked hard to improve the soil with good farming practices and did extensive refurbishing of the buildings. When he bought the Kittleson farm in 1913, there was no electricity. The house was lit by lamps and the barn by lanterns. The house was heated by wood stoves and there was no running water. Underneath the wash room was a cistern of rain water with a hand pump. A windmill pumped pure drinking water for the house and for the cattle. Soon after Dad bought the farm, he bought a milking machine that was powered by a gasoline engine but it caused so much trouble that when the boys were old enough to help with the milking, he discontinued the use of the milking machine and did not buy another one until the boys had left home and gone to college. During the Roosevelt administration, The Rural Electrification Association was established to provide electricity for farmers. What a day it was when we could just flip a

Paul Helgesen, progressive farmer, was the first in the county to adopt the new practice of strip cropping and contour farming to avoid soil erosion.

switch and the bulbs lit up!

At that time all of the farm machines were pulled by horses. Dad loved horses and always kept four beautiful ones. At one time he sold three of them who were getting too old to do hard work and bought three young ones that had not been broken. One day he came home from the field with his jacket in two pieces. He had hitched two of the young horses to the grain drill during spring planting. They were so difficult to control that he put the drill in the ground and never took it out until he finished, even when he rounded the corners. Around one corner his jacket caught in the barbed wire fence and he came home with it ripped in two. More stories could be told.

Because of his love for horses, he postponed buying a tractor until after the boys left home. Even then he put off the purchase until one hot day the horses were spooked by flies. They came racing through the barn and ran over sister Laurie who could have been seriously injured. Dad's brother, Albert, then convince him that it was now time to buy a tractor.

He had a strong sense that farming was a partnership between himself and God. One of his strong convictions which grew out of his religious background was that you never work on Sunday except to do the necessary chores. He would always say, "I'd rather let the hay rot in the field than haul it in on Sunday." On one occasion he made an exception. At that time, prior to raising hybrid corn, we picked our own seed corn. On one fall day which happened to be on a Sunday, the sky was clear and the corn was exactly ripe for picking. Dad had a dilemma: Should we pick the seed corn today or risk leaving it until tomorrow when there was a possibility of rain? "Boys," he said, "let's hurry out after milking and pick the corn. We can do it and still get to church on time." We picked a supply of beautiful ears and put them on the corn trees to dry. The next spring we planted the corn but to our amazement not a kernel grew! Dad was convinced that it was because we had picked it on Sunday. To this day I still wonder!

When Dad met and conversed with other people, he always wanted to be known as "just a farmer." To him farming was a profession which was not to be looked down on. As a farmer, he felt as good about himself as he did about his three brothers who were doctors.

As a person, his hallmark was "progressive." From his farm which was only 18 miles from Madison, he kept in close touch with the Dane County and University of Wisconsin Agricultural Departments. He always kept up with the latest developments in farming and usually put them into practice

The new thing in the late 1930s in Wisconsin was strip cropping and contour farming. It was a system whereby fields were laid out in strips so as to "farm on the level" and avoid soil erosion. He was the first farmer in the county to adopt the program. At about that same time he was also one of the first to plant and grow hybrid corn.

In working with the University of Wisconsin, he learned to know a number of the professors personally. His favorite story was about the day he entered an elevator in one of the University buildings and met two men who were both well known professors. He greeted them by name and one of them said to the other, "so you are [professor so and so]. I have always wanted to meet you!" to which Dad replied "so it took a farmer to introduce you two professors!"

Whenever a delegation from a foreign country came to the University on a study tour of American agriculture, they often sent them to visit Dad and learn about his methods of farming. Late in life when his health was declining, Dad was invited by one of the University professors to lecture his agriculture class. What a testimony—a farmer with a fifth-grade education ending up as a "university professor!"

Paul as Educator

High on his list of priorities was education. Having been orphaned at age eleven and receiving only a fifth-grade education, he read slowly with his lips always moving. Yet he was an avid reader who understood and retained what he read and loved to tell the stories to the rest of the family. After a busy day of farm work his evenings were always spent reading. In addition to the daily paper, he loved to read mystery stories and especially works by Zane Gray. None of us will forget the night while he had been reading *The Green Hornet* that he acted out the story in his dreams. In the morning Mother told us about being awakened in the middle of the night by Dad who was on his knees by the window with his shoe in hand waiting for the Green Hornet who he thought was about to attack him through the open window.

In keeping with his philosophy he always told us boys, "I don't care what you choose to do in life but whatever it is, you've got to get to the top and to get to the top you must get an education. I can't help you financially, but if you can figure out how to work your way through, I'll take care of the farm." For this he was criticized by neighboring farmers who thought he was stupid to encourage his sons to leave the farm just when they could be helpful and make life easy for him. Undeterred by the criticism, he continued to encourage the young boys in the community to further their education.

The Lukken School conveniently bordered our farm. Dad was always on the school board which involved him in all the affairs of the district including the hiring of teachers. The big issue for years was the question of whether to lengthen the eight-month school year to nine months. He felt that eight months was adequate and was concerned about getting the farm work done if the boys spent that much time in school. This concern was very real one spring when he was so sick that he couldn't sow the oats. He had to have Gil, who was in seventh or eighth grade, leave school early in the afternoon to come home and do the sowing. When Dad came home following the annual board meeting each year, the first question we asked was "Are we still going to have eight months of school?" As long as we were in school, the eight-month year prevailed. Yet the Lukken School students who went on to Mount Horeb High School kept up well with the city students who had a nine-month school year.

Besides our formal education, we learned so much from what transpired on the farm. The greatest lesson that I learned from my Dad was when I was about 13 or 14 years old. Our grain was harvested with a McCormick grain binder which was pulled by three horses. One day, when the time had come for me to learn how to operate this massive machine, Dad took me to the field. We oiled the binder and hooked up the three horses. I got on the seat, took the reins of the horses, shouted "giddyap," and off we went! Dad followed behind. He could have followed me all day long but half way around the field, he took off for home. This demonstration of confidence was one of the greatest lessons in my entire life.

Dad's greatest experience in education came late in life when the governor of the State of Wisconsin appointed a governor's committee to realign the rural school districts of the state. Because of the reputation he had earned, Dad was appointed as a member of this prestigious committee. The governor realized that this assignment was too emotional an issue to be settled by a vote of the citizens so he empowered the Committee to make final decisions. The Committee held hearings throughout the state so as to involve the citizens in the process. Understandably these meetings were at times explosive and most people did not believe that the Committee was really listening to them. This process took a toll on Dad's health. One day he went to see his doctor who told him that if this was affecting his health, he had better resign from the Committee. But then, on second thought he said, "if you are taking this work so seriously that it affects your health, we had better get you fixed up so that you can continue." Dad continued on the Committee and looked on this as perhaps the most difficult but significant assignment of his life. In the end, he also felt that it was the most satisfying. When the newly realigned rural school districts were completed, the plan had broad support and brought great benefit to the citizens of the entire state. My brother, Phil, who was a superintendent of schools in the state said that years later he heard people still extolling the benefits of the new arrangement.

During my high school years I was a strong competitor in the field of oratory. Though not a public speaker himself, Dad took an active interest in coaching me. I will never forget the night at home when he listened as I was practicing my oration. When I finished, he said, "Russ, you were perfect!" Wow, this made me really feel good until he finished his sentence, "Russ you were a perfect statue!" He had a lot of common sense and with his help in getting me to relax, I managed to win second place in the district speech contest and benefited from his help in my public speaking throughout my life.

Paul as Musician

Dad was not a musician. He never played an instrument and could not carry a tune. But he loved music and believed strongly that it was an important enrichment of everyone's life. Probably his greatest contribution to music, however was the part that he played in the organizing of a rural school band. Even before his children were in high school, he made sure that they never missed a local parade. He particularly enjoyed the marching band.

The Rural School Band. Russ was only 8 so was not in the picture but Ken and Gil are.

The Helgesen Band: Russ (left), Gil (back), Ila (right), and Phil (front).

He felt strongly that his children should be given an opportunity to play in the band someday but knew that they were at a great disadvantage because they could not begin lessons until they enrolled in high school.

Even though Dad had no children in the band, he learned to know Fred Hanneman, the band director. One day in conversation with him, he proposed that he organize a rural school band. Mr. Hanneman agreed that it was a good idea and that if Dad could recruit students, he would teach and rehearse with them on Saturday mornings without any cost to the students. The only requirement was that they would have to buy their own instruments. Dad began calling on parents of students in our school district and was successful in recruiting enough to make the venture successful. One of the prospects was Margaret, daughter of John Gronseth, a neighbor who was a Norwegian immigrant. After explaining the project to John, he replied, "Ya I tink dat I could buy Margaret a band!"

I don't know how long the band lasted but at least long enough for the four oldest in our family, plus many other students, to benefit from it. Thanks to Dad, the musician.

Paul as Statesman and Politician

Dad's concern for his neighbors and his conviction that he should help to make the world a better place in which to live led him into the field of politics. His greatest involvement was serving on the town board of the Township of Blue Mounds. When his neighbors pressured him into running for the Board after he had protested that he was too busy, they told him that they would come and help with his field work. After his election, only one farmer showed up. The main challenge at that time was the developing of roads within the township. Without engineers to lay out the roads, the men of the town did it themselves mostly under Dad's direction. They turned out with horses and road scrappers and cut and scraped until they had passable roads especially for the local farmers. In the process he was able to work out a plan to get the roads graveled.

Developing the roads and laying them out to please the residents was a sensitive and often nearly explosive issue. Dad used to tell stories of his experiences about dealings with the farmers where the roads were being built. When the construction crew moved in and began cutting the road for one of the farms, the farmer's wife became very upset. In her opinion they were grading the road in such a way that when it rained, the water would gush down the road and right into her house. Dad, with his sense of humor, assured her that there would be no problem. All she needed to do was to open both her front and back doors and the water would then run in one door and out the other! He ultimately satisfied her that the final project would work to her benefit.

I do not know the nature of the problem that was upsetting another resident of the township but one day he arrived in furious anger to confront Dad. At that time Dad was in the barn doing chores but took time out to hear his concern. When Dad did not agree with his point of view and would not grant what he wanted, the argument ended when the neighbor retorted with hot anger, "If you don't do this (whatever he wanted), I'm going home and coming back with my shotgun." To which Dad replied, "Go ahead and when you come back, I'll be here!" According to my recollection Dad was never frightened into submission, the man never returned and life went on for both of them.

Dad was always proud of the fact that he was a charter member of the Progressive Party of the State of Wisconsin. At that time Robert Lafollette was governor of the state and also involved in national politics. He was a very liberal and progressive Republican. Dad was a strong supporter and admirer of him and when he broke with the Republican Party and organized the Progressive Party, Dad followed him and actually attended the constituting convention. This Progressive Party had a long history but I will end the story here by recalling that when Robert Lafollette died, Dad attended his funeral in the Wisconsin State Capital and came home with a statue of the governor and other memorabilia which he highly prized.

Paul as "Doctor"

After Dad's mother died when he was 11 years old, he went to live with his brother Elias who was a doctor in New Glarus. For a number of years he worked in Elias's drug store which was on the ground floor of his office. During the time he worked there, he learned a lot about medicine that benefited him later in life.

When he was old enough, he drove the horse and buggy for Dr. Elias when he made his house calls in the country. Elias was considered a very fine doctor and had a thriving practice. As Dad sorted out his experiences in working with his brother, his favorite story was how he learned to eat lutefisk. During this time the doctor put in long days and often worked right through the dinner hour which meant that neither he nor his brother had anything to eat. They never carried lunch with them but depended on the generosity of their patients. Often when a housewife would ask if they had eaten, he not wanting to take time out, would reply that they had eaten when they actually had not. On one occasion when they had gone well beyond the dinner hour without eating, Dad was really starving. When the housewife asked if they had eaten and Elias responded that they had, Dad interrupted with, "no we haven't." She then apologized by telling them that she had nothing to serve but lutefisk. Both of them agreed that it would be just fine. Never having eaten lutefisk before in the German community of New Glarus, Dad remembers that that was the day he became a lover of this Norwegian delicacy.

During his years of farming he, like other farmers, had a lot of practice as a doctor treating their cattle as they faced a variety of challenges from birth to death. The medical skills which he had learned over the years were applied beyond the cattle and often to his children. The thing that we remember most as children was his treatment of our punctures caused by stepping on rusty nails while running barefoot. With the warning "this will hurt but we gotta do it!," Dad would take the square end of a toothpick, dip it in iodine, and probe till he got to the bottom of the hole. There was lots of pain and some screaming but never did any of us end up with an infection.

The ultimate medical challenge for Dr. Dad, however, was the time when infection invaded our farm. From the hogs it moved to us humans. It attacked the family in the form of boils. They were abundant and painful. They continued for an extended time and the longer they lasted the smaller but more painful they became. In the end Dad cured them. He bought a small bottle of carbolic acid, dipped the end of a needle in the acid and put one small drop on the center of the boil. His treatment soon ended the boils and when Dad reported to the doctor what he had done, the doctor replied, "Yes that was an effective treatment. It was a little dangerous, however, but it did the work."

His healing arts were very effective on his family as well as the cattle on his farm but they did not work well on himself. He was always hard working and (with Mother's help) managed to keep up the farm. But for most of his life he was in ill health. His greatest problem was ulcers which were common in his family but at that time were difficult to treat and cure. At times he was too sick to work. During one of his most extended times of illness, when he was bed ridden, Mother was his nurse in addition to doing most of the farm work. One morning he woke up deeply disturbed and so sick that he was trembling. That night he had had a horrible nightmare in which he dreamed that his brother, Albert, had been killed in a deadly accident. The dream was so real that he was sure that it had actually happened. He could not be comforted until Mother finally called Albert and asked him to come. Only when we saw his brother alive could he have peace.

On another occasion he was laid up for most of the winter with an arm that was immobilized. His greatest concern was that he was not able to split the firewood that was needed for heating the house. He was able to solve the problem by having his nephew, Irving, Henry Helgeson's son, come and stay until the work was done and he had recovered the use of his arm.

We remember with mixed feelings the time that he nearly needed a doctor. In our farm house, we entered through the back door. When Dad came in, he always sat down to take off his boots on a chair that was next to the door. One day when he sat down without looking, the chair was not there! To us it was hilarious until we realized that he had actually hurt himself.

Some years after he had retired from farming, and five years before he died, he was suffering severely from stomach ulcers and the doctor told him that he needed surgery to remove a portion of his stomach, which at that time was considered a very serious operation. When the doctor told him that his chances of surviving were only 50 percent, he responding by telling him that he was ready to face whatever came. "I have prayed," he said "that I could live until all my children are on their own. The Lord has answered that prayer, so now I am ready to go if that is the Lord's will. I can now face the future without fear." Then he confided that "last night I had a vision. It may have been a dream, but I believe that it was a vision. I was in the Garden of Gethsemane and Jesus was there kneeling at the rock in prayer. Every thing was so real except for one thing. The Olive trees were full of leaves which looked like huge drops of blood and on every drop were the words 'He died for you.' I am not afraid and I know that if I don't survive this surgery, I will be with Jesus in heaven."

Fortunately the surgery was a great success and his recuperation went well. He could eat things that he hadn't eaten for years without discomfort. At the beginning, he had to eat small quantities to help his stomach stretch.

The End Came and the Victory Was Won

After several years of relatively good health, he developed other problems. Doctors were unable to diagnose his condition and at one point he went to Mayo Clinic in Rochester, Minnesota. They, too were puzzled by his condition and could only determine what they thought was a kidney problem. There was no dialysis available at that time so treatment was limited. What followed is not clear but in retrospect it appears that Mother and Dad knew more than they wanted to talk about because they did not want to worry the family.

In the summer of 1959 they were present at the baptism of Laurie's daughter, Barb. As they were doing dishes, Mother told Laurie that Dad had a sickness that would only allow him a couple more years of life. She said she hadn't planned to tell her, but couldn't keep it any longer. It was possible that he was suffering from kidney failure. For a while he had shots to help get rid of the fluid buildup in his legs but after some time, the shots no longer helped. Some months later, after several week in the hospital in Madison, he said his final farewells to his family and on the 19th of August, 1962, at the early age of 72 went home to be with his Lord. Our family had hoped that there would be an autopsy so we could get answers to his cause of death and that the doctors might discover things that could be helpful in treating others, but Pastor Gunderson convinced Mother that, because Dad had suffered so much in life, she should not subject his body to that procedure. She accepted his advice and no more facts were ever learned.

When family and friends gathered at Lake Edge Lutheran Church in Madison, a beautiful service of remembrance was conducted by the Rev. Hector Gunderson. At Dad's request we sang:

> There is a fountain filled with blood
> Drawn from Immanuel's veins;
> And sinners, plunged beneath that flood,
> Lose all their guilty stains.
> E'er since, by faith, I saw the stream
> Thy flowing wounds supply,
> Redeeming love has been my theme,
> And shall be till I die.

The tune of that hymn was not familiar and we did not sing it well, but its message was unmistakable. How typical of Dad. He, who couldn't carry a tune, was not deterred by the unsingable melody of that hymn which was such a clear statement of his faith. Following the service six of us (sons and sons-in-law) carried him in his casket to his final resting place in Rose Lawn Cemetery in Madison. As we moved slowly in silence toward his grave, carrying him for the last time, we were filled with thoughts of sorrow and thanksgiving: It was sad to think that we could no longer spend days with a father whom we loved so dearly, but at the same time were thankful that the days that we had had with him were so full, and that in his time of living and dying he had given so much to others.

An appropriate ending to his life's story is a loud AMEN!

July 4, 2009

Paul and Helga had six children, 23 grandchildren, 46 great-grandchildren and, to date, countless great-great-grandchildren are being added to the lineage. Pictured here, c. 1960, are, left to right, Anita [Gil's]; Jane, Mary, and wife Lorraine [Russ's], Sonja, Ruth, wife Ginny, Rachel, Paul (front), [Gil's]; Jim, Becky, Tom [Russ's]. Back: Gil.

Book III

Russ Tells His Story

CHAPTER 14
_____

"Good Old Russell B"

Preface No. 1

All the world's a stage,
And all the men and women merely players:
They have their exits and their entrances;
And one man in his time plays many parts,
At first the infant,
Mewling and puking in the nurse's arms.
And then the whining school-boy, with his satchel
And shining morning face, creeping like a snail
Unwillingly to school. And then the lover,
Sighing like a furnace, with a woeful ballad
Made to his mistress' eyebrow. . . . Last scene of all,
That ends this strange eventful history,
Is second childishness and mere oblivion?
Sans (without) teeth, sans eyes, sans taste,
sans everything.

Excerpt from William Shakespeare's "As You Like It"

Preface No. 2

Who is "Good Old Russell B.?"

The name "Good Old Russell B" was a play on words for Pastor Russell Burnell Helgesen. It was coined by the men of St. John's Lutheran Church, Massapequa, Long Island, New York. During his seven years of ministry, the congregation had often heard him tell the dramatic story (told elsewhere in this document) of his crossing the Mississippi River by motor boat to serve two congregations in Wisconsin during the two years that the Mississippi River bridge was closed. When the congregation planned his farewell party in 1960, they did a humorous skit in which one of the men played the part of the pastor in a cardboard row boat which they named "Good Old Russell B."

The house on the Mount Horeb farm in Wisconsin, where Russell Burnell Helgesen was born on October 6, 1920.

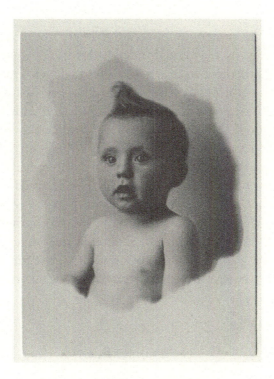

Tales of early childhood

Wednesday, October sixth, in the year of our Lord, one thousand nine hundred and twenty, was a great day in the farm home of Paul and Helga Helgesen near Mount Horeb, Wisconsin. On that day they were a happy couple with a family of two boys: Kenneth, who was five years old, and Gilford, two and a half. On that bright October morning, shortly after the sun had risen, the parlor of their home was converted once again into a "birthing room." Dr. Thompson, the family physician from Mount Horeb, had been alerted to the fact that this was the day that his services would be needed and that he should come as soon as possible.

In preparation for this long awaited event, Helga's half-sister, Crystal Kittleson, who was 15 years old at the time, had come to help out and made plans to stay as long as she was needed. By mid-morning the doctor arrived and after examining the patient, suggested that it would likely be a few more hours before the birth would occur. The doctor suggested that, inasmuch as he did not have other patients who would need him that day, he would just stay there until the baby had arrived.

At that point somebody came up with a bright idea. Instead of just sitting and waiting, they could make better use of their time. It was a beautiful day and there were lots of apples that were ripe and in need of picking. Why not get to work? So out to the orchard went the doctor, followed by Crystal and the two little boys, each with a bushel basket in hand. Throughout the day, as they continued to pick apples, the doctor checked regularly on the progress of his patient and before the sun had set, all the apples had been picked, the ordeal in the "birthing room" was over and a healthy baby boy had arrived.

On October 24, eighteen days later at the Sunday morning service at East Blue Mounds Lutheran Church, Russell Burnell was baptized by the Rev. S. Gunderson, "in the Name of the Father, Son, and Holy Spirit" and was "marked with the cross of Christ forever!" His God-parents were Mr. and Mrs. Gerhard Tollefson, Marie Kittleson, and Amos Stolen.

"Blunder Bus"

Everyone has a name and most people have nicknames which are acquired at an early age. This "cute and loving little boy" had gone through enough experiences at an early age to earn him the nickname "Blunder Bus." I don't know what "Blunder Bus" really means nor who thought it up and it is not in the dictionary. Maybe the best definition is "accident-prone."

The first experience that set the stage for the "Blunder Bus" was on a day when I was nearly a year old. Aunt Crystal, who had been with me the day I was born, was giving me my daily bath in the living room by an open window. On the living room side of the window was a stand on which sat a large bowl that served as the bath tub. A gentle breeze blew through that open window on that sunny day and Aunt Crystal could smell the beautiful scent of the yellow rose bush which grew just outside. Before the bath was finished, while I was still slippery with soap, Crystal lost her grip and out the window I tumbled, landing butt-end first in the rose bush. What followed wasn't funny. Amid the screams of a frightened baby, Crystal and Mother spent no little time removing thorns from their boy who never again was bathed in front of an open window with a beautiful rose bush beneath!

Monday morning was wash day in the Helgesen household and it was on a Monday that my second "Blunder Bus" story took place. I was two years old at the time and was accompanying my mother who was hanging out the freshly washed clothes. All was going well and I was enjoying the freedom and activity of the outdoors; that is until Mother finished hanging up the clothes and reached for me to go back to the house, only to discover that I was missing. Frantically, she began to search but could find me nowhere. "But he was here just a minute ago!" "He couldn't have gone far!" "He has to be somewhere around!" As these and a thousand other thoughts raced through her mind, she called for Dad and the boys who came on a dead run and joined in the search. Dad directed the search. Nearby were the woods. They were sure that I could not have gone that far but they began to search it anyway. Time went by; actually only minutes but it seemed like hours. Despair set in. Amid the panic they were praying, "Dear Lord, please lead us to our little boy!" Deeper into the woods they searched. Dad ordered the boys to be quiet and listen. No sound; no response. They all kept calling out, "Russ, Russ, Russy Boy where are you?" And then through the eerie silence came a piercing shriek, "I found him!" Out of the woods they came scrambling and behold, there was Mother standing over the clothes basket, tears streaming down her checks. There in the basket was "little Russy Boy" peacefully sound asleep.

Next comes story number three. Living on a farm at a time when there was no indoor plumbing, our outhouse was more than a necessary fixture: it was a virtual institution. Our outhouse was located behind the summer kitchen, about thirty feet from the back door of our house. The outhouse was a small building, perhaps six by eight feet, but what made it distinct was that it had three holes. Two were large to take care of adults, and one, which was small and raised about six inches with a foot rest, was designed for the use of children. Three holes which could be used at the same time was meant for both business and socialization. On the floor beside the holes was a Sears Roebuck catalogue. Most of the pages were very useful, but those that were printed in color were harsh and scratchy and only used when the softer pages were gone.

Beneath the three seats was a six foot deep pit. A short time prior to the day in question, the hole had reached its capacity, so Dad removed its contents and spread it on one of the farm fields where it served as

Real outhouse seats frame photos of Russ and Ken commemorating the infamous incident when Russ fell through the hole and Ken was lowered down to pull him out.

---

valuable fertilizer. With the pit newly cleaned and the outhouse back in order, I (aka "Blunder Bus"), who at the time was less than three years old, entered the outhouse and for some unknown reason decided to try one of the large holes. Like a streak of lightening, down into the pit I went! My predicament was promptly discovered, but the pit was too deep for me to climb out so there I stood, knee deep in trouble. Quick thinking saved me as brother Ken, who was about seven at the time, was quickly conscripted and carefully lowered down the hole where he picked me up, hoisted me as high as he could, while Mother brought me the rest of the way to safety. Not until many years later did I learn "the rest of the story" when Mother confided: "Yes, and I had to clean up both of you!"

In 1925, about two years after the outhouse incident, at the tender age of five, I lived through an ordeal that took me well beyond the realm of "Blunder Bus." It was feeding time for our cattle in our barn. I went with my Dad up to the hayloft to help him throw hay from the mow down the shoot and into the feeding trough below. With a fork full of hay on my favorite stub-handled fork, I went sailing across the slippery floor. As I gained speed, fork handle tight in my hand, the hay, the fork, and I went down the chute where I landed on the back of my head seven feet below on the bare concrete floor!

For the next three days I was unconscious and for an entire week was in and out of consciousness. The doctor came to see me at home, but without of the value of x-rays concluded that I had suffered a concussion. We later realized that it had indeed been a skull fracture. I was never taken to our local hospital; all of my recuperation was spent at home.

Tails of near disaster continued into my teen years. Two of them occurred in our milk house where we had all the milking utensils, including a cream separator. In the center of the separator was a spindle on which sat the bowl which, when spun at high speed, separated the cream from the milk. One day I got what I thought was a bright idea of replacing the bowl with a pop bottle. Because the bottle didn't fit tight, when it reached a high speed, it began to wobble and then crashed as the bottle shattered into a million pieces. Only one piece struck me and that was about a half inch below my right eye. The gash soon healed and fortunately my eye was not injured!

The next milk house incident actually began at the Lukken School. One day one of my classmates brought one of his dad's 22-caliber bullets to school. He gave it to me with the tempting idea that I could explode it by placing it on a concrete floor and hitting it with a hammer. It sounded intriguing so I took it to the milk house, placed it on the floor, and followed his instructions. The rifle shot told me that it had worked, but we never did find the hole it had made in the wall and once again, by the grace of God, I was still alive!

Tales of Violence

In a family of three robust boys with a sister tagging along behind, there was bound to be some violence, or shall we say "boys will be boys." One day Gil and I got into some kind of hassle which resulted in his taking my cap and refusing to give it back to me. In desperation I threatened him by picking up a stone and letting him know in no uncertain terms that "if you don't give me back my cap, I'm going to throw this rock and hit you square in the forehead!" He didn't and I did! It hit him square in the forehead but both of us survived.

Next I must tell you about the day the rooster died! Dad asked Gil and me to catch a rooster, behead him, and prepare him for dinner. We thought it would be fun. Because the rooster wouldn't cooperate when we stretched out his neck on the chopping block, we decided to whack him with a stick before we beheaded him. It worked after a couple tries and we had our chicken dinner. The humor of the whole thing, however, was to hear Dad tell his embellished version of the tale: "The boys decided to stun the rooster before cutting off his head. So Gil took the rooster by his legs while Russ took a big stick and swung with all his might. The stick missed the rooster but hit Gil in his legs. With that, Gil let out a yell and let go of the rooster who flew away and that ended the chicken dinner for that day!"

Fortunately, our next story averted a tragic ending. During our preteen years, my sister, Ila, and I were playmates. One Sunday after returning from church, I asked her if she would like a ride in our abandoned buggy. She was game and climbed in. The buggy had no tongue so I had to steer it by grasping the front axle with my back facing forward and my head toward the buggy which was perched at the top of a long hill. At the bottom of the hill was a drop of about fifteen feet over a creek. Shortly into the ride I lost control of the steering and the buggy took off down the hill. In panic, Ila shouted, "what shall I do?" "Just stay in; you might get hurt if you jump out." So I let go of the buggy, threw myself on the ground and let it pass over me. As it went down the hill, it gained speed, took off over the bank, across the creek and landed so hard on the other side, that Ila flew out and the two-inch steel axle of the buggy snapped. She ended up with a headache and instructions not to tell anyone. Of course, the next day the buggy was discovered. Instead of punishment, there was thanksgiving that neither Ila nor "Blunder Bus" was seriously hurt.

A Stalker in the Night

Sleepwalking can be humorous or in some cases tragic depending on whom you are. If a person who is sleepwalking is suddenly awakened, a serious accident can occur. During my preteen years I was a sleepwalker and to me it was very painful. Since boys will be boys, my brothers enjoyed teasing me about it but my parents were very concerned. The favorite story that was shared in our family was about the night that I got out of bed, walked out in the hall, climbed the railing that surrounded the stairwell and walked on top of it in my sleep. When my Mother was suddenly awakened, she rescued me and avoided tragedy by leading me gently back to bed without waking me. Because of the frustration that I was experiencing by this unsolvable dilemma, one night I took drastic action by tying myself to the spring of my bed with two of my belts. When Mother came to check on me before she went to bed, she discovered the belts, woke me and untied the belts. Never again did I walk in my sleep!

Notable Nicknames

Nicknames are common and I was "doubly blessed" with three of them. Family and friends, with two exceptions, have always called me "Russ." My mother-in-law, Grandma Mabel Sampson, always called me Russell which I accepted as her expression of respect. The other person who called me Russell was Dorothy Freeze, receptionist in the Southwestern Minnesota District office of the American Lutheran Church in Willmar. During the five years that I was assistant to Bishop Edward A. Hansen, she, on occasion with a stern tone in her voice, would call me Russell. When I heard her use that name I knew right well that I was in trouble!

As a child I earned my second nickname, "Blunder-Bus." The third was "Slow-Poke" which was bestowed on me by my mother and was really a reflection of the "genes" with which both of us were born. Mother and I were just wired differently. She always operated in high gear; I in low. When she was working in the kitchen, she always ran even a distance of just three feet. On our farm she was always the first one up in the morning and the first one out to the barn to start milking. Dad, who was often in poor health, followed closely behind and in due time "Slow-poke" arrived to join the family.

I really did have a wonderful mother who cared deeply for me but the speed with which I operated was always a source of conflict. She really didn't understand this about me and I was really hurt by the pressure she always put me under. When I sat down on a stool to milk a cow, I always heard, "Hurry up, Russell." She didn't mean to hurt me but it always did. I tried to work faster but I just couldn't function that way and the longer it went on the more the conflict grew within me.

This issue also carried over to my work in school where I usually did well except when taking "speed tests" which were anathema to me. I never got good grades on those tests because I was never able to finish them. The one thing that was encouraging to me, however, was that when I could move at my own pace, I did well. When all my grades were put together, I usually was at the top of my class.

CHAPTER 15

My Years of Growing Up

Lukken School

Lukken School, where I got my first eight grades of education, was located a ten minute walk from home just across the road from our farm. It was a typical one-room country school with only one teacher and about 25 students. The teaching was done by having the students for each grade come forward when it was time for their class and sit on a row of chairs facing the teacher with their backs to the other students. While the teacher led the class, the rest of us did a lot of learning by listening to what the other grades were covering in their lessons. We actually learned to listen and study at the same time.

During my first couple of years at Lukken School, when I was asked what I liked most about school, my reply was, "The last day of school because summer vacation was coming and the first day after Christmas vacation, because we could then find out what everyone got for Christmas."

Usually recess was the most exciting part of the school day. During noon hour and recess, we played games like Hit the Can, Hide and Seek, Fox and Geese, or Run My Good Sheep Run. The big event of the school year was Play Day. Near the end of the school year, about six or eight of the neighboring schools came together for a day of fun and competition. There were the high jump, the broad jump, sack races, three legged races, plus other activities for which the schools and

The Lukken School

students earned their blue ribbons.

From time to time during our school year, there were humorous incidents touched off by mischievous students. One that we didn't soon forget was the day that Rose Gobel, our teacher, left the school room to make use of the outhouse. She entered it not knowing that one of the boys, who was playing a game of hide and seek, was hiding behind the door inside the women's biffy. In Miss Gobel's rush to take care of business, she failed to close the door and didn't discover the boy until she was seated on the "throne" improperly displaying her apparel.

Oh yes, when we students had to go out to the toilet, we had to get permission from the teacher which we did by quietly raising our hand and holding up one or two fingers, depending on what we intended to do.

One day I was the victim of a dumb accident. That day, one of the boys brought a chain with him to school. He asked me to take one end of the chain so we could swing it like jumping the rope. After a few swings, he let go of his end and I was struck in the mouth by the chain. One of my front teeth was cracked and badly chipped. This set the stage for the day in our barn when I was about to pick up a pitchfork by stepping on the tines, instead of picking it up by the handle. The handle struck me on my damaged tooth and broke it off in the middle.

The dentist concluded that the best treatment was to pull the tooth, and so for years I suffered the sensitivity of a missing front tooth until later in life a very good dentist repaired the damage.

My first grade at the Lukken School was not a good year. The School Board had a difficult time finding a teacher that year and had to settle for Freddy Frame, a local resident who was not well qualified. For some reason which I have never known, Mr. Frame (but we never called him that) did not like me and with his normally poor discretion, used every opportunity to put me down. One day in exasperation, he turned to me and with a harsh voice said, "Russell, if you had as many brains as you have freckles, maybe you would amount to something someday!" My parents, who were very supportive of me and knew the problems of the teacher, used to enjoy telling the end of the story. My simple and spontaneous reply to the teacher was, "At least I don't have as many freckles as Alvin Thompson!" After one disastrous year, he was not rehired. He found a job pumping gas but did not work out well in that job and eventually depended on his wife for his livelihood.

Russ as a school boy

Mount Horeb High School

Moving from a one room country school house to a high school with over two hundred students was a great experience. Several families in our neighborhood took turns driving us to school which was only a little over two miles away. When we were snow bound in the winter, we walked cross country. One winter, when we had -40 degree weather for a week, we stayed with Knut and Lena Stolen, our uncle and aunt who lived a mile from the high school. We made this walk each day and froze our noses every time!

Mount Horeb High School

Mount Horeb was a highly rated school and we received quality education. We had a complete education including music and sports. Brother Gil and I both went out for football: he became a star and I kept the bench warm! I stared in academics. By the beginning of my junior year, I was number three in my class of fifty-three students. Jimmy Green was first and Eleanor Hustad, second. At the beginning of our senior year, to my joy, Eleanor (my cousin) moved away so I got the number two spot (commonly call Salutatorian). At the beginning of our last semester, she moved back so my "cloud nine" dream came to an end!

While I was serving on the Student Council, I was instrumental in developing a recognition program where students could earn honor awards in each of their activities and in turn were presented with a special badge which they wore on the sleeve of their sweater.

Several events of note occurred in the community during my high school years. One day a blast was set off in a rock quarry in near by Blue Mounds. The blast ripped a hole in the mountain side and the now famous "Cave of the Mounds" was discovered. Fred Hanneman, our band director, and Carl Buckner, one of the local bankers, teamed up to develop the cave and made it nationally famous.

The now famous "Little Norway" had its beginnings at that time also. Jimmy Green, my classmate, was a nephew of Isaac Daily who had purchased property north of Mount Horeb and began moving

Norwegian buildings, including a Stave Church that had been at the Chicago World's Fair. With Mr. Daily's permission, our class used to have picnics there before it was opened to the public.

The third major event that I recall was a tragedy that rocked the entire community. The high school freshman class, of which my oldest brother, Ken, was a member, had their class picnic in the park on top of Blue Mounds. Upon leaving the park one of the cars was struck by a train and three of the students were killed.

East Blue Mounds Lutheran Church

East Blue Mounds Lutheran Church was a cornerstone in the life of our family, not because it was conveniently located on the corner of

our farm but because religion was very important to my parents. We always attended services as a family. Because our church was part of a three or four point parish, we normally had services only every-other Sunday or even less frequently. The long standing tradition of our church was that the men and boys sat in the pews on the right side of the church and the women and girls on the left. We broke tradition and sat together as a family and soon others followed. At the time of my childhood, Norwegian services were discontinued except for a rare afternoon service in that language. I only attended one Norwegian service and that because we had misunderstood the schedule. It proved to be one of the most boring experiences of my life. Even my parents understood little of it because they seldom spoke Norwegian at home.

We never had Sunday School because of the multiple parish set-up but in lieu of that, we had Parochial School in the summer time. It was held in the Lukken School, a teacher was hired and we were in session from nine to four, five days a week for a whole month. That proved to be one of the great experiences of our lives. One of my favorite memories was that, when I was too young to attend, on occasion I would go with my two brothers. The teacher was Bertha Simely who was a real saint. She took a special liking to me and wanted to teach me Norwegian. Before she had class for the other students, she would have me come up to her desk and succeeded in teaching me four words: "cut" (cat), "moose" (mouse), "coo" (cow) and "hesten" (horse). We loved the fellowship of the students who were members of our church but attended other public schools, our wonderful teachers and learning all the Bible stories and memorizing many hymns. We never felt deprived because of not having Sunday School. We probably got more out of Parochial School than we would have from Sunday School.

Ladies Aid was important to Mother and Luther League for us kids. One of the most memorable events for me was the annual Mission Fest which lasted for the whole day and was held under an out door tent and often had a missionary as speaker. I especially remember the time when I was asked to participate in the program by reciting Psalm one. It went well except for my attempt to be dramatic. I used a handful of chaff to emphasize the line "the wicked are like chaff that the wind drives away." I opened my hand too soon and the wind blew the chaff away before I spoke the words!

The system of supporting the church financially was quite different

Russell B. Helgesen, back row, fifth from left, at his confirmation, 1935.

in those days. A committee was appointed to evaluate the financial potential of each family and decide how much each should give. The amount was determined by their ability to pay and the willingness of each family to give. Our family was always assigned to the top bracket, not because we had a lot of money but we were rated high in willingness to give. One year the big debate was whether unmarried young men who had jobs should continue to be assessed $1 a year or be expected to give $5. Shortly after Hector Gunderson became our pastor, he initiated the Fifty Cent (per family) mission offering. Another of the big events of the year was the Christmas Program. All of the children in the congregation recited Christmas pieces and received a bag of candy and fruit.

When I was in seventh grade, it was time for me to "read for the minister." That was the term that was used for confirmation instruction. Every Saturday morning for two years, Dad drove me into town to the parsonage where we met with him and other class members for an hour or more. Most of our time was spent on "Sverdrup's Explanation of the Catechism." That book consisted of over 200 questions and answers which we were required to memorize. Following the two years of instruction, I was confirmed with the rest of the class. On confirmation Sunday, before we participated in the sacred ceremony, we were all catechized in front of the congregation. This was a gruesome experience in which the pastor asked questions from the Catechism of each of us and we were expected to give the memorized answers.

About ten years later, after completing my Seminary education and being ordained into the Holy Ministry on January 28, 1945 at Central Lutheran Church in Minneapolis, I preached my first sermon to my home congregation at East Blue Mounds Lutheran Church.

Christmas

Christmas was very special in our home; both as a religious festival and a time for ceremonies and gift giving. My Dad believed very strongly in Santa Claus. To him Santa Claus was the embodiment of the spirit of Christmas. Even during the Great Depression when money was scarce, he felt strongly about doing their best to make Christmas a happy time for us children with as many gifts "from Santa Claus" as possible.

To me Christmas began long before December 25. Weeks ahead of time, I would lay on my stomach on the living room floor with the Sears Roebuck catalogue making up my wish list. When Mother would inform me that the list was too long and that I could not get all those things, I would reply, "yes, but I wish I could!" When Christmas finally came, it was always a disappointment to me, perhaps because my expectations had been set too high and for some reason, if something went wrong, it seemed to happen to me, like the year that the mail truck which was carrying my present, burned up and I had to wait weeks for its delivery.

For us Christmas began at 3:00 P.M. on the day of Christmas Eve. At that time the shades in our living room were pulled to prepare for the arrival of Santa Claus. Then at 4:00 P.M. our church janitor, Ole Jevne, made his way across our farm to the church where he rang the bell. Then we headed for the barn to do the chores. On that special night the cattle were fed the best second crop Alfalfa hay. Because it was such a special night, we did the milking and chores before supper.

The meal on Christmas Eve was oyster stew which we all loved.

The table had to be cleared and dishes done before Santa Claus could arrive. Following the meal, Dad would peek through the keyhole of the living room door. When he reported that Santa had come, we all celebrated around the Christmas tree by opening our presents. Our big lutefisk dinner with lefse and all the trimmings was always reserved for Christmas Day.

Some time during the Christmas season, there was always a Christmas Program at church in addition to the worship service. The Christmas tree was a large, freshly cut evergreen with real candles that were lit and burning during the service. Because of Dad's concern about fire, he provided a five gallon bucket of sand as his personal fire department. Following Christmas he took the tree down and before disposing of it, cut the top off and made it into a Norwegian stir stick which Mother used when she made milk mush or rumagrout. On the days following Christmas we did a lot of visiting with relatives and neighbors. One of the things that we enjoyed most with our neighbors was the Norwegian ritual of ragamuffing. This Norwegian name means "a ragged disreputable person." We would all dress up with homemade costumes, including masks to cover our faces, and would call on our neighbors unannounced. We would do silly things and talk in strange voices until the neighbors guessed who we were. When they guessed our names, we would then remove our masks. When all our faces were uncovered, they would treat us to home made root beer and Christmas goodies.

Fourth of July

Growing up on the farm the 4th of July was an important day of celebration for our family. We always had watermelon, ice cream and firecrackers. The day began with a morning trip to town. The watermelon we bought was put in a wash tub under the windmill pump where the cold well water chilled it and made it delicious for eating. With no refrigeration, we seldom had ice cream except on the 4th when we either bought a gallon in town or made it in our hand-turned ice cream maker. In town we bought our fire works: fire crackers, canon crackers, and sparklers. Under Dad's careful supervision we made noise with the fire crackers, blew tin cans into the air with the canon crackers, and lit up the sky at night with the sparklers.

The one 4th that I particularly remember was when brother Ken drove us to town and back in our old Essex Super Six. After shopping, we headed for home. I was sitting on the front passenger seat. In my attempt to cool the hot car, I reached for the window crank, but by mistake took hold of the door latch. On the Essex, the front doors were hinged on the back and when I unlatched the door, the wind caught it, the door flew open, and I went tumbling out head first onto the street. Fortunately we were traveling very slowly when it happened, Ken quickly stopped and I climbed back into the car, none the worse for wear. This was a 4th of July to be long remembered!

CHAPTER 16

My Personal Ten Commandments

1. **You shall not steal**

   Every Saturday night our family went to town. While my parents were visiting with friends I would browse through the stores. In one store a 10¢ cigarette holder caught my eye. I couldn't resist and when no one was looking I put it in my pocket. All week long my conscience tormented me. I didn't have the courage to tell anyone or to return it, so one day I put it on the ground where a wheel of our wagon crushed it. My conscience paid a heavy price but never again did I steal.

2. **It is more blessed to give than to receive**

   In some ways the Great Depression was difficult, but at least we always had enough to eat. It was at times when we needed something extra that we had to sacrifice or go without. I remember the time when one of our horses developed a bad sore on her neck from her collar. The sore was so bad that we could hardly use her for field work. A special collar was needed but Dad did not have the $1 that was needed to buy one. On one of our Saturday night trips to town I left the family and sneaked into the harness shop. In my pocket was a dollar which was all the money I had saved up. With it, I bought the collar. It made me feel very good and Dad was in tears. Things like that you never forget.

3. **Trust has great value**

As a kid of 13 or 14 years of age, I learned the value of trust. One day when the time had come for me to learn how to operate our McCormick Deering grain binder, which was powered by three horses, Dad took me to the field. Together we oiled the binder and hooked up the horses. I climbed up on the seat, took hold of the reins of the horses, called "giddyap" and off we went with Dad following closely behind. Because this was my very first experience, he could well have followed me all day long, but when we got half way around the field on my very first trip, he took off for home. This demonstration of trust was one of the greatest lessons of my life.

4. **You shall not curse, swear, lie, or deceive**

Dad never swore and Mother made sure that we didn't. We were taught that "gosh" and "darn" were abbreviations for "God" and "damn" and to this day, I have not added them to my vocabulary.

5. **Gambling doesn't pay**

On one of our visits to the County Fair during my preteen years, Dad gave each of us a dime to spend for the day. I headed for the Midway and watched all the activity at the gambling booths. It really intrigued me and finally I spotted a booth where no one could lose. Just pick up a ball, have it opened, and you get whatever the number indicated. I gave the attendant my dime and picked up one of the balls. They opened it and I got my prize which was a green drinking glass. I could have bought the glass for a nickel. When Dad found out about it on the way home, he felt very badly and said, "You should have told me sooner and I would have given you another dime so that you could at least have bought an ice cream cone." That was the end of my gambling career!

6. **Sunday is a day of rest**

   The Third Commandment, "Remember the Sabbath Day to keep it holy" was taken seriously in our home. We never considered missing church on Sunday and Dad always said, "I'd sooner let the hay rot in the field than bring it in on Sunday." Resting on Sunday is also good for one's health.

7. **Mid-day naps are healthy**

   Brother Ken recalls that when we roomed together in college, every day I would say, "I'm lying down to take a nap, call me in five minutes!" I still depend on mid-day naps to replenish my energy.

8. **You must get to the top**

   My Dad only had a fifth grade education but in keeping with his philosophy of life he always told us boys, "I don't care what you do in life but you've got to get to the top! To get there you need an education. I can't help you financially, but if you can figure out how to work your way through college, I'll take care of the farm."

9. **Set your shoes straight at night**

   One of the little things I learned from my mother was, "before you go to bed at night, set your shoes together straight or you won't be able to run in your dreams." To this day I still have to set my shoes straight when I go to bed.

10. **Don't make a boy wear his mother's shoes**

    When I was a kid, my Mother bought a new pair of shoes which proved to be too tight for her. When it was determined that my feet were a size larger than hers, I was given the assignment of stretching her shoes by wearing them. I would not have survived the embarrassment I was experiencing if a reprieve had not been granted me.

Lessons I Never Forgot

All of us have learned some things that we have carried with us throughout life. Sometimes the learning process was painful but in the end they have proven to be helpful.

1. **Don't leave your keys in your coat pocket**

   When I was in my teens, our family went on a trip to Madison. When we entered a restaurant for lunch, Dad hung up his overcoat in which were his car keys. When we got ready to leave, Dad's coat was missing. Later he received his keys in the mail but his coat was never returned. I don't recall how we got the car home without his keys, but ever since, I have never put my car keys in my coat pocket when I hang it up in a public place.

2. **Count how many notice**

   We all make mistakes and think that everyone notices them. During our years on Long Island, we bought a piece of land in Shirley, Long Island, and built a modest vacation home. I had no trouble framing the house but I didn't know how to frame the roof. In our congregation was an old experienced Swedish carpenter who agreed to come and help me. When I got to that point, he showed up ready to go to work but before we began, I felt compelled to take him on a tour and point out all the mistakes I had made. He listened patiently and when I was finished, he simply said, "count how many notice!"

3. **No shame, no shame**

   While spending time at our summer place in Shirley, we became friends with a lovely Italian family next door. Her beauty was in her personality and likely did not count her calories! While picnicking with them one day, she treated us to an abundant spread of delicious food. When we had eaten all our stomachs could hold, she insisted that we have another helping and urged us with her favorite expression, "no shame, no shame!"

4. **What difference will it make five years from now?**

All of us have done things that we regret and wish that we could do over. When we lived in Uniondale, Long Island, we had a neighbor that belonged to our church and with whom we had become good friends. One day he felt free to call me and ask if he could borrow our car for a few hours while his was in the garage. I told him that I would be very happy to loan him the car but unfortunately I needed it at that time. The fact was that I had planned to call on some prospective parishioners of our church that afternoon but had not made any appointments and could easily have adjusted my schedule to accommodate him. I don't remember the results of the calls I made that day but I do remember that he never asked me for a favor again. The lesson I learned was that it is important to ask the question "what difference will this make five years from now?"

5. **Always be honest, but . . .**

It was Easter Sunday: The service at Our Savior's Church, Lansing, Iowa, progressed nicely and I was about to preach my Easter sermon. I began with the usual greeting, "Dear friends in Christ," but altered it by adding the words, "and hypocrites." I proceeded to explain that anyone who had not been in church since Christmas but came on Easter Sunday, was a hypocrite. That could be defended as honesty but good judgment prompted me to never use it again. In the congregation was a farmer's wife who was always in church but her husband never came. Following the service she came to me and said, "Pastor, I have tried and tried to get my husband to attend church with me and finally today he agreed, but after that sermon, he will never come again!"

CHAPTER 17

My College Years

The Journey Begins

How three brothers (including me) and one sister got to Eau Claire State Teachers' College (now the University of Wisconsin—Eau Claire) is a story in itself. The unfolding of that drama began in 1934 which was at the height of the Great Depression. My oldest brother, Ken, had just graduated from high school and wanted to go on to college but knew that he could not because there was no money. So he found a job which paid him $1 a week.

Two years later, my brother, Gil, graduated from high school. He also wanted to go on to college but knew that, of necessity, he would have to follow the same track that Ken was taking. At that time our cousin, Alvin Stolen, was Superintendent of Schools of Eau Claire, Wisconsin, and his intervention changed our lives. Near the end of that summer, he and his family came to our home for their annual visit. In the course of conversation he asked Gil what he planned to do. His reply was that he would like to go on to college but had no money. Alvin knew that Gil was a good football player and knew that he could enlist the help of his good friend Bill Dorn who was the college football coach and would be willing to find work and housing to make it possible for Gil to work his way through college.

With only three weeks notice, Gil had packed up, was on his way to Eau Claire, and had enrolled in college. With the help of Bill Zorn, he found an apartment and lined up a dish washing job at the Savoy Café. With Gil's ability and connection with the football coach, it looked like he was on his way to a football career. However, at the last practice before the team's first game of the season, he tore a cartridge in his knee which ended his football career, but he proceeded on his track for a college education.

By the end of his first year of college, Gil knew how to line up jobs and make enough money to meet college expenses. With Gil's help, Ken enrolled in Eau Claire State Teachers' College the next year and a year later, in 1938 when I graduated from high school I, too, was off to Eau Claire. My sister, Ila, followed two years later. During the time the three of us brothers were in college, we shared housing and helped each other finding jobs. For a long time, we kept washing dishes at the Savoy Café, but in addition to that had paper routes and other jobs at the going rate of 15¢ an hour.

A Good Academic Education

With the help of a full academic scholarship of $26 for my first semester, I had a successful freshman year. Sports was not my forte but I had a good experience playing alto saxophone in the college concert and marching bands. Public speaking proved to be one of my strengths and my academic career was very positive. My major was in history and minors were in social science and English. Because my college education was designed as preparation for seminary, I took two years of German and, as a Teachers' College student, I was required to do practice teaching which was done at Elk Mound High School. Upon graduation, I received a Bachelor of Science degree, a teaching certificate and was inducted into Alpha Kappa which was the National Honor Society.

Russ in his band uniform at Eau Claire State Teachers' College.

College Life Was Work, Work, Work

If you want something badly enough, you have to be willing to pay the price. Even though college in 1938–42 was inexpensive, it took a lot of hours at 15¢ to pay the cost of board and room and to have some spending money beside. For the first part of my college career, I earned my way mostly by washing dishes, cleaning houses, and putting on and taking off storm windows, plus washing inside walls with Dic-a-Do which was a very effective cleaner (but slow work when all I could afford was a 1½-inch paint brush!) These jobs left me with enough time each day for a paper route.

The best job I had during college was with E. M. Hale who was president and owner of the very successful Eau Claire Book and Stationery company. The Hales lived in a modest mansion with a golf putting green across the street from their house. I was engaged as chauffeur for Mrs. Hale and their teenage daughter and as grounds keeper for their property. I enjoyed the work and the occasional nap in the basement when I was especially tired from my high pace of activity!

During college years I was a member of First Lutheran Church where Dr. Seth Eastvold was pastor. He was very aggressive and legalistic and under his leadership, the congregation grew rapidly with many people who became either his loyal friends or aggressive enemies. It was said that "people either swore by him or at him." I was one of those who highly respected him and "swore by him." At that time he built a new parish house that included a gymnasium and then applied to the Federal Government for a grant with which to hire a youth athletic director. When the grant was approved, he hired me to the position and in that capacity I was Scout Master of a scout troop (though I had never been a Boy Scout) and basket ball coach (though I had never played basketball). During my time there I organized a basket ball tournament for a number of the churches in Eau Claire and our team ended up winning the championship!

When Ken and Gil were still at college, the three of us lived together and did our own cooking but when they graduated, I was left to fend for myself. I was able to work out various arrangements for housing but the most interesting was living in the Eau Claire Hotel. The owner was a friend of Mr. Hale's and for business purposes gave him two coupons,

Russ's championship basketball team from First Lutheran Church.

each of which was good for six weeks of free hotel occupancy. Because Mr. Hale could not use the coupons, he gave them to me and the owner agreed that I could use both of them which gave me a free hotel room for three months. The one drawback to that arrangement was that during that time I had to eat in restaurants which proved to be expensive. Because I had so little money I couldn't afford dessert. I satisfied the problem by starting to drink chocolate milk. By saving a good swallow of it until the end of the meal, I satisfied my craving for dessert.

A Blessing from Tough Times

This chapter is dedicated especially to our five children: Becky, Jane, Tom, Jim, and Mary who, except for a quirk of fate (or shall we call it a blessing of God) would not be here today. This chapter tells how the parents of these five children met, fell in love, and married. Mom, who 65 years ago was known as Lorraine Sampson, loves to tell the story of how her parents' (August and Mabel Sampson) house burned down and then lost their farm in the Great Depression, and if that had not happened, our children wouldn't be here today.

It was a sad day in 1936 when Mom came home from school to their farm near Winchester, Wisconsin, and saw only a heap of ashes where their house had been that morning. Grandpa and Grandma had no insurance and no money with which to rebuild the house and like so many others at that time, were not able to make the mortgage payments. So they packed up the few possessions they had and left. Grandpa Sampson's brother, who had a farm near Elk Mound was in poor health and needed help on the farm so Grandpa and Grandma decided to go and live with him and help out. Some months later, when Mom graduated from Winneconne High School, she went to live with them.

In the fall of 1936 Mom enrolled in Stout Institute, Menomonee, where she majored in Home Economics. After one year, she did not have the money to return to college so she moved to Eau Claire and enrolled in a business school. After a few months, she felt adequately prepared for secretarial work and was hired by the Eau Claire Sand and Gravel Company.

So if her parents' house had not burned down and if they had not lost their farm, your mother and I would not have met! The moral of the story is "a tragedy can be turned into a blessing."

You have already read the other half of the story of how your Dad, one of the three farm boys from Wisconsin, got to college in Eau Claire. Now we will find out how he and your mother met.

Two Lives Converge

The academic aspects of college prepared me for life but romance gave me a life partner. You have learned how two people, unknown to each other, were brought to Eau Claire in a near miraculous way. But the city at that time had a population of 30,000 and now we must find out how these two people found each other and fell in love. For clarity at this point, I shall call this couple Russ and Lorraine.

When Lorraine moved to Eau Claire and got her job at the Eau Claire Sand and Gravel Company, the first thing she did was to attend and join First Lutheran Church where she sang in the choir and was active in the LDR (Lutheran Daughters of the Reformation). Upon her arrival she looked for an apartment, but being a student she had no money for rent. Fortunately she found a home in which she could live and work for her board and room. When she finished business college three months later, she was introduced to Louise Hultgren who was looking for a roommate. The two of them moved into an apartment in the home of a Berg family near downtown Eau Claire. When she left her job at Sand and Gravel, she went to work for radio station, WEAU Eau Claire. In addition to her secretarial duties, she co-hosted a radio commercial once a week with Marie Hilmer for a local women's clothing shop. The program was called "News of the New with Marie Hilmer and Lorraine Sampson." About a year later, her roommate, Louise Hultgren, was married so Lorraine had to give up the apartment. She found a new roommate and was able to stay in the same house in a single room and had her meals with the Berg family.

About this time, three college students, Ken, Gil, and Russ Helgesen, "the three farm boys from Wisconsin," were looking for an apartment and, as luck would have it, moved into the one that Lorraine had just vacated. For some time their relationships were friendly but casual. They were all pleased to have such "nice" people under the same roof. Sharing the same bathroom seemed to present no problems. In casual conversations we learned that we all were members of First Lutheran Church and sang in the choir. Russ seemed to be too busy (or maybe too shy) to engage in much conversation. Gil was bold enough to invite Lorraine to join him in the kitchen one night when he was eating pop corn. Familiarity increased but it was only casual among "nice" young people who were not having any problems.

Romantic Days and Nights

On a spring morning in 1941 a spark was lit, but it was neither a flash nor an explosion. Russ was leaving the house to go downtown on his bicycle and at the same time Lorraine showed up on foot for the same destination. Trying to be a gentleman, he asks her if she would like a ride downtown with him on his bike. When she graciously accepted, there was really nothing he could do but try to fulfill his invitation. In less than a block they both recognized that this was not a "bicycle built for two" and each proceeded on their way with their own means of transportation. From the start Russ knew it was a dumb idea and only intended it as a joke. After that he learned to be more careful with his offers. In retrospect it was apparent that their relationship had not suffered any damage.

Soon another problem or opportunity presented itself. At that time Russ's brother Ken was engaged to Esther Hendrickson and despite his desire to spend the summer with her, he volunteered to go home and help Dad on the farm. Before leaving, he gave Russ the assignment of taking care of Esther. Several weeks went by and Russ began to realize that he should do something about his assignment. So he called Esther and they agreed to go roller skating. Lest they be misunderstood, they thought it best that she invite her girlfriend, Lorraine, to go along. Late in the afternoon of the appointed day, Esther called to apologize. She was stuck at work and would have to beg out. So Russ called Lorraine and explained the problem but suggested that, if she wanted to go anyway, it was all right with him. She thought it would be a good idea (not knowing that he had never skated before!). When they got on the roller rink, she found out. It was probably at that moment that Russ concluded the she was the one that he would like to skate with throughout his life and she knew for sure that he could not make it without her! and a few weeks later, on the 10th of August, 1941, they had their first official date. Russ invited her to go with him to the Chippewa County Fair and they agreed that this would be a good time to invite Esther to go with them. During their time at the fair, Esther informed them that it was Ken's birthday and she would like to call him to wish him a Happy Birthday. They found a phone booth and the call was successful. In fact the whole day was delightful and Russ concluded that Lorraine was the right choice.

In the next six weeks their relationship grew. Then came Halloween! Dr. Fox, who was one of Russ's college professors and the one that all the students chose to pick on, was facing the dilemma of "Tricks and Treats." Knowing that students would descend on his house that night, he hired Russ to guard it. At that time Ken had his car at college and was willing to loan it to Russ for the evening and, in turn, Lorraine accepted the invitation to join him. Ken's car was small, which was just fine with them. Because it was an oil guzzler, Ken kept a five gallon can of oil in the trunk of the car which did not have a lock. When darkness descended, the tricksters arrived as expected. When they saw the two of them in the car, they chose to leave the house alone but proceeded to attack the car. The four of them each grabbed a corner of the car and gave it, including Russ and Lorraine, a good shaking and in the process ran off with the five gallon can of oil.

Neither Russ nor Lorraine remembers whether it was before or after the shaking, that Russ proposed to her, but neither of them will ever forget that he did. When he proposed, she made it clear that she highly respected him BUT she needed more time. After all it was only six weeks since their first date and she hadn't yet had time to decide if she could fulfill the role of pastor's wife. When she said YES a few weeks later, they both were sure about their commitment to each other which now has lasted for more than 65 years. During the next two years, while Russ was in college and Lorraine was working in Eau Claire, they spent a lot of time together as their love deepened and their relationship grew.

One night about six months after their engagement, Russ dropped a "bomb." He shared with Lorraine a letter that he had just received from his Mother, explaining that his Dad's health was such that he would need help on the farm again that summer! The previous summer of 1941, Ken had left his "beloved" in Eau Claire to help Dad on the farm. It seemed only fair that Russ should do the same this year. Both he and Lorraine were disappointed because they had been looking forward to a wonderful summer together. As they thought about the matter, Lorraine came up with a bright idea: "I have not yet met your parents and I would also love to see the farm where you grew up. If you go home for the summer, I could do both of these things."

As they parted that night, Russ's mind was still in turmoil. As he walked slowly and thoughtfully on his way home, the April air was clear and crisp; the star studded sky was bright and the Milk Way was a canopy of beauty. While he struggled to clear his thoughts, an awesome feeling came over him. It was as though God himself were speaking. He saw no light nor heard no voice but the message was clear. It began like a paraphrasing from *A Tale of Two Cities:* "Come home dear son, your Father needs you; come home dear son, while it still is day" and then concluded with what seemed to be the final words of Charles Darnay, "It is a far, far better thing that I do, than I have ever done; it is a far, far better place that I go to, that I have ever known."

Russ went home that night and slept well and during the summer that followed, Lorraine visited him and the Helgesen farm at Mount Horeb where they had a wonderful time and his parents agreed that "this was a match made in heaven!"

Lorraine Theona Sampson: Russ's sweetheart.

Later we will talk about the wedding but for now we will tell the story of the diamond ring. Since they wasted no time in becoming engaged, Russ had not had time to save money for a ring but now his goal was to buy one as soon as possible. He discovered that he would have to spend $30 for an acceptable ring. At 15¢ an hour, it would take 200 hours over and above his regular work. A short time before he was about to leave for the farm for the summer, he bought the ring. He planned an appropriate presentation. One evening shortly before Lorraine was scheduled to leave for church for a Mother/Daughter banquet he found an excuse to call on her. He came early enough so they had adequate time to sit and enjoy each other while they held hands. As Russ played gently with her fingers, he casually slipped the ring that she was wearing off and replaced it with the diamond. When she finally discovered the diamond, she was surprised and excited. At the banquet that night, she really enjoyed showing it to her friends! The ring served her well until their 25th Wedding anniversary when Russ replaced it with one which was of a more appropriate size. The new one didn't require 200 hours of work!

"With This Ring I Thee Wed"

After nearly four years of courtship, our wedding plans were set. We had planned to wait until I had completed seminary, but settled on the big event to be held between my last two years of school. When I enrolled in Luther Seminary in St. Paul, Lorraine continued for a while to live and work in Eau Claire but it didn't take long to conclude that it would be much better if she moved to Minneapolis and got a job there. She made the move shortly and lived temporarily with my Aunt Margaret and cousin Mona Mae Helgesen and got a job at Cargill Company. We loved the arrangement and made use of the street cars in getting back and forth to spend time with each other. After two years we set May 26, 1944, as the wedding date and began our serious planning.

The wedding would be at Grace Lutheran Church, Winchester, Wisconsin, which had been Lorraine's church and the home of her extended family. Oliver Berglund, pastor of Grace, and Hector Gunderson, pastor of East Blue Mounds Lutheran Church, which had been my home church, would perform the ceremony. Some months before the wedding, Lorraine, with the help of her mother, made her own beautiful wedding gown. She borrowed the veil from my sister-in-law, Esther. The veil was very old and had been used by her mother when she was married.

The wedding would take place during my break from seminary which would allow us time for the wedding and a week's honeymoon. Because Lorraine was working, she arrived at her parents' home in Winchester a few days after I did. What a beautiful experience it was to meet her at the train station in Neenah, Wisconsin, before the sun had risen. The first task on our list was to go to Oshkosh to get our marriage license. I had no problem getting the license but, to our

Russell Burnell Helgesen and Lorraine Theona Sampson were wed on May 26, 1944, at Grace Lutheran Church in Winchester, Wisconsin.

Russ and Lorraine Helgesen's wedding party: Gill Helgesen, Phil Helgesen, June Christianson, Virginia née Ganther Helgesen, a cousin, and Laurie Helgesen.

surprise, they would not issue Lorraine a license without her father's signature, even though she was 25 years old, because she was not a resident of Wisconsin. So back to Winchester we went to get her father and with his help, the document was issued without a problem.

On the 'to do" list was the matter of flowers. A florist in Neenah provided the corsages but flowers with which to decorate the church were beyond our budget. However, on our way home form the florist, as we were driving out of Neenah, we discovered a home with beautiful white lilac bushes in full bloom. We were bold enough to stop and present our case to the owner who graciously offered us as many as we needed to beautify the church. The ceremony that evening was beautiful and proceeded without a hitch. We had requested that the pastor use as his text, Psalm 84. The words and thoughts were uplifting: "Behold our shield, O God; look on the face of your anointed. I would rather be a doorkeeper in the house of my God than live in the tents of wickedness. No good thing does the Lord withhold from those who walk uprightly. O Lord of hosts, happy is everyone who trusts in you." In advance of the wedding, I located someone who had an 8mm movie camera and was willing to loan it to me to film the wedding. It was a bit tricky being both groom and photographer. We solved it by repeating the ceremony after everyone else had retired to the church basement for the reception. It was an awkward and lengthy process but we have always cherished this film and long ago the family has forgiven us for the

Russ and Lorraine eventually made it to the reception to cut the cake after staging a second ceremony for purposes of filming it. Helga Helgesen and Mable Sampson also pictured.

long wait. Once we got started, the reception was very nice and the wedding cake was beautiful.

Following the ceremony and reception, we borrowed Lorraine's parent's car and took off for the Valley Inn in Neenah where we spent our wedding night. The next day we drove to Waupaca where we spent the next week in a cottage on the lake. It proved to be a wonderful week of fishing and honeymooning. Our long awaited dream had finally come true and following that week we headed back to Minneapolis to seminary and job as Mr. and Mrs. Russell Helgesen.

Russ gets his fill of fishing on their honeymoon in Waupaca, Wisconsin.

CHAPTER 18

When God Needs Help

In the days of the Prophet Eli when the boy Samuel was living with him, one night he heard what he believed was a call from God. After the third call, Samuel answered, "Speak, for your servant is listening." It was then that Samuel realized that he was to be a prophet of God.

When God calls, sometimes he does it through other people and at times he uses strange and even miraculous circumstances. In my life I have experienced both of these kinds of calls. When in the hymn "I, the Lord of Sea and Sky," God asks "whom shall I send?" I reply by singing with gusto, " Here I am, Lord. Is it I, Lord? I have heard you calling in the night. I will go, Lord, if you lead me. I will hold your people in my heart."

As a little child, when people asked me what I wanted to be when I grew up, my reply was "I want to be a pastor and a cheese maker. I will make cheese during the week and preach on Sunday!"

The First Time the Lord Called Me

My very first call came in baptism when God call me to be his child. His call to service came later. As time passed, that call to be a cheese maker and a pastor did not materialize and my interests turned to wood working. By the time I reached high school, I decided to be an industrial arts teacher. That goal continued for three years until one day my life was changed forever. It was the summer of 1937 when the severe drought which followed the Great Depression was at its worst.

The crops on our farm, as well as those of our neighbors, were drying up and everyone at church and at home was praying for rain.

On one of those hot days in the middle of the summer I harnessed the horses, headed for the corn field on the back forty, and hitched them to the cultivator. After a short time of cultivating what little corn there was, I saw the sky becoming cloudy. Quickly the clouds turned black and I knew that a storm was coming. I unhitched the horses as fast as I could and headed for home in a dead gallop. In the pouring rain I offered up a prayer, "Thank you God for answering our prayers. Because you have sent this rain to save our crops, I will dedicate my life to serve you as a pastor." From that day on, when the Lord called me, I have never wavered from my promise and now, 65 years from the day of my ordination, I'm still fulfilling that call which the Lord laid on me.

The Lord Called Again

After receiving my college degree, I enrolled in Luther Seminary in St. Paul, Minnesota. At that time all of the costs, including board and room, were paid by the Norwegian Lutheran Church. What a treat to eat in the Boarding Club where we could have all the food we desired after our "starvation diet" during college years. At that time I was 6 feet tall and weighed 125 pounds. During the first six weeks in the Seminary Boarding Club where we could eat all we wanted, I gained twenty pounds!!

My Seminary years were during World War II. The Government agreed to defer seminary students from the draft on condition that we complete our education as quickly as possible. At the end of the first year, which included summer vacation, the seminary continued in session for the balance of the time we were there, with no internship and no vacations. So instead of four years, we completed our education in just over two and a half.

I was ordained into the ministry of the Norwegian Lutheran Church of America at Central Lutheran Church in Minneapolis on January 28, 1945. Shortly thereafter, the name of the Church was changed to the Evangelical Lutheran Church (ELC).

Then the Lord called again. In fact I received two calls, one from a small town and country parish in Clinton, Minnesota, and the other

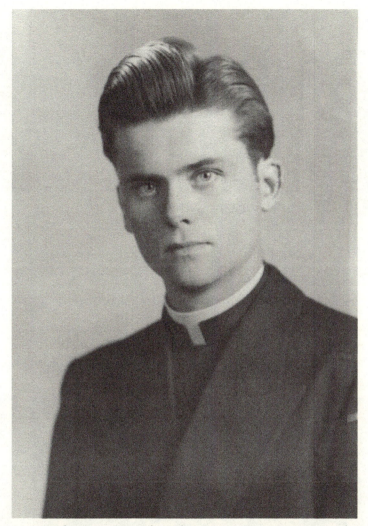

Russ Helgesen was ordained January 28, 1945, into the Norwegian Lutheran Church of Amercia.

from the Norwegian Lutheran Church in Lansing, Iowa, and two small churches in Desoto and Ferryville, Wisconsin. I accepted that second call, believing that it was God's will for me at that time and was excited by the challenges it offered. Lansing had not had a resident pastor for many years and the last pastor to serve it said, "there is no shame in serving a dying congregation if it must die!" Desoto was a small rural church east of the Mississippi River and the plan was for me to organize a new congregation in the little river town of Ferryville.

Luther Seminary, St. Paul, Minnesota, where Russ began in 1942, during World War II.

On January 28, 1945, Russ was ordained into the ministry of the Norwegian Lutheran Church of America at Central Lutheran Church in Minneapolis, Minnesota.

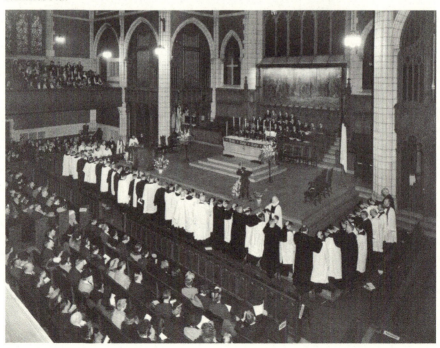

Three brothers ordained: Russ, Gil, and Ken Helgesen.

Columbia South America Calling

When I was in Seminary, our mission professor, Dr. Rolf Syrdal, said, "don't accept a call to a foreign mission field if you can help it!" After one year in the Lansing parish, I had a very strong feeling that the Lord was calling me to Columbia, South America. The call persisted and in due time I wrote Dr. Syrdal offering my services. In his reply, he informed me that violence had broken out in the country and the doors for missionary work had now been closed. The deep sense of missionary calling persisted but it turned out to be Home Mission work.

Lord: New York Is Calling

In the midst of an exciting ministry at Lansing, I thought I heard the Lord call again. One day Pastor Herbert Hanson, my good friend and classmate who was serving a congregation at Glen Head, Long Island,

During their time in New York, Russ and Lorraine recieved a visit from family members: Russ's sister Laurie, sister-in-law Esther, and parents Paul and Helga. Lorraine is center front and Russ on the right.

and was also part-time Home Mission director for the New York area, approached me with the question, "How would you like to come to New York and start a new congregation?" He explained that the potato fields of Long Island were being turned into housing developments and were in need of new churches. This seemed to me to be the new direction of the missionary call that I had previously experienced to Columbia, South America. I told him that this would interest me very much and he assured me that I would soon be receiving the call.

For several months I heard nothing, so I inquired of him. He then explained that he had talked to Dr. Martin Anderson, the District President, who did not think that I was capable of handling this challenge. After a short time, I did receive the call and with it my career in Home Missions was launched. During the next twelve years I started two new congregations on Long Island and spent most of the balance of my ministry in administrative work in American Missions for the national church.

Five years after starting Grace Lutheran Church in Uniondale, I accepted a call to move seven miles and start a new congregation in Massapequa. Because we had no building and could not find any facilities in which to hold our services, it was necessary to delay the start of the

Becky helps her dad, Russ, install the sign on the new church in Massapequa.

congregation until the first unit of the church building was completed. While waiting, I spent six months in interim ministry. The Evangelical Lutheran Church (ELC) had just voted to establish a Home Mission Trust Certificate program. Dr. Philip Dybvig, Mission director, asked me to come to Minneapolis and begin the new fund drive in that area. The project had not as yet been publicized and no literature had been printed. So, for several weeks, I stayed with my parents on their farm in Cottage Grove, Wisconsin, and teamed up with Olaf Gilderhaus, a highly respected layman in that community. He drove me around and introduced me to potential donors for the new fund. Since raising the first dollar for that new Home Mission Trust Certificate Fund over fifty years ago, the fund (now called the Mission Investment Fund) has grown to over $700 million. After several weeks of fund raising, I decided to return home to my family and I spent the next six months as Interim Pastor of Good Shepherd Lutheran Church, Levittown, Long Island.

Lord: Florida Calling

Early in 1951 we were ready to start St. John's Lutheran Church in Massapequa which proved to be a very positive experience. But after two years, I was confronted with a new call. Dr. Dybvig, the director of Home Missions, wanted me to go to Florida where the ELC did not have any churches. My assignment would be to move there with my family and spend six months or more exploring the state for mission opportunities and then start a new congregation. Though the call had exciting possibilities , I declined because I had been in Massapequa for only two years and felt that my leaving so soon would be detrimental to the congregation.

Lord: Minneapolis Is on the Line

In 1959, after 7½ years of very exciting ministry in Massapequa, New York, I experienced a strange phenomena. When we returned home from a very good vacation that summer, I should have been full of energy and ready to delve into another exciting year of parish activities but instead, I was listless and lacking in focus. I had no enthusiasm for continuing at St. John's but had no thoughts of any other ministry. After continuing in that state of mind for some days, a letter arrived from Dr. Philip Dybvig who had just been elected Mission director for the newly formed American Lutheran Church.

His letter to me, dated October 21, 1959, read in part: "I am writing to find out whether or not there would be any possible chance, whatsoever, of interesting you in becoming a member of our staff for the new Church. You have a background of experience and you have such ability and imagination, that I would like nothing better than to recommend you to the new Board for election." If this would happen my responsibility would be to serve as regional director of the Upper Midwest. As I read the letter, it was clear to me that this was the Lord that was calling and the thought of it excited me.

I informed him of this by return mail, and on November 19, 1959, I received the following reply: "When I returned to the office, I was very happy to find your letter on my desk. I say this because it is still true that I can think of no pastor in our church that I would rather have on our staff." Shortly thereafter I received the call, accepted it, and began work in the spring of 1960. I spent 14 years of very exciting ministry in the national office: the first seven of those years as regional director and the last seven as director of the newly created Department of Special Ministries.

Lord: The Bishop Wants You

My ministry in the office of American Missions was very fulfilling but came to an unhappy ending. It was a time of major turmoil in the Church. One of our new board members took the position that "unless there is conflict within a staff, they cannot be productive." He succeeded in fostering conflict and our staff became divided and unproductive. As a result of a "political" move, my position was eliminated and I was without a job, which in retrospect was fortunate for me as it opened up new paths of ministry. Within a short time, I was called by the Southwestern Minnesota District of the ALC to be the assistant to Dr. Edward Hansen, bishop. After five very happy years in Willmar it was time for the Lord to call again.

Lord: Minneapolis Is Calling Again

The time was now 1978 and with the election of a new bishop, my call had come to an end. In seeking a new call I felt an inner urge to return to the parish ministry but the Lord had other plans. In retrospect it was clear that administration has been my forte. At this same time Bishop Hansen's term was completed. Both of us received calls from Golden Valley Lutheran College. We loaded our furniture on the same moving van, moved to Minneapolis and joined the staff of Golden Valley Lutheran College. I was treasurer and financial aid director for one year and development director for the next six years until I retired at the age of 65.

But Lord: I've Got Another Idea

When I retired in 1985, I established my own business called Stewardship Counseling Service and worked with congregations in fund raising for the next two years. In the winters we went to Arizona where we worshipped at Victory Lutheran Church in Mesa. There we developed a close relationship with Fred Moberg, Pastor of Victory. After one year, he asked if I would consider joining his staff as part time visitation pastor. I told him that I loved what I was doing and would not consider a change at that time.

But again the Lord intervened in a very strange way. At the end of the second winter, Pastor Moberg asked me the same question and I gave him the same answer. We returned home for the summer and I began soliciting work for my Stewardship Counseling but things did not go well, so I began thinking and praying about Arizona. In the meantime Victory had not filled the position and Pastor Boral Bjorn who was filling in temporarily, was growing weary of waiting to be relieved. One day he asked Pastor Moberg what he was doing about his replacement. Moberg's answer was, "nothing, I'm just waiting for the Lord!" The next day he went to his mail box and found my letter telling him that if he was still looking for a pastor, I would consider the call. The rest is history and after seven years of gratifying ministry, Victory bade me farewell.

At this point I had an idea: "God, after 50 years of answering your calls and after retiring three times, I want a change of pace. Let me know what you want me to do but on one condition: No pay. If I get paid, I can be told what to do. Now I would like the freedom of being my own boss. (Of course, God, I still plan to listen to you!). For the last decade I have been experiencing an exciting and "productive" list of volunteer opportunities. In many of these, I am thankful that I have been able to use my God given talents and in many ways have made a difference.

CHAPTER 19

Russ as Entrepreneur

At various times during my life, I have had a yen to get involved in a variety of business ventures. Like anyone who deals in venture capital, some succeed while others fail. Here is a bit of my story.

Honey Bee Keeper

My very first business venture was as a child of about twelve. One of the joys that our family experienced was in the winter when very few dairy cows were producing milk, the Lukken Cheese Factory was closed and we processed our milk through the cream separator. We then ate Mother's delicious homemade bread with rich cream and golden honey. Our supply of honey came from our neighbors, the Ranums, who were in the honey bee business. At that time, my dream was to develop a bee business of my own. One day it happened. Mysteriously out of nowhere a swarm of bees arrived and settled in our garden. With Dad's help I got a hive from the Ranums and the bees promptly entered their new home. Three days later they departed as mysteriously as they had arrived. The Ranums concluded that it was a swarm of good honey bees but without a Queen. Thus ended my first business venture.

Seminary Barber

I grew up in a home where Dad was our barber and I learned the trade from him. I never really did anything with that skill until I got to Luther Seminary where there was a barber chair in a little room off the gymnasium. Since no one else was in business, and to earn personal spending money (10¢ for a movie or 5¢ for a street car ride), I became the seminary barber. I set up shop and advertised by word of mouth. During my nearly three years at Seminary, I gave haircuts for 35¢. Every body paid cash except brother Gil, to whom I gave haircuts for free. My records show that I gave as many as eight haircuts a day for a total of over 1,100 during my seminary years. Most of the students used my services and even some of the faculty are listed among my customers.

The Chinchilla Business

Many years after my first business venture, during the years that I traveled for the Church and had time to dream as the miles rolled by, I fantasized a lucrative chinchilla business. In the sixties the big rage was raising chinchillas. One could start with just one pair, they would multiply rapidly, and big money was to be made. I found a friend who was in the business and doing very well. He encouraged me and was happy to sell me a pair for $1,500. Measured against my annual salary of about $10,000, that was big money. As headquarters for the operation, I built a room in the front end of our garage, equipped it with an optimistic number of cages and installed air conditioning (which we did not have in our house in Burnsville where we lived at the time).

Things went well. The pair began to multiply and the time arrived when I was ready to market the first pelt. Before removing the pelt, the animal, of course, had to be killed. This was a simple process and was done by attaching an electrical cord to the animal with one end to its ear and the other to the end of its tail and plugging it into an electric socket. The process work as planned and five pelts were sent off to market. The marketing firm dressed the pelts and sold them for me. After deducting their costs, they sent me a check for 46¢ for all

```
Hair Cuts – 1942

 1. Sept. 25    Otis Lee                    .35
 2.  "    31    Art Olson                   .35
                              Total         .70

 3. Oct. 1      Olaf Torvik                 .35
 4. Oct. 1      Jack Prenn                  .35
 5. Oct. 1      Lloyd Refsel         (64)   .35
 6.  "    2     Albert Halverson            .35
 7.  "    3     Richard Nelson       (4)    .35
 8.  "    6     Ernest Nelson               .35
 9.  "    7     Orville Heipler             .35
10.  "    7     Al Selid                    .35
11.  "    7     Elmo Agrimson               .35
12.  "    7     Richard Larson              .35
13.  "    7     Clifford Grenneberg         .35
14.  "    7     Erling Erickson             .35
15.  "    7     Carsten Orien               .35
16.  "    8     Clifford Swanson            .35
17.  "    8     Robert Berthelson           .35
18.  "    8     Harold Masted               .35
19.  "    9     Joe Luther                  .35
20.  "   10     Joel Njus                   .35
21.  "   10     Morris Ulring               .35
22.  "   10     Sterling Johnson            .35
                                           5.25
23.  "   12     John Suvaag                 .35
24.  "   13     Powell Swanty     (exchange)
25.  "   13     Dr. Tang                    .35
```

Some of the over 1,100 35¢ haircuts Russ gave throughout his seminary career.

five pelts! In due time I sent additional pelts to the same firm which I learned was a cooperative located in New York City. Shortly I was notified that they owed me $2.78 but no check was enclosed. Then the bad news came. The bottom had fallen out of the market and the cooperative had gone bankrupt. Because the company was involved in a reported scandal, my pelts were never recovered and the $2.78 they owed me was never received. So I liquidated the business and took Lorraine on a trip to Europe! Yes, we did go to Europe in 1969 but not with any proceeds from the chinchilla business. Later I learned that the last money that my friend made from his business was from the two chinchillas he sold me for $1,500.

Real Estate Business

When we built our new home in Burnsville in 1963 our kids began to leave for college. While designing the home, it occurred to us that it did not make a lot of sense to build a bigger house when our children were leaving home. We decided to take the walkout-basement bedrooms which they were planning to occupy and convert them into an apartment which would give us funds to finance their college education. For the ten years that we lived in Burnsville, the plan worked well. We built our next home in Willmar, Minnesota, and included a basement apartment which gave us extra income for the next five years. We also built homes in Edina, Minnesota, and Voyager Village, Wisconsin, and finished their basements but without apartments.

Investments Go North and South

In 1952 we bought a small piece of land in Shirley, Long Island, for $625. We built a summer home on it for $2,535 and sold it four years later with a 44 percent profit of $1,128. Over 50 years ago that was good money. We won't go into details about other projects that were less profitable such as Winds' Crossings (a 52 town-homes project) and a Robert Trail Building Limited Partnership which were projected to put us on easy street. When all was said and done, we survived the South Wind!

Ray Nell, Inc

Our next business venture was in Owatonna, Minn. Again, during my work and travel with the Church, I discovered an opportunity which I thought had the potential of turning a profit and could be a service to that community. Several acres of land on the growing edge of town were for sale for $14,000. The only hitch was that we had no money with which to purchase the land. I discussed the matter with Mother (Helga), who agreed to loan me the money on a signed contract with the going rate of interest. Our plan was to plat the land and build homes which in turn would be sold. We decided to build very modest homes which could provide housing for low-income families. Before proceeding with the project, Lorraine and I decided to set up a corporation. This was done by an attorney friend who agreed to do the legal work and defer payment until we had realized a profit from the sale of homes. We chose the corporate name of Ray Nell, Inc. The word Ray was inspired by "Lorraine" and Nell was the last part of my middle name, Burnell. We bought the land, platted it under the name "Ray Nell Addition" and built and sold about 25 homes within five years.

Surveyors, engineers, and architect all agreed to do the work and also defer payment until the project turned a profit. When I attended meetings of the City of Owatonna to take care of legal matters, I was always known as "Mr. Ray Nell." Normally cities require that sewer, water, and other utilities be installed before the building of a project begins. Our project, fortunately was the last one approved in Owatonna before they adopted their new policy of requiring all utilities before building. If the requirement had been in place when we built, it would have made it impossible for us to manage the project. In the end we were proud of the relationship that we developed with the city officials and the Ray Nell Addition homes that we built. All those who had trusted me to wait for their pay were paid in full and, oh yes, Mother was repaid the entire amount of the loan with interest and we in the end turned a profit which helped to offset our losses from the chinchilla business!

Stewardship Counseling Service

During the two years after my retirement, I established my own business in which I worked with congregations in stewardship counseling and fund raising. As a result of the programs, most congregations experienced a doubling of their income which made for a lot of friends. With fees ranging from $4,500 to $10,000 it gave a very good supplement to our Social Security income. One of the most satisfying programs was with a Roman Catholic Church in Litchfield, Minn., where I preached at their masses on Sunday morning and gave a bible study between each service. I had the satisfaction of doubling the income for their parish which included a parochial school.

Travel Business

While I was director of the Department of Special Ministries, which included vacation and leisure ministries, I represented the Church at a world conference on tourism in Tutzing, Bavaria, in 1969. Lorraine traveled with me and we incorporated the meeting into an extended vacation tour which included Rome. While in Rome, we walked the Apian Way. The experience of walking in the footsteps of the Apostle Paul was so moving that we thought of how great it would be to walk in the footsteps of Jesus. We set a goal of taking a trip to the Holy Lands within two years.

With the help of brother Gil who had already led tours there, we co-hosted a trip to the Holy Lands in 1972. Because we did not have the money for the trips which followed, we turned them into a business and earned our way by recruiting and leading tours for people who had the money to travel but did not possess the know how. Over the next 30 years we made 20 trips including 18 tours which we led, which included nearly 500 people:

           1972   Holy Lands (the original trip with Gil)
           1973   Holy Lands
           1974   Scandinavia
           1975   Europe/Germany/Switzerland/France
           1976   Scandinavia

1977 Hawaii
1980 Holy Land/Jordan/Passion Play
1983 Holy Land/Egypt (with Al & Gretchen Quie)
1984 Italy/Greek Island Cruise/Passion Play (with the Quies)
1985 Holy Lands/Egypt/Jordan
1986 China
1987 Alaskan Cruise
1989 Australia/New Zealand
1990 Holy Lands/Egypt
1991 Scandinavia
1993 British Isles/Norway (with our family)
1994 Russia
1995 Baltic Countries (went as passengers, not leaders)
1997 Holy Lands/Rome
2002 Norway (for a family reunion)

Russ and Lorraine at the Garden Tomb during their first tour of the Holy Lands, which they hosted with Gil. This began a 30-year career of leading tours around the world.

CHAPTER 20

Secrets of the Heart

My Role Models

Each of us has one or more role models after whom we have consciously or unconsciously patterned our lives. There have been three people who have significantly shaped my live. All three had some characteristics in common which have been important to me. They have all been hard-working, religiously-progressive people with drive motivated by vision and concern for the welfare of others. Proverbs 29:18 describes them: "Where there is no vision, the people parish."

My Dad

Having written a whole chapter about my father's life, I shall only make a few summary statements. When he left me alone and headed for home on my first trip around the grain field with the binder and three horses, he gave me a sense of trust that has stayed with me all my life. His progressive nature was part of his very being. As a progressive farmer, he literally beat a path to the University of Wisconsin to learn the latest in farming and was a charter member of the Progressive Party. He taught me that it was up to me to choose what I wanted to do with my life but to succeed I needed education and with it had to get to the top. He lived by the philosophy that "you should always leave things better than they were when you acquired them."

Dr. Seth Eastvold

Dr. Eastvold, who was my pastor during college years, had a strong impact on my life. When he became pastor of First Lutheran Church, he inherited a congregation that was dying on the vine. Within a short period of time he built it to a congregation of over 3,000 members which at the time was the largest congregation in the Norwegian Lutheran Church of America. His leadership style was to set forth bold plans and proceed with them whether people agreed with them or not. The biggest project that he proposed was the building of a parish house which included a gymnasium, which was a new and bold venture at that time. His concern was primarily to have a strong youth program. When he submitted the plan to the Church Counsel, they turned it down. So he cancelled his vacation and single handedly went out and raised the necessary money and built the building. His next step was to get government funding and, when he did, he hired me to be the youth director.

Dr. Philip Dybvig

Dr. Dybvig was director of the Division of American Missions during the fifteen years from my graduation from seminary (1945) until I concluded my call as regional director of American Missions. He was a very creative thinker and developed a new mission program which I had the privilege of helping to shape. Working under his direction significantly shaped my ministry. The one thing that I remember most about him was that he literally taught me how to think. When I would come to him with a question, he never answered it, but by the time he had asked me a number of questions I knew the answer. I remember on occasion standing at his door prepared to knock but returning to my office because I suddenly thought of a question that he would ask me for which I did not yet have the answer!

A Thorn in the Flesh

The Apostle Paul, following his conversion, lived the rest of his life with a "thorn in his flesh." He described it this way: "To keep me from being too elated, a thorn was given me in the flesh. Three times I appealed to the Lord about this, that it would leave me but he said to me, 'my grace is sufficient for you, for power is made perfect in weakness.'" (II Corinthians 12:7–9)

Most everyone has a thorn in their flesh (whatever that thorn may be.) I am telling you about three of mine. To whatever extent the Lord has chosen to remove or not remove these thorns, I am thankful to my family and friends for the extent to which have been patient with me.

Thorn N° 1: A Poor Self Image

Little needs to be said about this as most of us at times feel that we are not as good as other people and when we have a successful experience, we too often still think we have failed. As pastor of St. John's Lutheran Church in Massapequa I had many experiences which others judged as being very successful (e. g. instructing and confirming over 600 adults in the seven years I served the parish). However, despite the scores of classes I taught, I used to tell Lorraine that I never felt confident in my teaching unless my shoes were polished and my trousers pressed. Over the years I have learned to think less about myself and to keep my head up and smell the roses.

Thorn N° 2: Legalism

I grew up in a culture (mostly Norwegian and Lutheran) which taught that drinking, dancing, and card playing were sins and Christians should not engage in them. In college I belonged to First Lutheran Church when Dr. Seth Eastvold was pastor. He personified legalism and would not, for example, confirm any young people until they promised that they would never dance. So they made the promise and proceeded to break it. This did not contribute to their well being. I accepted Dr. Eastvold's preaching and attempted to follow it to the letter of the law: Lorraine and I gave up leading the Grand March at the college prom, accepting the position that it would not be compatible with our Christian witness. That legalism had a negative affect on my ministry and it took many years for me to mellow and develop a more moderate life style which lead to a more positive Christian life.

Thorn N° 3: Reading Limitations

Do you remember the story about Freddy Frame, my first grade teacher who told me that "if I had as many brains as I had freckle, I might amount to something some day"? As long as I can remember, I have had problems with my reading. An easy out would be to blame my first grade teacher who may well have been a contributing factor.

I have dealt with this all of my adult life but all the prayer and work has not removed the "thorn." Reading is mostly my personal problem. I am not an avid reader because I find it especially intimidating to tackle a big book when I know it will take me forever to read it. My Dad would well understand my problem; he was a very slow lip-reader which did not deter him from reading.

In most of my school days I used one criterion for choosing books to meet reading requirements, namely, which book had the fewest pages or largest print! Thankfully I remember well the things I read. Perhaps my most profound experience in reading was in my high school English class when the class was required to read *Uncle Tom's Cabin* by Harriet Beecher Stowe. The book was just too big and I couldn't get myself to tackle it. When the day came for the test, the teacher announced that anyone who had not read the book must leave the room and could not take the test. I didn't move! After a second announcement, I still didn't leave and my anxiety reached a high level. I stayed, took the test and passed. To this day I am not sure how I had learned enough about the book to pass the test.

During the years in my first parish at Lansing, Iowa, I worked hard at improving my oral reading skills. Every day when I went to my office I would take my Bible, go into the church sanctuary and read aloud for fifteen minutes. It helped but the problem did not go away. At one point I responded to an ad for a Rapid Reading kit. Spending time daily on this program for years helped but, again, the problem did not go away.

Few people know about this "thorn" in my flesh. I am often asked to read the text for the day at our church worship. Actually I would find it easier to preach the sermon than to read the text. People think I read well and so do I—because in order to do the task well I rehearse the reading many times before I read it publicly. St. Paul says that a thorn can be good because it keeps one humble!

Honors and Awards

In life, all of us have received some honors and awards. These come to us because someone who thinks highly of us wants to recognize some good that we have done. Most people, and especially those of us of Norwegian heritage, are hesitant to receive compliments. I had an old friend who has since gone on to glory who used to say, "If you don't toot your own horn, your horn will not be tooted." Whether this philosophy was good or bad is not for me to judge, but I shall share a few of my awards which have been framed and hang on the wall above my desk or have been tucked away. For whatever good I have done with the gifts that God has given me, to God I give the thanks.

The America Lutheran Church

When I concluded my ministry with The American Lutheran Church in 1973, I received a plaque with the following inscription: "Pastor Russell B. Helgesen has rendered faithful and consecrated service to his church for 13½ years as Mission Director and Director of the Department of Special Ministries. It would be difficult to count the number of congregations that have been touched and the lives that were affected by his ministry."

Candidate for Bishop of Southwestern Minnesota District

When the Southwestern Minnesota District elected a new bishop in 1978, they chose five candidates for this office. I was assistant to the bishop at the time and was one of the five. When the campaign was finished and the final vote was taken, I was number three. On May 3, 1978, Dr. David Preus, president of The ALC, wrote: "congratulations to you for your selection as a nominee for district president. That is a singular honor."

Candidate for President of St. Olaf College

Really? No, not really! But the fact is that I did receive a letter from the St. Olaf College selection committee which read: "Your name has been submitted as a candidate for president. Do you want to be considered?' Very quickly, they received my answer which was NO!

Internal Revenue Service

For ten years of volunteer income tax service, I received the following plaque: "For outstanding public service to your community through VITA and TCE (Volunteer Income Tax Assistance) 2000–2010"

The Knight of Yorke Award

Each year at 7500 York Cooperative, the Men of Yorke choose "one man whom they believe is the single greatest one among them who contributes most to the way of life at 7500 York" and award him the title of Knight of Yorke. "For the year 2007, we confer upon Russ Helgesen the honorary title of Knight of Yorke."

Board of Directors of 7500 York Cooperative

Plaque: "Certificate of recognition to Russell Helgesen for his six years of service on the Board of Directors. 2001–2007"

Russ (front row, second from right) with the 7500 York Cooperative Board of Directors.

Who's Who in Religion

In 1976 The Marquis Who's Who Publication Board published their First Edition of *Who's Who in Religion*. In that Edition three pastors who were staff members of the American Lutheran Church were included. One of the three was Rev. Russell B. Helgesen. "Inclusion is limited to those individuals who have demonstrated outstanding achievement in their own field of endeavor and who have, thereby, contributed significantly to the betterment of contemporary society." My name continued in the publications until my retirement in 1985.

Trinity Lutheran Seminary Faculty, Columbus, OH

In 1973, when I was director of Special Ministries for the ALC, Dr. Fred Mouser, President of Columbus Seminary invited me to design and teach a rural ministries course for their summer 10-day special session. The course was a combination of classroom lectures, workshops, and learning how to live and minister in small town and rural communities. The session was well received by the dozen or so students who attended and was affirmed by President Mouser. More than a year later he told me that they had not continued the course because they were "not able to find anyone else in the Church qualified to teach it."

Instructor at Land Grant Colleges

While director of the Department of Special Ministries, I worked with rural staff members of several other Lutheran Church bodies. Each summer we conducted Great Plains Church Leadership Schools for rural pastors at Michigan State and Colorado State Universities which were both Land Grant Colleges (meaning that they were established by the Agriculture Department of the Federal Government). In each of the schools I taught one of the courses.

Electric Chair at Sing Sing Prison

This was not exactly an award or an honor but I have in my possession a letter with the personal signature of the Warden Wilfred L. Denno of Sing Sing Prison, Ossining, New York. His letter approved delivery of my letter to inmate George Miller, #111019. In return Mr. Miller, a member of St. John's Lutheran Church, wrote to me on March 3, 1958, thanking me for lining up a job for him which made it possible for him to be released from prison and particularly for playing a part in his accepting Christ as Savior. While visiting him, I was given a tour of the prison and the "privilege" of sitting in the electric chair. I am likely one among a very few who have had the "honor" of sitting in the electric chair at Sing Sing and have lived to tell about it!

A Communist? Not really!

In the late 50s when Senator Joseph McCarthy of Wisconsin was doing his "communist hunting," he claimed that he had documents proving that a number of pastors were communist sympathizers. One day I received a letter informing me that I was among that group and that they had now determined that the signatures in the documents, which Senator McCarthy was using, were forged. The letter asked whether I would like to request my right to appear before the Senate committee. Nothing ever came of the matter but some years later it was reported to me that a pastor in California, at a public meeting called for the purpose of criticizing the American Lutheran Church, held in his hand a book which contained the names of two ALC pastors who were communist sympathizers, one of which was Russell Helgesen. Now, after all these years, the rumor has apparently died.

Grandmother Clock Award

In 1987 I ordered a Grandmother clock kit from Emperor Clock Company and assembled and finished it. The next year I entered the beautifully finished walnut clock in the creative arts competition of the Minnesota State Fair and received a blue ribbon.

Preacher at Eastern District Convention

As pastor of St. John's Lutheran Church, Massapequa, I was a member of the Eastern District of the Evangelical Lutheran Church. The district included all the congregations east of the Mississippi River. In 1958, Dr. Myron Austinson, president of the district, invited me to be the preacher for the convention worship service. This was considered a high honor.

Commencement Speaker, Burnsville High School

In 1963 when Jane and Tom were in the graduating class of Burnsville High School, I was invited by Superintendent Metcalf, to give the commencement address. When he introduced me, it was obvious that he had a totally exaggerated opinion of my professional position with the church. An exact quote is as follows: "Pastor Helgesen, I should say Reverend Helgesen, excuse me, Reverend Helgesen is one of eight of the directors of The American Lutheran Church, supervising the activities of this church in all of the United States and Canada. His work is very important!"

In my address to the class I quoted the great theologian Dr. Paul Tillich as saying, that "freedom is the right to be what you ought to be and not to do what you want to do." After developing that thought, I closed the address with the following words: "if freedom is the right to be what you ought to be, then the price of freedom is the willingness to live under restraints. Graduates, as you leave these sheltered halls and go out from the protective canopy of your homes, we hand to you the torch of freedom. If you throw this torch to the wind it will destroy you with a cruel and consuming fire, but if you carry the torch with restraint, it will light the pathway of your life so that you can be what you ought to be and live in a land that under God shall indeed have a new birth of freedom."

Entertaining a Celebrity

While serving a parish in New York, it was my privilege to entertain Dr. Philip Dybvig who was the director of Home Missions for the ELC. For entertainment, I used a connection to get tickets to a New York Giants baseball game. Things went well and late in the game during the roar of the crowd, he turned to me with the question, "how far is it to Washington?" When I replied that it was 237 miles, he got a very quizzical look on his face and only then did I discover that I had misunderstood his question which really was, "how far is it to the washroom." A few years later he became my boss!

Tributes to a "Celebrity"

On April 3, 1959, the Plainedge Baseball League wrote a letter to me which read in part "This year we have expanded our program . . . to include 750 boys. Consequently we are expecting a very large turnout on our Opening Day, and if you could find the time in your busy schedule, we would like very much to have you with us to be introduced to the assemblage and also to take part in the ceremonies."

On April 20, 1950, the Board of Education of the Union Free School District of Uniondale wrote a letter to thank me for my "kind and thoughtful participation in the cornerstone laying ceremonies at our Goodrich Street School."

The president of the Kiwanis Club of Uniondale wrote me on April 20, 1951, "I write this letter with a personal desire and wish, to have you enrolled as an honorary member of the newly organized Kiwanis Club of Uniondale. An opportunity to meet you personally will give me great pleasure."

And the "ultimate" letter arrived on April 30, 1949, from the president and musical director of the Long Island Philharmonic Orchestra. "An orchestra of professional stature, led by a competent conductor, bringing the best programs directly into Long Island communities and cooperating with Long Island civic and school organizations will, we are confident, be warmly received. It is proposed that such an orchestra be established now. Would you be willing to serve on the organization committee?"

My Highest Honor

In 1971 when Dr. Norman Borlaug received the Nobel Peace Prize for developing his Miracle Wheat, it was my privilege to interview him in his office in Mexico City and write a cover story for *The Lutheran Standard* entitled "No. 1 Hunger Fighter." What was a near miracle was that the Lutheran Church—Missouri Synod bought the article from *The Lutheran Standard* and ran it as their cover story with the name "Mainspring in the Green Revolution." The picture which had been taken of Dr. Borlaug and me together was included in the Missouri Synod story but not in *The Lutheran Standard*. To sit in his office, across the table from this great man of faith, was like one farmer chatting with another. Dr. Borlaug died in 2009 at the age of 95. What a privilege to have known him.

Dr. Norman Borlaug, Nobel Peace Prize winner, with Russ Helgesen.

Last But Not Least – My Golf Record

Hole-in-one—Yes, I did make a hole-in-one! I remember it like it was today. It was on the Par 3 course at Voyager Village in Wisconsin. The date was August 6, 1991, on the first hole which was 126 yards.

Other Voyager Village Geritol League Awards

1989	Sr. 3rd Flight Champion
1991	Sr. 3rd Flight Champion
1992	Geritol League Champion
1998	Geritol League Runner-up (Green Jacket)

Miscellaneous Golf Records

1988—Oak Knoll Golf League Team Champion
Eagle—on 257 yard hole in Arizona (But it was winter, the grass was dry and the ground hard. A good drive reached a hill where it rolled half way to the green and then I sank a 20-foot put for two strokes on a par 4 hole.

Russ with golfing companions, brother Gil, a pastor friend, and wife Lorraine.

Longest drive—311 yards! The drive was good but landed on the cart path where it rolled over 100 yards. It has never happened again!

My Musical "Career"

When it comes to music, once again I inherited another one of my father's genes. When I wrote his story, I said: "Dad was not a musician; he never played an instrument and could not carry a tune. But he loved music and believed strongly that it was an important enrichment of everyone's life. He went far beyond his natural talent in his musical career. Of our five children, at least four of them have good, if not outstanding musical talents. Maybe, because of their musical ability, they have been less than complimentary of their father's musical accomplishments. As a result, they never went out of their way to encouraging their father in his attempts to use what musical talent he had. But there is a bright spot. Recently our grandson, Nate, who exceeded the rest of the family in his musical ability, "tested" me, and deemed me, teachable. "You can match notes," he said "and if you had been given more help over the years, you could have done OK." Thanks, Nate, for the encouragement! The following facts (as I remember them) will be left with you to judge.

Instrumental Music

At Lukken School we had no instrumental music program. Because of my father's interest in music, he worked with Fred Hanneman, the Mount Horeb High School band director and organized a rural school band. My two older brothers and I had an opportunity to learn to play an instrument before enrolling in high school. From the beginning, I played a B-flat clarinet which I inherited from brother Ken. Gil played a trombone and both of them did very well. Though our high school was small with a total enrollment of about 200, it was highly rated in the State of Wisconsin. Our band competed with the state class A bands such as Madison East, Wausau, Stevens Point, and Eau Claire.

When I got to high school, Mr. Hanneman had high hopes for me based on his experience with Ken and Gil. As a result, I was admitted into the concert band as soon as I entered my freshman year and placed in the first-chair clarinet section! As the year progressed, he began to recognize that I was not meeting his expectations and so moved me to the third-chair section. I continued in the band all four years of high school. After the first year, I played alto clarinet in the concert band and snare drum in the marching band.

On May 22, 1937, during my senior year, I enrolled in the Wisconsin School Music Association at Mineral Point and won second place with my clarinet in the solo contest. When I got to college, I played in the marching band all four years. My instrumental music terminated with my graduation from college.

Vocal Music

Though my family support for my vocal music was a bit (considerably) lacking, following are some of my ups and downs. At Luther Seminary the story was simple; I tried out for the seminary chorus but didn't make it.

When I was a student at Luther Seminary, all the students were required to take a class in liturgics. On the assumption that everyone could sing, we were all taught how to chant the liturgy for the church service. Beginning with my first Sunday, I chanted. Everyone seemed to be pleased with what they heard from their new pastor and no complaints were registered. After a few weeks, my kind and supportive wife, Lorraine, managed to muster up enough courage to suggest,

"Russ, maybe you shouldn't chant. Some of your notes are a bit off key." Being a little defensive, and confident in my abilities, I thanked her for the suggestion but reminded her that Lansing was just a little river town and if a few of my notes might be a tad off, likely no one would notice it anyway. A few weeks went by and I continued chanting. Finally one night we invited our organist to our home for dinner. In the course of conversation, she shared with us the fact that she had perfect pitch! I never chanted again!! Not for all these sixty-five years!

Having said what I have about my vocal "musical career," I will now give my theory of choir directing. Obviously, ability is important but, if one is deficient at that point, an outgoing spirit and positive camaraderie can take its place and lead to success. Now for a few facts about my choir directing career.

When I organized Grace Lutheran Church in Uniondale things went very well. From a musical standpoint, the most fun thing I did was to produce and direct the operetta, "Hansel and Gretel." The children loved doing it and the audience was supportive.

An adult choir at Grace was organized and directed by a member of the congregation. Following a picnic put on by the director in his home, one of the choir members felt compelled to inform me that the director had served beer at the picnic which was against the "moral standards" of the congregation. Being supportive of the legalistic policy which was likely more mine than that of the congregation, I informed the director that he was being relieved of his duties. Because no one else was available, I took over the directing and the choir which continued in good form.

The peak of my choir directing career (if I may call it that) was at St. John's Lutheran Church in Massapequa. This congregation was the highlight of my parish ministry and a place where everything (well, nearly everything) went well. One of the first needs when this new congregation was organized was to find a pianist. Shortly I found one who was top notch in the person of Peggy Downer. After a short time we got a church organ so I asked her to be the organist. She had never played an organ and so declined. I was not able to understand that a good pianist could not play an organ so my persistence prevailed. She did an outstanding job for a number of years. When she finally moved to upstate New York she continued her service and was recently honored for her 50 years as church organist. On that occasion she expressed her gratitude to me for refusing to accept "no" when I asked her to become an organist at St. John's.

Because we could not find a choir director at St. John's, I assumed the responsibility of organizing and directing both youth and adult choirs and a hand-bell choir. In 1950 we were one of the first congregations in the country to purchase and play "English hand bells." Never having directed a bell choir, I simply took hymnals, circled notes in red and told the kids to strike their bell when their note was circled in red. Three of our children (Becky, Jane, and Tom) plus a few others loved playing the bells and the people loved hearing them. According to an article in *The Lutheran Standard,* ours was the first congregation in the ELC to have English hand bells.

Our senior choir grew and they loved singing in a group that had such a wonderful spirit (even though the director wasn't the greatest musician!). Upon leaving church one Sunday, a visiting couple shared with me the fact that their reason for coming to our church that day was that they had heard that we had the best choir on Long Island.

One of the members of our congregation was Dan Slick who worked for NBC radio in New York City and was musical director for Robert Shaw. One Sunday Dan approached me, "I know it's selfish of me to ask but would you be willing to let me direct the choir. I get tired of working with tapes all the time; I would like to work with people." What a find, and he expected no pay. When I conducted my last rehearsal, the members of the choir gave me a much cherished card which read, "You have been our inspiration and will always be among us as we continue to sing our Lord's praises." The story, however, had a sad ending. Under his direction the joy and spirit that had really built the choir began to diminish. One by one the choir member began to leave and within two years of my leaving the parish, he was asked to leave. The problem, they said, was that his goals were so high and he was so demanding in his attempts to achieve perfection that it was no longer fun to sing.

At about the same time, while I was directing the youth choir, Dan Slick came to me with another request: He had a friend who was a fine young director, would I be willing to let him direct? Again he would not expect any pay; he only wanted experience. Sadly, within a few weeks I had to ask him to leave. The children were unhappy with him. He knew the music well but the spirit, that was so important to them, was lacking in his leadership.

Long Island Junior Choral Union

Two more highlights from my ministry on Long Island will now be shared. My leadership among the churches of Long Island and my interest in church music was fairly well known. One of the finest musicians in the area was Betty Ann Ramstad, wife of Ruddy Ramstad, pastor of Trinity of Alden Terrace Lutheran Church, Valley Stream, Long Island. She responded positively to my idea that we plan a Choral Union for the Junior Choirs of Brooklyn and Long Island. This, we believed, was an opportunity which had not previously been explored. Together we planned and carried out the project which resulted in a very successful concert with more than a hundred children singing under the direction of Betty Ann and myself. This event was repeated for several more years.

Once in a Lifetime Christmas Concert

The year before I completed my ministry at St. John's Lutheran Church in 1959 we planned a Christmas concert for all of our St. John's choirs. Because of our limited seating (about 200) at St. John's, we were able to acquire the auditorium of the Massapequa High School. It proved to be a great event with our senior, junior and bell choirs participating plus some of our outstanding soloists. With upwards of a thousand people filling the auditorium, it was one of our greatest opportunities to present the message of the birth of our Savior.

Book IV

A Career and a Family

CHAPTER 21

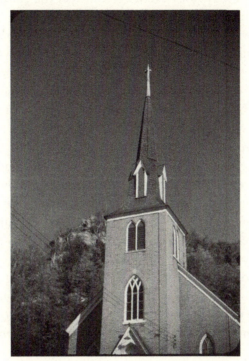

Our Savior's Church in Lansing, Iowa

Years of Committed Service

Lansing, Iowa

Following graduation from Luther Seminary and my ordination on January 28, 1945, my first parish was at Lansing, Iowa, a small town on the Mississippi River twelve miles south of Minnesota. This was a new parish arrangement which included Our Savior's Lutheran Church in Lansing, and Desoto and Ferryville in Wisconsin. The three-point parish was set up by the Home Mission department. The Lansing congregation was 75 years old and had fallen on hard times. The last pastor to serve it had no faith in its future and had said, "there is no shame in serving a dying congregation, if it must die." When I accepted the call I said, "I may not be able to resurrect the congregation, but at least I will get it to turn over in its grave!"

Before moving to Lansing, there were certain preparations that needed to be made. The first was to buy a car. This was war time, no cars were being manufactured and even used cars were hard to come by. The best we could do was a small, old model Chrysler which proved to be a headache for the three years that we owned it. On a salary of $1,800 a year, we averaged $25 a month in repairs.

Mother came to Minneapolis for my graduation and volunteered to help us in the move to Lansing. At the time, Lorraine was six month pregnant and we did not deem it wise for her to make the trip to Lansing in January, especially in an undependable car with an unreliable heater. So she took the bus to Madison which was near Mount Horeb where my parents lived. She stayed with Dad and I was to pick her up the next day.

Mother and I managed the trip to Lansing pulling a trailer behind our car. Arriving after dark, we unloaded our belongings and stayed overnight. The next day we drove the 135 miles to Mount Horeb.

The following day, Lorraine and I made the trip back to Lansing and prepared to settle into our new home. The parish had no parsonage but the congregation had arranged to rent a house from parishioner Merty Ruud who agreed to live on the second floor and we would have the use of the first floor. Again, out of a salary of $150 a month, we had to pay rent of $25 and all of our own car expenses. It was not possible to meet all our expenses from that meager salary, but with the help of some generous parishioners who brought us food from time to time, and Grandma Sampson who sewed most of the clothes for the girls, we managed. Even the 5¢ toll on the Mississippi River Bridge was a burden but the Mission Board agreed to reimburse me for that.

In many ways, a pastor's first parish is the most important one considering that he comes without experience, is full of enthusiasm, and too often learns by making mistakes. So now let the story begin.

The Lansing Ministry

It was the middle of February 1945 when Lorraine and I arrived in Lansing. Church facilities consisted of a lovely brick church with an impressive steeple but no basement (except for a furnace room), no sacristy, kitchen, or Sunday School rooms. A very high quality outhouse had recently been constructed behind the church! When we arrived, it was the beginning of Lent and a midweek service was held in addition to the regular Sunday service. Attendance at worship was minimal and about 30 children were enrolled in Sunday School. I found it exciting, however, to take up this challenging ministry.

Amid the excitement, my first blooper occurred on the very first Sunday. A choir of about 6 or 8 people sang at the service. It was obvious that more members were needed and I made a plea for new recruits. I spotted one teenager in the congregation who would obviously make a good addition. Following the service I proceeded to enroll her. She persisted in her claim that she could not sing but I would not take no for an answer so she dutifully showed up at the next choir practice. Following the practice the director came to me with the exclamation, "what have you done to me? This girl was a member of our choir but is a monotone. I finally succeeded in easing her out of the choir and now you got her back in!!"

Our home in Lansing, Iowa

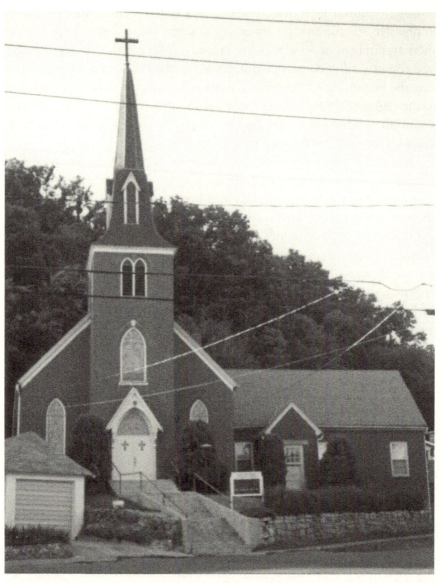

Our Savior's Church

Though the number of worshipers was small, many dedicated members were committed to doing what was necessary to make the congregation grow. I believed without a doubt that if we reached out to people in the community, they would respond. With the help of members who provided me with names of unchurched people in the community, I began calling on them in their homes. Our worship attendance began to increase, I offered an adult instruction class for non-Lutherans, children joined our Sunday School and within a year the Sunday School had doubled to sixty students.

The increased attendance in worship and Sunday School began to present a problem. How could we adequately care for this growing congregation in our limited facilities? The Church Council agreed that we must somehow expand our building. In April 1945, just six weeks after our arrival, a building committee was chosen to explore the needs and carry out the project. For some years the congregation had been holding an $1,800 education fund that had been given by Chris and Pete Smedsrud. The fund was still in tact except for $100 that had been used to build the new outhouse. Apparently there had been agreement that this much-needed outhouse met the criteria of the "Education Fund" (maybe because it was a critical need and would be used by the Sunday School children.) The Council agreed that the balance of this fund should be used for building expansion but it would not be adequate for the needed facilities.

Some miles from town was the abandoned church building of the former Faegre Prairie Lutheran Church. When the congregation disbanded some 20 years before this, the remaining members had joined the Lansing Lutheran Church. The final business meeting of Faegre Prairie had failed to transfer the property to a new owner so the building was simply abandoned. Our Building Committee decided that it would be to everyone's advantage to tear down this deteriorating building before it fell into ruins and use the lumber to construct the proposed parish house addition to our church. Because the congregation had "died" there was no one to give us permission to carry out this plan. Just before we were ready to dismantle the building someone in the community objected to our plan and threatened our congregation with a law suit. In consulting with our local attorney, he advised us that since there were no longer any remaining members, no one legally owned the property and therefore no one could give us the necessary permission to dismantle it. We then asked, "If we go ahead and tear it down, what is the worst thing that could happen to us?" His answer was "someone might make you rebuild it!" At that point there were 12 members of our Lansing congregation who had previously been members of the Faegre Prairie congregation. We proceeded to draw up a statement which all 12 signed giving us permission to dismantle the building. We were well aware that the document had no legal standing but we concluded that if all the former Faegre Prairie members agreed to our plan, there would be no one to sue us. The plan was carried out and no objections were ever raised.

To carry out the building program, which was to consist of a parish house, kitchen, new furnace, and pastor's study/office, we agreed that most of the work would have to be done by the men of the congregation. Work proceeded and on October 7, 1945, (less than eight months after my arrival) the cornerstone was laid. While the men were digging, laying blocks, and constructing walls, Jim Peterson, who ran the local book store and could not do manual labor because he had only one kidney, was out calling on members and friends to raise additional money. In the midst of a very successful project we suffered one major set back. The laying of the basement block walls was completed but unfortunately no one thought of bracing them while they cured. The first night after they were completed we had a very heavy rain that washed dirt behind the back wall and in the morning we found that the whole wall had collapsed! But we picked up our spirits, redid the wall, and in less than a year the entire project was completed. On Pentecost Sunday, June 9, 1946, it was dedicated.

Because the Smedsrud gift and the lumber from the Fagre Prairie church provided the major resources for the new parish house, it was decided to name it the "Fagre-Smedsrud Memorial" That name was then carved in stone over the entrance to the Parish House. Pastor and congregation all rejoiced that we now had such wonderful facilities for our growing congregation.

In keeping with our changed and more ethnic community and congregation, in 1947 we agreed that the name "Norwegian Evangelical Lutheran Church" was too restrictive so it was changed to Our Savior's Lutheran Church.

This I Remember

Personal stories are important when history is written. Following are some that are important to me.

I remember John Bjerke who owned a garage in the south side of town. He had been treasurer of the church for many years. He fully recognized the need to improve our finances and was very cooperative in helping to carry out a new stewardship program. He told me about the time, not too many years before, that the church treasurer came to him "collecting" money for the church. When John gave him $5 for the year, he objected because he thought it was too much. So he gave John $2 back and said that if they needed more later, he could come back. When I proposed a new stewardship program, the congregation cooperated fully and the giving of our members increased substantially.

I remember Alex and Margaret Knutson who were such wonderful people. They lived on their farm and did butchering each year. They were aware that our family was having difficulty getting along on the very limited salary. The last year we were there they rented a locker in the local freezer and kept it stocked with meat for us for the entire year. What a great blessing from those saints!

I remember the "bats in the belfry." There have always been bats in Lansing. Lots of them. In fact one could hardly live without them. They told me that bats eat their weight in mosquitoes every day. For that we were grateful, but for years the bats had made their home in the church steeple and the aroma in the church was unpleasant. So one day Oscar Kerndt and I climbed up in the steeple with shovels in hand and cleaned out the huge piles of manure. In the process we screened all the openings and, at least as long as I was there, we experienced no further problems with the bats.

I remember serving on the Lansing volunteer fire department, not as chaplain but as a "real fire fighter." There were two calls I still remember. The first came in the middle of a bitter cold winter night. The hardware store on Main Street was on fire. It was so cold the fire hoses froze up. We did not succeed in saving the building but we did prevent the fire from spreading to adjacent buildings. The second call was in January of 1948. I had just resigned as pastor of Our Saviors Lutheran Church and was packed and ready to leave with my family the next day to start a new congregation on Long Island. The sun had set and it was past twilight when we heard the fire siren and immediately the fire department responded. A thirteen-year-old Ellefson girl was missing. She had left school but never arrived home. Our search began along the creek leading to the Mississippi River. Before long a glove was discovered and near it a hole in the ice. Her body was soon recovered but she could not be revived. Though her family did not attend our church, the children had attended our Sunday School. I still remember the pain of having to leave town the next day without being able to give help and comfort to the family.

I remember George Ashem who owned the local grocery store. He did not belong to our congregation but we were good friends. He had a beautiful voice and was invited to sing at most of the funerals in the several Protestant churches in town. He always sang the same song, one that I had never heard before and have never forgotten since: "Go'ng down the valley one by one; go'ng toward the sett'ng of the sun!"

I remember one Palm Sunday service when Lilah Kerndt came to me after the service and in her blunt way said, "well, you sure made a liar out of me today! I brought my little nephew with me to church today and promised him that he would hear the Palm Sunday story but you never told it!" Since that day, whenever I preach a festival sermon I have never failed to "tell the story."

I remember that when we moved to Willmar, Minnesota. In 1974, we soon began to hear from town's people that "Dr. Sadd makes us glad!" What they were saying was that they had great love and respect for Dr. Milton Sadd, the local dermatologist. When I went to visit him, I asked if he had come from Lansing, Iowa. He affirmed that he had indeed been that little boy in my confirmation class. His family lived on a small farm, they were very poor, his father never attended church but his mother came faithfully and brought her three children to church and Sunday School. Milton was a very shy little boy but responded to my encouragement to go to college and in due time graduated from St. Olaf and became a very fine and respected medical specialist.

I remember the day the Black Hawk Bridge went out. For people in the Lansing community, March 17, 1945, was a day "that will live in infamy!" To hasten the barge traffic on the Mississippi an icebreaker was sent up the river too early that spring and the resulting heavy ice flow damaged the bridge making it unusable until it was finally restored and reopened twelve years later. This changed the community forever.

The Black Hawk Bridge went out on March 17, 1945, changing the Lansing community forever and creating a dramatic story of the birth of Russ and Lorraine's first child!

High School children could no longer be bussed across the bridge from Wisconsin; Lansing merchants lost all their Wisconsin customers; and the Lansing, Desoto, and Ferryville Lutheran Parish was cut in two.

For our family that was a double red-letter day! It was the day our first daughter, Becky, was born at the Lutheran Hospital in La Crosse, Wisconsin, 40 miles up the river from Lansing. When we arrived at the bridge at 8:00 that morning, with Lorraine in labor, the bridge was closed. Though we insisted that it was necessary to cross, the guards told us that it was impossible because one of the bridges was out completely. As a result, we had to drive down the river to Prairie du Chien, Wisconsin, where we could cross the bridge to reach the hospital in La Crosse 105 miles away. The trip took more than four hours on nearly impassable mud and gravel roads. Thankfully we arrived at the hospital several hours before our daughter made her entrance into this world.

For our parish at Lansing, Desoto, and Ferryville the closing of the bridge made a significant impact. To continue serving the Wisconsin churches it was necessary for me to cross the river by boat in the summer and go downstream via the Prairie du Chien bridge in the winter which made a round trip of 160 miles.

Angels on the Mississippi

Being determined to continue serving the Wisconsin churches, I concluded that the only way to make the trip across the river was by motor boat so I made a deal with a local fisherman for an old fourteen-foot wooden boat and a nearly worn out motor. For the next two years, while I was making the river crossings, it seemed that I spent half of my time repairing, cranking, and coaxing the motor to complete the trip. As a farm boy from Wisconsin, I had never owned a boat, traveled on a river, nor even learned to swim.

My trip by boat began at Lansing on the west bank of the Mississippi and continued five miles up the winding river channel to Desoto on the east. My usual Sunday schedule included conducting services at Lansing in the morning, going by boat to Desoto for afternoon services, and completing the day with evening services at Ferryville. One of my parishioners would meet me at Desoto and drive me to the scheduled services. Following the last service, which was usually quite late at night, I would return home by boat. Though the river was dark, I was not afraid of it. The channel was clearly marked by lighted buoys. The old experienced fishermen, however, who knew the dangers of the river were very uneasy about my night travel and were relieved when they heard my motor pull into the dock and knew that I was safely home.

I still shudder when I recall that one dark night on the river when I sighted the lights of an approaching barge. At that inopportune moment my motor stalled. I worked frantically to get it started and finally, just as the motor fired and the boat took off, I heard the swish of the barge passing within feet of my boat!

But the most memorable of my river experiences occurred on a Sunday night after I had completed my services in Wisconsin and prepared for my return trip home. As my driver and I headed for the boat which was docked on the river, the sky began to darken and lightening was flashing in the west. My driver was aware that a dangerous storm was approaching and urged me to stay with them for the night. He knew that I had a wife and two little children at home and that my boat would never weather a dangerous storm on that river. Being young and foolish and not really understanding the danger that awaited me, I insisted on returning home.

By the time we arrived at the boat, the storm had increased in intensity but I still insisted on going home! In preparation for the return trip, I put the motor in place and prepared for fueling. When I tried to remove the gas cap, it would not budge! Being unsuccessful I grabbed my pliers but the gas cap still would not budge. At that moment the storm struck with a furry, one of the worst storms ever on the Mississippi! The decision had been made for me. My only alternative was to stay for the night.

In the morning we drove back to the boat landing. I found the boat completely swamped. After bailing it out, I tipped up the motor, unscrewed the gas cap with my hands, filled up the tank, and made the trip safely home.

As I reflected on that stormy night, I realized that if I had been successful in removing the gas cap, I would have been out on the river at the moment the storm struck and my boat would have sunk. Being unable to swim and without a life preserver, I would have gone down with my boat and been drowned in the depths of that angry river. What really happened? Why wouldn't the gas cap budge that night when at all other times I unscrewed it easily? I have no problem believing in angels and miracles and am convinced that God used one or the other that night to save my life! Each day since that eventful night I have asked, "Lord, what do you want me to do for you today in thanksgiving for saving my life that fateful night on the river?"

Desoto Lutheran Church

Until 1945, the small white country church near Desoto, which was now part of my parish, had been served for forty years by one of the pastors from La Crosse. Because of the extensive travel involved for the pastors, they had worship services only once a month or, in later years, twice a month. When I began my ministry there, I took it for granted that all three congregations would have services every Sunday. Several weeks after I began serving the parish, I was in the sacristy at Desoto preparing to begin the service and the three Deacons were with me. After a period of puzzling silence, one of the Deacons said to the others, "What should we do about this?" To this strange question I responded, "What should we do about what?" He then explained that they were used to having services only every other Sunday and they felt that every

Sunday was too much!" I was not prepared for such a question and spontaneously replied, "I don't know what you will do but I will be conducting services every Sunday. If you would rather not come, that's up to you!" Nothing more was ever said about the matter and weekly services continued as long as I was serving the congregation.

Though my ministry at Desoto was short because of the problems resulting from the bridge going out, it was a very good and pleasant experience. I do recall the one stewardship program that we had. For years the members had supported the congregation through "assessments." When I proposed that we give the members the opportunity to pledge whatever they chose, the congregation agreed. One young man, however, was quite apprehensive. "We have had a difficult time getting enough money when we tell our members how much they are expected to give; but how will we ever make ends meet if we let them give what they choose?" He and all the other members were pleasantly surprised when the new system resulted in a very substantial increase in their income.

A New Beginning for Ferryville

As part of the new parish arrangement, I was responsible for organizing a new congregation in the little river town of Ferryville which was just across the river from Lansing. Some years before I arrived, the town's people had built a modest cement block building that was intended for use as a church by any group that chose to use it. For a number of years the Lutherans had been conducting services but had never organized a congregation. Upon my arrival it was announced that we would be conducting services every Sunday. In addition to the services, I began calling on all of the residents of the town. The response was very positive. Services were well attended and I began a ten-week adult instruction program for those who had not been baptized or confirmed Lutheran. After several months, we announced a special service at which we would formally organize the congregation and receive new members. What a thrill that service was when 14 children and adults were baptized!

The story that I remember best that was told by the congregation was about a funeral service that had been conducted some years before my arrival. The residents of this fishing village were referred to as "river rats." One of the residents who had died was known to be a very unsavory character and possessed more than his share of unacceptable traits. For the funeral service, his casket was placed in front of the chancel over the large grill of the Pipeless furnace. For better or for worse the presiding pastor decided to use his sermon time to extol the virtues of the Law and make it clear that those who are under the Law will suffer its condemnation. Just as he reached the point of telling the congregation that the deceased "river rat" would not be going to heaven, the wind created a strong down-draft in the furnace and a large puff of smoke surrounded the casket. Those who were present testified to the authenticity of the story and assured me that they would never forget it.

The Closing of a Chapter

When the Black Hawk Bridge went out, we experienced significant and difficult changes in the parish as well as in the towns. For two years we made the most of the situation and kept going with the assumption that the bridge would soon be repaired and reopened and life would return to normal. As time passed, we came to recognize that this would likely not happen. The bridge was privately own and went into bankruptcy. Eventually the states of Iowa and Wisconsin took over the bridge and after twelve years it was finally reopened.

In due time we came to realize that the parish arrangement had to be changed. It was finally agreed that, with financial help from the Board of Home Missions, the parish would be divided. Desoto and Ferryville would share a pastor and Lansing would have one full time. This placed me in a very difficult position. I thoroughly enjoyed my associations with all three churches and the entire parish was thriving. However, after much prayer, I came to the decision to resign from the Wisconsin churches and continue serving Lansing.

Less than a year later I received a call from the Home Mission Board of the Evangelical Lutheran Church to move to Long Island, New York, and organize a new congregation. So in January 1948 our family left Lansing with heavy but joyful hearts, satisfied that a wonderful chapter in the service to our Lord had been fulfilled and indeed, Lansing, instead of dying had been very much resurrected.

Following my departure from the parish, Lansing bought a parsonage and called a full time pastor. Several years later they formed a two-point parish with Waterville, Iowa, and the work still goes on to this day.

Desoto continues as a congregation in a new arrangement with rural Freemont Lutheran Church, an arrangement which still continues.

The Ferryville congregation concluded that it would be to everyone's best interest to close their building and join with the Freemont church. This new arrangement resulted in the entire area being well served.

Uniondale, Long Island, New York

The years during which I served the Lansing parish were in some ways difficult because of World War II. Sugar, gas, tires, and other items were rationed. Automobile travel was restricted and assembly lines were building war machines rather than cars. The old Chrysler we had gave us no end of trouble but new cars were not available. When the War ended in 1945 things began to change and, most importantly to us, automobile assembly lines began building new cars. In the summer of 1947, despite horror stories about the new cars that were being produced, we were fortunate enough to be able to buy a new Ford that gave us wonderful service. The first major trip we took with it was to the Lutheran Hospital in La Crosse, Wisconsin, on the day that our first son Tom was born.

Three months later, when we completed our ministry in Lansing, we were off to New York. On a cold day in January, 1948, we left Lansing and drove to my parents' farm home near Mount Horeb where we spent the night. It was 10 degrees below zero on the morning of January 23 when we left on the two day journey to New York. In retrospect, I can understand the anxiety that Grandma and Grandpa Helgesen felt as they said goodbye to us with our cargo of three little children—Becky, less than 3 years; Jane, 1½ years; and Tom, just 3 months.

The trip went well in our shiny new Ford and near the end of our second day we found ourselves in New Jersey stopping for supper at a small restaurant. While there, Lorraine discovered that Tom's formula had soured. The cook was gracious enough to share the kitchen so she

Lorraine with Becky, Jane, and Tom in front of their new Ford, built in 1947, two years after the War ended.

could make new formula. While she was busy in the kitchen, I was engaged in conversation with another customer who advised me not to attempt driving through New York City but rather to cross the Bay by ferry which would get us onto the Long Island Parkway to Uniondale. We followed his directions and found ourselves on the Parkway but going in the wrong direction and pulling a trailer, not knowing that trailers were not permitted on the Parkway! We got ourselves turned around without the help of the police! About 11 P.M. we arrived at our destination to find that our good friend and neighbor, Pastor Joyce Ranum, had set up the beds, which had been shipped ahead of time by rail with the rest of our furniture. How great at that hour of the night, with three little kids, to have the beds made and waiting for us.

On the 24th of January, 1948, when we arrived, there was no congregation to welcome us and no friends to greet us except two neighboring pastors (Joyce Ranum and Herb Hanson.) After a good night's sleep, we awoke the next morning to the first day of our new and exciting lives. Pastor Herbert Hanson, who was serving as

Mission Director of the area, had purchased a portion of a potato farm which included a large farmhouse for the new church. He had made arrangements with a local contractor to remodel the farm house so that the first floor and basement could be used for church services and Sunday School, and the second floor for our family living quarters.

We wasted no time in getting the church going. The first thing we did was to erect a large sign announcing that a new Lutheran Church (Grace) was coming and that the first service would be on February 15, 1948. When one young girl in the community saw the sign she was so impressed and excited that she announced to her family: "You know what? There is going to be a great big Lutheran church in Uniondale!" Right she was. Our parish worker, Mildred Dybvig and I began knocking on doors and the first service was held just three weeks later. Someone described that first service this way: "Sunday morning was a mild winter day and the ground was covered with snow. A Sunday School staff of eight people greeted 38 children who attended the first session at 9:30 A.M. Long before 11:00 A.M. 150 worshippers filled the chapel and overflowed into the pastor's living quarters, the side rooms, and the basement. A loud speaker system carried the service throughout the building. "Yes, Uniondale is going to have a great big Lutheran church!" Within one month we added a second worship service.

With the help of committed residents, the outreach to the community brought a significant response. One of the first persons we met was Bill Keller who worked for Liberty Mutual Insurance Co. and was their top salesman in the United States. He agreed to be Sunday School superintendent and was a great asset to our new congregation. On May 3, just 2½ months after our first service, we enrolled the 100th child in Sunday School. By July we had organized a Luther League and Ladies Aid and the congregation had unanimously voted to proceed with building the first unit of our church.

The start of a career in Home Mission work. Uniondale, Long Island, New York.

Grace Lutheran Church, Uniondale, Long Island, New York.

For the next five years, the Lord continued to bless our ministry, deepen the spiritual life of our members and add to our membership.

Before concluding details of this ministry, I shall share a few significant stories. Because we could not find anyone to play, nor could we afford to pay anyone to play the piano, Lorraine did the playing during the first few months and the parishioners were more than gracious in helping her with our three little children. One Sunday Lorraine was playing a prelude while I was in my study just off from the sanctuary, just ready to begin the service when suddenly I heard a thump on the floor above us (our bedroom with Tom's crib in it.) With both Lorraine and I both on duty, I grabbed one of the ushers and said, "Tom just fell out of bed. Will you go up and put him back in." He did and the service began on schedule!

Next to the sanctuary on the other side was what had been the kitchen of the old farm house. We used it for Sunday School and Lorraine used it as her laundry. In one corner stood the washing machine. One Sunday, well before worship time, I went down to the sanctuary and heard children's voices in the laundry. When I went in to check on what was going on, I discovered two little kids who had come early for Sunday School. They had been engaged in a deep theological argument which the little girl proceeded to present to me. "Pastor," she said, "isn't it true that God is everywhere?" When I assured her that this was indeed true, she turned to her little friend and said, "See, I told you that God was in the washing machine!"

One of our most meaningful experiences while at Uniondale was the sponsoring of several displaced persons in the aftermath of World War II. The resettlement program was conducted by the Lutheran Inner Mission Society of Brooklyn and the refugees were from Estonia. When the Russians captured Estonia, they came into the homes and took the husbands who in most cases were never seen again. The remaining family members were put in concentration camps in Geislingen, Germany, while they awaited resettlement in other countries. Our responsibility as sponsors was to find housing and a job for those who were approved for resettlement. As part of this program we brought six people to our community. Two of them, Leida Unt and her nine-year-old daughter, Tiiu, were sponsored by Lorraine and me personally. They stayed in our home for about six months and did domestic work for us for their room and board until Leida found a job which made it possible for her and Tiiu to get their own housing. To get to the United States, they sailed on the General Blatchford and arrived on September 24, 1949. With them on the ship were her sister, Elfiide Rehesaar and her nine-year-old son, Teet. The two of them were being sponsored by a member of our congregation and would stay in their home while she worked at a job which they arranged for her.

During the six months that Leida and Tiiu were in our home, we developed a very good relationship with them. Often as the two of them would do dishes each night, we sensed that they were dealing with some frustrations by talking Estonian which we could not understand. In Estonia, Lieda was used to upper class living where Tiiu was treated like a "little princes." Lieda understood her plight and was willing to make the best of it, but still wanted Tiiu to live the good life. This produced an undercurrent of resentment that her daughter had to be a "domestic."

In preparation for their coming, I finished off the attic with a nice bedroom for the two of them. As they looked out the front window, they looked down on the busy street and a tavern. One night there was a fire in the tavern. When the fire trucks and police arrived with flashing lights and sirens and they saw the tavern on fire, they were both terrified and came running down to our bedroom. To them it was a reliving of the nightmares which they had experienced so often during the bombings of their homeland. After they left our home, they continued to attend our church so we saw them often and for years kept in touch by mail. In due time, Leida received word from someone who had witnessed her husband's death. In all our contacts we sensed that they were grateful for what we had done for them, but it was not until nearly 50 years later that she really poured out her heart in gratitude for what we had done to make it possible for them to live the good life in America. Tiiu married and has a family. In 2008 she wrote to inform us that her mother had died.

In the mean time, Leida's sister, Elfriide, experienced tragedy. After a ten year separation from her husband, she had accepted the reality that he was dead. Then, like a bolt out of the blue, came the news that he was still alive! And nearly at the same time her son, Teet, who was then 19, was killed in an automobile accident. We attended Teet's funeral but never did hear the rest of the story about her husband but are reasonably sure that she chose not to correspond with him. World conditions at that time were such that it would not have been possible for them to get together nor continue their lives where they had left off. Elfriide has since died. So ends another story of tragedy. This now concludes a satisfying chapter of ministry at Uniondale, so now we move on to Massapequa.

The Massapequa Story

Seven miles to the east of Uniondale was an area called Plainedge which in 1952 was the growing edge of the Long Island building boom. On April 24, 1952, I accepted a call from the Board of American Missions to establish a new congregation in that area. Our plan in starting the new congregation was to rent public facilities for worship until the first unit of our proposed church could be built. The parsonage was already under construction and in the fall of that year our family moved into our new home in time for the children to start school in Plainedge.

When we were not able to find rental facilities for worship, and I had already resigned as pastor of Grace Lutheran, I found myself without a job. In consultation with Dr. Dybvig he suggested that I come to Minneapolis and begin raising funds for the newly established

St. John's Lutheran Church, Massapequa, Long Island, New York

Home Mission Trust Certificate program. I decided to do this and had the satisfaction of raising the first dollars for the Fund. Since that time over fifty years ago, the fund (which now is called "The Mission Investment Fund) has grown to over $700 million. After several weeks of fund raising, which unfortunately kept me away from family for an extended time, arrangements were made for me to serve as interim pastor of Good Shepherd Lutheran Church in neighboring Levittown for a period of six months.

In the meantime the first unit of what was to be St. John's Lutheran Church, Massapequa, was under construction. By spring is was sufficiently completed so that we could begin using it. As a result of the "door knocking" of parish worker, Ingrid Johansen and myself, we found that only 11 percent of the community residents were Lutherans so we could not depend on a lot of transfers from other Lutheran congregations. That fact did not deter our efforts. The residents of this new community were young people with large families and responded positively to our invitations. From the very first worship which was on Sunday, May 3, 1953, they began pouring into our church.

During the years that we spent at St. John's everything seemed to go just right and it proved to be the greatest parish experience of my ministry. The historical notes of the congregation reflect the positive tone of this ministry. It describes the beginnings of the church this way: "By the first Rally Day in September, an additional 68 new pupils were enrolled in Sunday School. During the next two Sundays, 25 more new ones came for a total enrollment of 209."

At the same time scores of new adults were coming to church and responding to our invitation to learn about the teachings of the Lutheran Church and "by October, 52 adults had enrolled for the pastor's adult class which met weekly for 10 weeks." The historical notes continue to say: "The pastor is now conducting three classes concurrently: Sunday, Tuesday and Friday evenings." During the 7½ years that I served the congregation, I instructed and confirmed over 600 adults and performed over 500 baptisms. There were normally several baptisms every Sunday, except on communion Sunday because of time constraints. The record was the baptism of 99 children and adults for one year.

Shortly after we began using the building but before it was finished, one of the young Sunday School pupils who had come from a large and beautiful church with multiple staff was not impressed by the unfinished building. He went home and said to his mother, "I don't like this church, it has no wall paper and only one God." Then later,

Easter Sunday, 1957, was St. John's Lutheran Church's all-time record with 1,597 people attending the one service which was conducted in the newly built Frog Hollow garage.

reacting to the name Helgesen, he added: "That's an awful name for a pastor to have, it has both hell and sin in it!"

The Fifth Anniversary of St. John's

We will now skip ahead and look at what this rapidly growing congregation was like on its fifth anniversary. During that time one additional classroom had been built to help accommodate the 800 children and a staff of nearly 100 teachers. Four separate and complete Sunday Schools were conducted every Sunday morning. Because of the large turnover of Sunday School staff, mainly caused by mothers on maternity leave, it was necessary to recruit about fifty new teachers each year. To meet this goal I did all the recruiting myself. During the month of August each year, I made about 100 calls on likely prospects in order to recruit the fifty teachers needed. Because most of the people who agreed to teach had no previous experience, I conducted a four week teachers' training course for them.

Before the congregation was five years old we were conducting four church services every Sunday morning to accommodate the congregation which had now grown to over 1,500. Our all-time attendance record was set on Easter Sunday, 1957, when 1,597 people attended the one service which was conducted in the newly built Frog Hollow garage. By its fifth anniversary, we had a full-time staff of six people: senior pastor, student intern, two parish workers, office secretary and custodian. We also supported Pastor Donald and Grace Flaten who were missionaries to French West Africa (now Cameron).

During the first five years St. John's grew to be the second largest congregation in the Atlantic Circuit of the American Lutheran Church. We were a "Mega Church" but we didn't know it! We just looked on ourselves as a cadre of people committed to Christ's command to go and make disciples. We had scores of trained people who every year made about a thousand calls on the people of our community.

Numbers were important because they represented people who were touched by the Gospel. For now we will tell just one of the many stories. Hazel Gay was one of the many people whose lives had not been touched by the Gospel. She called herself an atheist. One day our parish worker knocked on her door. In response to her invitation to attend our church and bring her children to Sunday School, she replied that she was an atheist, had no interest in church, and would not permit her children to attend Sunday School. But the story did not end there. The Spirit of God was at work. Her children kept pleading with her to let them go to Sunday School. She finally got tired of their pleading and said that they could go on condition that they would not come home and try to fill her with what they learned at church. But the children did not keep their promise. They were so excited by the Bible stories they learned that they had to share them with their mother.

My first contact with her was the night that she showed up at my adult instruction class. Later she shared that she came because she got so tired of hearing what the children were telling her that she decided to come and learn firsthand what this was all about. She came faithfully and during the class which dealt with the person and work of Christ, she had an unusual experience. The class was over, everyone had left the building and as I was locking the doors and turning out the lights, Hazel returned. Bluntly she told me that she had gone home but knew that she would not be able to sleep, so she came back and then simply asked, "Is it true that Jesus died for me?" "Hazel," I replied, "If you had been the only person ever born into this world, Jesus would have died just for you!" And with that she gave heart to the Lord!

She was so excited about her newfound faith that she immediately wanted to teach Sunday School; not just one class but two and on condition that they be different grades. This would involve double preparation which would enable her to learn more of Scripture. Now, some 50 years later, she is a trained and commissioned deacon at Grace Lutheran Church, Uniondale, New York.

A Tragic Ending to a Beautiful Story

The story of St. John's Lutheran Church eventually came to a tragic end. It was really a process that lasted for more than 20 years. Here is a brief sketch. During my ministry at St. John's, John Hove served a year as intern and did such a fine job that following his graduation from seminary he was called as my assistant. When I resigned, John was called as senior pastor and in May 1961, his seminary friend, Jack Hickman, who had been brought up Baptist, joined the staff as Hove's assistant. Later the two of them became co-pastors and finally, Hickman became senior pastor with John as his assistant. Jack Hickman was very charismatic and people began to follow him in "blind faith."

The first indication of change in the congregation came at a retreat when one of the women, claiming to have received the gift of prophecy, began to prophesy. This incident grew to the point that the congregation became largely charismatic with the gift of prophecy and to this was added the gift of speaking in tongues. For a period of years there was growing unrest in the congregation as Jack Hickman gradually replaced the charismatic aspect with a different phase of activity.

At this time John Hove was playing a very low-key leadership role. I have only good things to say about him but his mother once shared that he tended to be a bit naïve and at this time, most things were under Hickman's leadership. Jack Hickman now began to let the congregation know abut his interest in the Jewish faith. By 1970 he began to wear a Jewish prayer shawl at worship services. The congregation was puzzled by this change but considered it rather harmless. However, during the next few years he gradually abandoned the Christian faith and led the congregation into being a Jewish community living under Jewish laws. At this time he changed the name of the congregation to **The Shoresh Yishai Congregation** (which means "The Holy Congregation of the Root of Jesse). Local Rabbis, however, refused to accept any of these people into membership because they said that their teachings were not in compliance with Judaism. In 1979 the congregation, under Hickman's leadership, slaughtered seven goats in the church parking lot on the Jewish Day of Atonement and as a result was expelled from membership in the American Lutheran Church. On August 15, 1982, the New York Sunday addition of *The Newsday Magazine* devoted the cover and a major portion of the edition to telling the Massapequa story under the title "The Fables of Abba: A Prophet's past shakes the sect he founded."

We lift up just two points made in the article. The first was that Hickman was a homosexual and that he had been having sexual encounters with boys in the congregation. He did not deny the charges but explained that this was indeed an ancient Jewish ceremony of "the passing of the seed." He was so convincing that some of the mothers were offended that he had not chosen their sons for this important sacred ceremony. A second story in the magazine was about the congregation buying a new parsonage for Hickman (a bachelor) in 1980. It was a mansion set on 22 acres on the Great South Bay in East Islip, Long Island, for $275,000.

The following is taken from the *Newsday* article. "With the revelation of these and other unbelievable tales in 1981, the "Hickman Sect" began to crumble. In the wake of these disclosures, hundreds in Shoresh Yishai now found the contradictions intolerable and they fled. By summer, perhaps half the community had departed and in the next several years the exodus continued until there were not enough members left to sustain the ministry. The church building was sold to a Pentecostal congregation and those who were left in the congregation began having small group meetings in their homes on Friday nights." On last report only one such group was left which consisted of John and Darlene Hove and Frank (president) and Joan Utting. This ends the story of St. John's Lutheran Church.

During this long and painful road we kept in touch periodically with John Hove's parents and sister in Minneapolis and with a few friends of the St. John's congregation. It was a very painful process to see what was happening to so many of the wonderful people who through our ministry had come to know Christ as Savior. For a long time the question haunted me, "was there something that I did while I was their pastor that made this tragedy possible?" The best answer that I could come up with was that during my ministry, I had led the members to trust their pastor and when Jack Hickman came as "a wolf in sheep's clothing," their trust in him made all this possible.

At one time after John Hove had embraced the Jewish faith, our daughter, Mary, was on a trip to New York and wanted to visit them. She called John and asked if he would pick her up at the train station. His reply was, "I'm sorry than I cannot do this because it is on Saturday, and I cannot drive my car on the Sabbath Day."

Lorraine and I had only one personal contact with the Hoves following their embracing Judaism. We were in New York and were invited to their home for lunch. John appeared at the table with his yarmulke and gave the blessing in Hebrew. When the group could no longer afford to pay Hove's salary, he got a job teaching math at nearby Farmingdale College until he retired and they moved to Corinna, Maine, where they still reside. Jack Hickman disappeared! When I asked Hove where Hickman was, he said, "I do not know." Knowing that they had been friends for 27 years, he knew that I had a difficult time believing him so he repeated, "Honestly, I do not know." I believe he was telling the truth and chose not to know where Hickman was because, if he knew, he might be forced to tell. With the weight of the law upon him on his sexual charges, it is understandable that he would go into hiding. Now, nearly 30 years later, I occasionally ask myself, "I wonder where Jack is?"*

The American Lutheran Church (American Missions)

In 1959 I received a call from the Division of American Missions to become the regional director of the Upper Midwest Region which would give me the responsibility of the Home Mission work in Minnesota, Wisconsin, and North and South Dakota. My work would consist of doing the research necessary to determine where new congregations should be started and then buy land, build the church first units and parsonages, and guide the pastors and congregations during their first years of development. During my seven years in that call, I started 40 new congregations in the region. All but two of those churches are still alive and thriving after these nearly fifty years.

Director of ALC Department of Special Ministries

In 1967 the Board of American Missions called me to become the director of a new department which the Board had just voted to create. As such, my portfolio would include the responsibility of directing the ministries of Church in Town and Country, Indian Ministries, Eskimo Missions, Mexico Missions and Vacation and Leisure Ministries for the American Lutheran Church. To carry out this responsibility would require extensive travel throughout the United States and Mexico.

In considering this call and knowing its challenges, I went to see Dr.

---

*Note: At the time of publication of this book, it is possible to find more information on the Internet about the cult that Jack Hickman began at St. John's Lutheran and that, apparently, still continues today. According to a blog about Jack Hickman, with posts by many of his victims, he died in 2004 in Colorado and was burried in Maine.

Dybvig who at that time was retired and working for Luther Seminary. Respecting his wisdom and experience and his knowledge of my qualifications, I wanted his help in determining whether this would be the best use of the talents that God had given me. He was very affirming and helpful in thinking this through and I still remember one thing he said: "Remember that the higher you climb, the harder the wind blows!" In the seven years that I served in this office, the wind, at times, blew very hard, especially in my dealings with the American Indians.

I still remember the first day on the job. I sat at my desk with no mail to open, no phone calls to answer, and no meetings to attend. What a luxury to start with a clean slate and design a new program. I determined that the first thing that I needed to do was to study the issues and challenges that were confronting the programs that I was responsible for. Shortly, I planned two trips to accomplish this goal. The first was a trip by car through the deep south and back to Minneapolis to study rural poverty. My contacts on the trip were mainly with groups of Blacks who were recipients of government grants for self-help programs. The other was a trip through the San Joaquin Valley of California to study the grape strike issues. These were important issues for the church and gave me a good understanding from which to work. The five ministries that I was responsible for needed to be taken one at a time. At this point I shall give a brief resume of the things that I accomplished during the next seven years.

Church in Town and Country

The greatest challenge for the rural churches at that time was the mechanization of the farms that resulted in decreased population, which in turn was causing the demise of small towns and, therefore, the country churches. I met with many church councils to help them think through their problems. I would often remind them that the farmers were now pulling 12-bottom plows that were made up of 12 individual lays that had not changed since I was a kid and plowed our garden with one horse pulling a one bottom plow. They were challenged to do the same with their churches by linking them together to form parishes consisting of several churches.

During my time with Special Ministries, I did a lot of writing for

The Lutheran Standard and publishing of literature for the Church. *The Lutheran Standard* published a number of major articles that I wrote such as:

"*Is the ALC a Rural Church?*"
"*Good Samaritanism—By the truckload*"
"*Tractors Don't Go to Church*"
"*God Calls Politicians, too*"
"*The Myth of Rural America*"
"*No. 1 Hunger Fighter*" (Norman Borlaug cover story)
"*Mainspring in the Green Revolution*" (LCMS/Borlaug)
"*Love Reborn*" (Marriage Encounter story)
"*None of the Pallbearers Wore Gloves*" (Indian Ministry)
"*O Master, Let Me Walk with Thee.*" (101 year old pastor)
"*The Bells of Massapequa*" (Church hand bells)

Two things stand out among the many things that were accomplished for the rural churches in my Special Ministries Department. The first was for the rural pastors' wives. Many young women who were brought up in the city who became pastors' wives were having serious problems adjusting to life in small towns. With the help of professionals, I conducted a number of "rural pastors' wives retreats" throughout the country. Those who attended found the experience very helpful. The second was a number of "Listening Conferences" which we conducted in rural areas throughout the country. The church leaders who attended were instructed to do no talking but only ask questions and listen to what the rural people had to say. These conferences proved to be very helpful experiences for rural people who felt that the church had not been listening to their concerns.

Following the conferences our committee arranged a meeting of personnel from the ALC national staff and reported to them the concerns of our rural churches. The most significant, was that they wanted biblical Sunday School materials. Only then did I learn that there had been a serious conflict between the director of Parish Education and the president of Augsburg Publishing House. The education director won out and proceeded to publish materials that only dealt with life issues and had no biblical stories in them. As a result of this meeting, Al Anderson, president of Augsburg Publishing, had the necessary backing to enable him to change their whole Sunday School curriculum and produce the biblical materials that the rural congregations were demanding. Thus our department brought significant change to the educational program of the ALC.

Migrant Ministry

Many Hispanic people and Mexican workers were coming to the rural areas of our country to work on fruit and vegetable farms. Because these workers migrated with their families as the seasons changed, there were many problems relating to education, medical care, religion, and discrimination that needed to be addresses. Our department worked with the rural congregations in the impacted areas to help them minister to these families.

Indian Ministry

During the seven-year ministry of our department, we were on the firing line of the unrest in the Native American communities. I took the position that we should now turn the leadership of the Indian ministries and programs which had been in the hands of Caucasians, over to the Indians. This created no small conflict and at times the wind blew very hard. At this time the American Indian Movement (AIM) was born and I became close friends (or enemies?) with Dennis Banks and Floyd Belcourt. They tried to accomplish change through the use of violence which I could not support. At one time I asked Dennis Banks why they were on **my** back all the time rather than putting pressure on other churches. His answer was that "you are the only one that responds to our pressure so why should we bother with other churches and groups that won't respond?"

I could write a book on my relationships and activities with the Indian community (particularly AIM) but I shall simply headline a few incidents.

1. At one time I arranged for a Conference of Indian Workers at Augustana College, Sioux Falls, SD. Though AIM was not invited, Dennis Banks and friends showed up. As the meeting began, Dennis stepped to the podium and took over the meeting. Most of the attendees thought it was just a joke but when they found out that it was for real, they were sure that we all would be scalped. We did have a couple rough days but all of us (even I) did survive.

2. We were later involved in a more serious event in the Sioux Falls court house. Judge Bottom was conducting an Indian trial. When the personnel in the court room were asked to stand when the judge entered the room, the Indians refused on the basis that he had no respect for the Indians, so they would not show respect for him. A number of Church executives were meeting in Sioux Falls at that time. Dennis Banks met with us and urged us to come to the trial the next day to show support for the Indians. When he promised us that there would be no violence, we agreed to attend. When the trial began we and the Indians did not stand. The four bishops present conducted long negotiations with Judge Bottom who refused to budge on the basis that "the Indians want violence and if we don't give it to them today, it will come later." When the Indians again refused to stand, the room erupted into bloody violence. At that moment I decided that this was not the day nor the cause for which I was ready to die, so I leaped over several pews and ducked out the back door where I waited until it was quiet inside and was permitted to reenter the room which was in bloody shambles. There were serious injuries, but fortunately no one died.

3. I did a good deal of work with the Lutheran Indian Missions at Rock Point, Arizona, and Tokio, North Dakota.

4. On the fun side, I attended an Indian Powwow with a tribe at Omaha, NE. They made me an honorary member of their tribe and invited me to the high privilege of dancing with them during the Powwow.

Vacation and Leisure Ministries

With the increase of tourism throughout the country, my department was given the responsibility of assisting congregations whose worship services were overflowing with winter visitors. The first congregations that I worked with were St. Peter's Lutheran Church in Mesa, Arizona, and several churches in the Rio Grande Valley of Texas. I also was elected to the board of Christian Ministries in the National Parks which planned and provided worship opportunities for National Park visitors.

The most interesting experience I had in this ministry was to represent the ALC at an International Conference on Leisure and Tourism which was held in a castle in Tutsing, Bavaria. We were guests of the Bavarian Tourist Society which sponsors the famous Oberamergau Passion Play. On this and one other visit to Oberamergau, Lorraine and I had the privilege of attending the Passion Play.

In connection with the conference, I was able to arrange a vacation trip for Lorraine and me which was our first international travel. Along with Tutsing, it also included Oslo, Copenhagen, Berlin, Rome, Paris and London. This put us on a path that resulted in our leading 18 tours to many and varied countries, including seven tours to the Holy Lands.

Eskimo Missions

The ALC had done mission work among the Eskimos in Alaska for many years and had established several congregations. The work was started in 1894 by Norwegian missionary, Pastor Tollef Brevig. It is of interest to know that he never learned to talk the Eskimo language but taught the Eskimos to speak Norwegian.

In writing her book *Of Eskimos and Missionaries* for the ALC, Henriette Lund, on page 137, pays tribute to work that I was doing: "the Rev. Russell B. Helgesen, speaking for the Division of American Missions, expressed the thought that in the new approach [to Eskimo missions], the development of native leadership will be stressed."

Normally I made one or two trips to Alaska a year to meet with the missionary pastors. The most interesting was the trip where I never got there! Bishop Clarence Solberg and I had arranged to meet with the pastors. Solberg got there on time. I never made it. I flew to Seattle and the next morning went to the airport for my 8:00 A.M. flight. After a long wait, I was told that the 8:00 A.M. plane did not fly any more and the 8:30 flight had already gone and the only flight to Alaska would be the next day. So I called the bishop and told him that I would be a day late. No problem, the Alaskans have plenty time. The next day everything went fine and after many hours in the air we were on our descent into the Nome airport. When we were about 500 feet from the ground, fog suddenly rolled in and the plane took off. An hour later we landed at the US Air Base where we were given an option of flying to Fairbanks and waiting another day for a flight back to Nome or to go home. When I reported all this to Bishop Solberg, he indicated that the two days he had spent with the pastors waiting for me to arrive proved to be a very valuable time and they really had nothing more to talk about so he agreed that I would do best to go back home.

Mexico Missions

The Mexican Lutheran Church was established some years ago when a group of Pentecostal pastors who were dissatisfied with their church negotiated with the ALC to become Lutheran. Once a year I met with the eight pastors and attended their annual convention. On one occasion I traveled with the president and vice-president and visited all of their congregations. As I visited each church it was evident that they looked on me as a dignitary and were highly honored by my visit. Unfortunately their work did not go well, their congregations were mostly family affairs and experienced little growth.

In Mexico City there were two American Lutheran churches that were doing well and I did some work with them and also the seminary which was being conducted together with other Protestant Churches. When my department was phased out, the work was turned over to the World Mission Department and eventually the ties were severed with the Mexican congregations and from there on I have no knowledge of their fate.

Southwestern Minnesota District

After fourteen years on the staff of the Divisions of American Missions, I was called to be the assistant to Edward Hansen, bishop of the Southwestern Minnesota District of the ALC in Willmar, Minnesota. The five years that I spent with him were very satisfying. We had known each other for many years and had a very congenial relationship while I was on his staff. He had served as bishop for nearly two decades and had grown weary of the many meetings with call committees and with congregations and pastors to arbitrate their disputes. While he spent much of his time in meetings outside of the District, he was very content to let me be (for all practical purposes) the bishop. I thrived on the many pastor/congregation meetings and enjoyed doing a lot of preaching especially in connection with the installation of pastors and the dedication of new buildings.

During my time in Willmar, I was elected to the Board of Bethesda Homes. Because I knew that my District call was limited to five years and there was a possibility of change in administration for Bethesda Homes, I took the necessary training and received my certification for Nursing Home Administration. The plan did not materialize but the procedure was of help and interest to me.

Five years after I joined the staff it was time to elect a new bishop as Ed Hansen was not eligible for re-election. I was one of the five candidates chosen and came in third, so my call, which was coterminus with the bishop, came to an end. Both Ed and I accepted calls to Golden Valley Lutheran College and in December of 1978 loaded our furniture on the same moving van and took off for Minneapolis.

Golden Valley Lutheran College

On January 1, 1979, I became treasurer and financial aid director for Golden Valley Lutheran College, a two year Christian college which was the successor to the Lutheran Bible Institute. After one year, I was given the position of development director of the College, which put me in charge of the fund raising with a staff of about ten people under me. During the next six years, I carried out two major fund appeals.

Golden Valley Lutheran College, Golden Valley, Minnesota.

The first was "Thanks a Million" and the goal of the second was four million dollars. Prior to these appeals, the largest gift that the College had received was $5,000. In our second appeal, the pace was set with an initial commitment of $250,000.

The president at that time had limited administrative skills and depended much too heavily on borrowing funds with which to balance the budget. Finally in 1985, with interest rates of 18 percent and a declining student enrollment, the College tragically was forced to close and since it coincided with my 65th birthday, I retired.

My Years in Retirement

During my years with the Division of American Missions, I had been trained in professional fund raising which I then used with congregations in the Southwestern Minnesota District and were carried out extensively at Golden Valley Lutheran College. Upon retirement I established my own business which I called "Stewardship Counseling Service." For two years the business went very well. Many congregations wanted my services and I was able to earn all the money that I was allowed under

Social Security. Because most congregations wanted the programs in the fall, it left me free to spend the winters with Lorraine in the sunny South. Congregations paid me fees of from $4,500–$10,000 and in most cases the program resulted in doubling their annual income. Most programs were with Lutheran congregations but the most interesting was with a Roman Catholic church in Litchfield, Minn., where during the program, I preached at Mass and conducted a half-hour Bible study between each Mass. The priest was doubly satisfied with the results and said that it had saved him from becoming a janitor!

During the first year of retirement Lorraine and I went to Florida where we spent two month, saw all the sites, and had good fellowship with friends. The next winter we went to Arizona for most of the winter and found many friends, especially at Victory Lutheran Church in Mesa.

Victory Lutheran Church

Fred Moberg, pastor of Victory Lutheran Church, had once served Atonement Lutheran Church in Jamestown, North Dakota, a congregation which I had started while with American Missions; so we were well acquainted. After two years I decided to give up my Stewardship Counseling business and join his staff at Victory as part-time visitation pastor. After 27 years, it was good to be back in parish ministry. The seven years I spent on the Victory staff were among the best in my ministry. We spent eight months in Arizona and the summers in Voyager Village in Wisconsin.

Victory at that time was a great congregation. The area was flooded with winter visitors from the Midwest. In the summer Victory had

After retiring at age 65 after 27 years in Church administration, Pastor Russ had the chance to enjoy parish ministry once more as part-time visitation pastor at Victory Lutheran Church, Mesa, Arizona.

Victory Lutheran Church, Mesa, Arizona

worship attendance of about 500 and in the winter over 2,000. On an average winter Sunday we had as many as 40 new families who attended and visiting with them in their homes was my responsibility. After seven years, I retired again and for the next two years we spent winters in Arizona and summers at Voyager Village in Wisconsin.

Russ on his way to enjoy a game of golf, in front of their summer house in Voyager Village, Danbury, Wisconsin.

Finally 7500 York, the Ultimate!

In 1972 we bought a lot in Voyager Village, Danbury, Wisconsin. For $3,800. We looked on this as a good investment and a place where we could spend time camping with the family. For some years we used it for a limited amount of camping and some wonderful games of golf. When we sold our home in Plymouth in 1988 and moved to Arizona, we needed a place where we could spend our summers so we built a modest home on the lot which we had owned in Voyager Village for seventeen years.

Finally, on September 20, 1997, after ten years on the waiting list, we moved into 7500 York Cooperative. The twelve years that we have spent at York are the closest that we have come to having a dream realized. Being fully retired at the time we moved in, we were eager to become involved in this cooperative community. The first obstacle to overcome was the two homes we owed in Arizona and Wisconsin where we were still spending most of the year. Our Condo in Arizona was rented out and finally sold. After a year we sold our place in Voyager Village and since that time we have been spending the entire year at 7500 York.

Being full-time residents, I have been able to contribute substantially to life here. The list is long: Chairman of the Worship Committee, head of the Bible study program, "Lieutenant" of the Geranium Brigade, caretaker of the apple trees, gardener, member of the sound system task force, etc. etc. But at the head of the list, I must put my six years on the Board of Directors and two years as president. During that time we accomplished two major projects: refurbishing our corridors and installing in-house mailboxes. On both of those projects, the "wind at times blew mightily" but the wind has ceased to blow and by now we hear only affirmation.

But there is one more wind (actually, hurricane) that has blown, but now is like a calm breeze in the cool of the day. It all began about five years ago (2005). I was on the treadmill in the exercise room when "it came to me!" What we need for 7500 York was to add assisted living. When the Board approved moving ahead on the project with Ebenezer, I was appointed chair of the Assisted Living Ad Hoc Committee. As the project advanced, the violence of the wind increased. Since I got the original idea, residents have looked upon it as my project and opposition focused primarily on me. Though there have been tough times, I never lost faith that it would come to pass. Finally on April 3, 2009, the members of the co-op cast their ballots with 75 percent voting in favor of the project. Much more could be said about this experience but sufficient to say that necessary financing was approved December 30, 2009, construction began on March 1, 2010, official ground breaking took place on April 22, 2010, and completion is scheduled for the spring of 2011. What a thrill it was for me to put on a hard hat and be one of those who put the golden shovel into the ground. For all this, we give thanks to the Lord.

The Crowning Touch

Mark Thomas, president and CEO of Ebenezer, and I have had a very positive working relationship throughout the entire assisted living project. In mid August, 2009, he called me with the question: "Would you be willing to serve on the Ebenezer Board?" This was like a bolt out of the blue! Ebenezer is considered the Cadillac of the Senior Housing Industry. Their reputation is impeccable and to be on their Board is considered a distinguished honor. My answer was yes, my nomination was approved by the Fairview CEO and on August 20, 2009, my nomination was approved by the Ebenezer Board.

My first Board meeting was on November 19, 2009, at which time I was warmly welcomed by the Board, doubly so because they were so pleased to have a board member from 7500 York. In the course of the meeting I had the personal satisfaction of being the one who made the motion that we authorize the officers of the Ebenezer Board to sign the documents that finalized the $16,000,000 loan arrangements with the banks. With this, the financing of the "York Gardens" was put in place. When construction began on March 1, 2010, it was to be the event that marked the fulfillment of the dream that I had five years ago! Again, thanks be to God!

22

Time to Meet Our Family

The Story of Five Birth Days

Lorraine and I were blessed with a family of five children. The first three were born at the Lutheran Hospital in LaCrosse, Wisconsin, which, though 40 miles away, was the hospital that serviced our area. As we were about to leave the hospital after the birth of Becky, our first child, I asked Dr. Harmon how much we owed him. To my amazement, his answer was "Nothing. We don't charge pastors!" This was especially good news since we had such a limited income in those days. I really don't think that his generosity influenced our family planning but we did use his services two more times in the next 2½ years, and each time we were grateful for his generosity.

Rebecca Lynne, born Saturday, March 17, 1945

There is always extra excitement when your first child arrives, but with Becky, it is a story that has been told and retold every St. Patrick's Day for the last 65 years. Because of nearly impassable roads in the spring of the year, Dr. Harmon advised coming to the hospital a week early to have labor induced. We did but it didn't work so we returned home with instructions to come back in a week for another try. When we returned home that afternoon, we found that the bridge across the

Mississippi River which we needed to get home had been closed. After a close inspection, the guards permitted us to cross.

Early the next morning labor pains set in and by 8:00 A.M. we were at the bridge again for our trip back to La Crosse. With barriers up and guards in place we were told that we couldn't cross. When we insisted that we had to cross, they informed us that a portion of the bridge was completely gone and that crossing was not an option (see p. 198). We quickly concluded that our only alternative was to drive down the river 80 miles to Prairie du Chien where we could safely cross. After driving two hours on muddy and nearly impassable roads, we found ourselves just across the river from Lansing where we had started. At this point Lorraine said, "I think the pains are letting up!" to which I replied, "no way" and continued on our journey. By noon, after four hours of driving, we safely reached our destination. After checking her in at the hospital, I returned to the parking lot to find the car sitting with a flat tire! By six o'clock our darling baby had arrived and all was well.

Skip ahead about three years. Our first baby had finished her "terrible twos" and had done and was doing everything that normal children do. One day Lorraine took her hand and led her across the alley to Schafer's grocery store. As they entered the back door, Becky tripped on the threshold and would have fallen if her mother had not been holding her hand. Lorraine looked at her and said, "Becky, pick up your feet" to which she replied, "I can't, I has to walk!"

Jane Marie, born Tuesday, June 25, 1946

It was late spring and the roads to La Crosse were now in good driving condition. The trip went well and the delivery of our second daughter went smoothly. I still remember Dr. Harmon announcing to me that "you have a beautiful daughter." After a few days in the hospital, Lorraine was ready to be discharged but baby Jane could not go home because she had not regained her birth weight. Though the news was disappointing, we were assured that she was perfectly normal and it would likely be only a couple days before she could leave.

Because Lorraine had a need (or urge) to do some shopping, we headed for the department store. Shopping went fine but Lorraine was uneasy because of the fear that she might meet someone who knew her and would be critical of her going shopping so soon after having a baby. All went well. She met no one we knew and baby Jane was home a few days later.

Skip ahead a few months. After adjusting to a very active first baby, we were amazed that this one could be so good and contented. We called her our Carnation Baby. At the time the Carnation Company ran radio commercials urging people to "buy Carnation Milk from contented cows." Jane was our "Carnation Baby."

Thomas Russell, born Tuesday, October 21, 1947

As we awaited the birth of our third child in Lansing, our other big excitement was the fact that the War was over and the auto industry was again producing cars. We were so relieved to have gotten rid of our old jalopy which had caused us so much grief the last three years and now were the proud owners of a shiny new Ford.

As we set out on our third trip to the Lutheran Hospital in La Crosse

Lorraine holding Jane and Russ holding Becky

on that Saturday morning in October, John Bjerke, our favorite garage mechanic, waved us goodbye and told us afterward that he could tell that this was going to be a boy. And so it was. Again all went well and, after the delivery, as I was about to leave for home, Dr. Harmon put his arm around me and in his fatherly way suggested that after having three children in 2 ½ years, it might be well to take it a little easier. I was so pleased that I now had a son who would carry my name.

Skip ahead about two years. We were now living in Uniondale. Tom was a typical healthy and active little boy. Because he couldn't be kept in the house all the time and could not be left out side alone only a block from a busy highway, we resorted to tying a long rope around him and fastening it to a large tree. Horror of horrors. One day we came out and found him missing. After some anxious moments, we found him in the grocery story, having safely crossed the busy highway.

Skip ahead another couple years. I had in my possession a beautiful leather bound New Testament. One day when I reported it missing, Tom, who like George Washington could never tell a lie, came up with it and handed it to me. In examining it, I found that a number of the pages of Psalms in the back of the book were missing. In answer to my dismay, Tom replied, "well Dad, you always tell us in your sermons, that we should always spread the Word, so I tore out pages and gave them to my friends!"

James Philip, born Saturday, April 28, 1951

By the time Jim was born we had moved from Lansing to Uniondale, Long Island, and were starting over with most everything including our medical care. Dr. Harmon was no longer our doctor but likely would have been pleased to know that it was nearly four years before our next child was born. The event took place on a Saturday morning. A friend and parishioner, Jessie Andresen, had agreed to take care of the other children when Lorraine went to the hospital. When we called her out of bed at 6:00 A.M. on a Saturday morning, she was not a happy camper. But we deposited the three children with her and took off to the hospital in Seaford, Long Island.

We arrived safely, and I entered the hospital with Lorraine at my side and her suitcase in my hand. We checked in at the front desk and headed down the hall intending to go to the delivery room. At the door we were met by a nurse who informed me that fathers were not permitted beyond that point and that she would take good care of Lorraine! Things went well and in due time I was informed that we had a new bouncing baby boy.

In the meantime back home more permanent arrangements had been made for the other three children. Tom was deposited at the home of our good friend, Margaret Ranum, who gave him tender, loving care until he returned home. But with Becky and Jane the story was different. They went to stay with another friend, Margaret Horst, at near by Valley Stream. Her "loving care" included their eating oatmeal for every breakfast. They both hated oatmeal and refused to eat it but were not allowed to leave the table until they finished their dish. Cold oatmeal is not tasty and they told us in no uncertain terms that they would never stay with this "friend" again.

Skip ahead two years. Jim was a loving baby and got everything he wanted without asking for it so it was not until he was two years old that he began to talk. He didn't asked for another sister, but soon got one that he loved very much. He and baby Mary really loved to played together, especially in their favorite corner kitchen cabinet.

Mary Lorraine, born Sunday, October 25, 1953

Mary arrived on a very eventful Sunday morning. It was just five months after our first service at St. John's Lutheran Church in Massapequa. I had gone down to the church early that morning to oversee the Sunday School. Soon I was called to the phone only to have Lorraine inform me that she was experiencing labor pains. What should I do? I couldn't leave the Sunday School, much less abandon the church service. Everyone in the congregation was so new to me that it was not easy to know who to ask for this very personal assignment. I looked around and grabbed the first couple I saw which was Ray and Olive Sosnoski who, as fortune would have it, seemed to be the most likely candidates. They agreed and hurried off to meet Lorraine. A short time later as I stood in the chancel about to begin the church service, I glanced out the window and saw the Sosnoskis and Lorraine on their way to the hospital. Later Lorraine reported that Ray really didn't know the

The Helgesens: front l–r, Mary, Lorraine, Russ, Jim; back l–r, Becky, Jane, Tom c. 1959.

way to the hospital and had it not been for her help, they would have gotten lost. Back at the church, I finished the service, pronounced the Benediction, greeted the parishioners as they left, and rushed off to the hospital. Upon arrival I received the good news that we had a new and beautiful baby girl.

Skip ahead just a bit. Everyone in the family loved her, she and Jim were playmates, and Becky and Jane treated her like a doll in their beauty parlor.

Skip ahead again about seven years. In 1960 we left New York and moved to Edina, Minnesota. Soon after moving into our new home we had a very scary experience. Sometime after Mary had gone to bed, we heard a strange noise coming from her bedroom. We rushed in and found her in the midst of a seizure. A visit to the doctor the next day confirmed that she had epilepsy. He assured us that it could be controlled with medication. Some days later we sat down with Mary and explained her problem to her as tenderly as possible. She did not seem to be upset by what she was hearing and when we finished she simply replied, "does that mean I die?"

During the next few years she had only a few more seizures and only when she was asleep in her bed. Fortunately she was spared the embarrassment of having any seizures in public. After a few years, the doctor suggested that she try going off medication which she did and never again had a seizure.

There is much more to be told about our five incredible children but those stories will have to wait until they decide to write their own edition. To date, however, they have blessed us with twelve grandchildren and nine great-grandchildren.

A precious moment for Mary as she gets to share breakfast in bed with Mommy and Daddy, c. 1955.

In 1979 Russ had the joy of baptising his granddaughter, Britt Elise Vennie.

Russ and Lorraine in 2009 at Lorraine's 90th birthday celebration with many of their twelve grandchildren (plus spouses) and nine great-grandchildren.

23

A Family that Loved Camping

Our First Camping Experience

From 1948 to 1960 we lived in New York and most every year took a trip back to Wisconsin to visit family. In about 1958 we got the idea that we would like to try camping. We had no experience nor any equipment but that didn't deter us. Tom's good friend, Russell Jones, who lived next door to us had a Boy Scout pup tent and was happy to lend it to us.

At the end of the first day of our journey from Long Island to Minneapolis on the Pennsylvania Turnpike, we found ourselves at the Harrisburg exit. When we asked the attendant at a nearby gas station if he knew where we could find a place to camp, he pointed to a big alfalfa field surrounded by woods and was sure the farmer who owned it wouldn't mind if we pitched our tent back near the woods. As we started unloading our equipment and setting up the tent, lightning began to flash and rain began to fall. We hurried the set up and Tom, Jim, and I got inside the tent, which incidentally had no floor.

As the rain began to pour, we discovered that the tent was not waterproof. We hurriedly tore down the tent, loaded all the wet equipment into our luggage carrier on top of the car and drove all night in rain pouring so hard we could hardly see to drive. We vowed that this would not be the end of camping for us and next year would be better.

Thee Camping Experience of a Lifetime

Following our first catastrophe, we had a whole year to prepare for our next camping trip. It was 1959 and our five children were 14, 13, 12, 8, and 6 years of age. We went to Sears Roebuck and bought a good tent with all the necessary equipment. Following the Church convention of the ELC in Minneapolis, we set out on a six-week journey which would take us to Yellowstone National Park and eventually back to New York.

Our plan was to travel to Billings, MT, where we would meet our good friends, Orv and Judy Bilstad, and go on to Yellowstone National Park where we would spend a week with them and their boys. We left Minneapolis and drove west all day. Following a good night's sleep in our new tent, we continued west through the Dakotas and into Montana. The day wore on and the sun was sinking low in the west and then it happened! A stone in the road; an attempt to straddle it; the front tire hit it and sent it flying. Nothing seemed to have been damaged so I drove on. Some miles later I smelled gas, looked at the gas gauge and, horrors, it registered empty! A quick stop and inspection revealed a gash in the tank with what was left of the gas pouring out.

Earlier, our map had indicted that we were about 150 miles between towns and so we were now at about the half-way mark! Our quick decision was to drive as fast as we could, as far as we could and when we ran out of gas we would then decide what to do. Thankful that there was no speed limit in Montana, we roared on. Finally we spotted a car ahead. As we passed it we observed that it was full of Indians. I knew that by passing them, we would have one car behind us when we eventually ran out of gas. It worked; going up a long incline, we heard the inevitable chug as the motor went dead.

Only minutes later we saw the car of Indians coming and thankfully they stopped. Expecting that we were at least 75 miles from the next town, we asked the inevitable question, "do you know how far it is to the next gas station?" "It's just about 150 yards just over this hill and we will be glad to push you there!" At that point we were aware that God's angels were watching over us. At the gas station one of the Indians took out his knife, whittled a wooden plug which he drove into the hole in the tank. It seemed to work so we filled the tank with very expensive gas and exercising great care in driving, we reached Billings

Tom, Mary, and Jane in front of the seven-person tent that sported a blanket hung down the middle to divide the "boys" from the "girls" side.

safely before dark. The next day was a holiday, but our friend Orv found a garage that was willing to repair our tank and the next day we were on our way.

The week at Yellowstone was wonderful, including the camping. Our teenagers hung a blanket down the middle of our tent to give the girls some privacy and though they did a lot of teenage fighting, they loved the experience. We enjoyed singing, "Bless this tent, O Lord we pray, keep us safe by night and day" our own translation of the tune, "Bless this House."

We left Yellowstone and headed for Omaha, NE, for a week's stay with my sister Ila and family. When we left Omaha, we took cousin Jackie (age 14) with us for a visit in New York. After a long day of driving on the Ohio Turnpike, we agreed that six weeks of camping was enough and seeing a sign "Lorain, Ohio" we decided to turn off and try to find a hotel. With no delay, we found the Lorain Hotel. When I went in and inquired about a room, they asked about our family and how many rooms we needed. When I told them there were six children, all 14 or younger, they began to find excuses why they could not accommodate our family. My persistence won out and with

Russ helps Jane wash her hair in the great outdoors. Becky manages her own shampoo.

the help of our sleeping bags and two back-to-back rooms, we spent a very restful night. On leaving the next morning, I asked for the bill and was told that it was a total of $3.75! Then I learned the problem: Their policy was "children fourteen or under free!" They were very gracious but I am guessing that the next day they changed their advertising to "Children fourteen or under free in the same room as their parents."

When we got home and the children were back in school, Becky was given an assignment of writing a theme on "The kind of husband I want to marry," she wrote, "One who loves camping!"

Our Final Camping Trip

It was nearly ten years later that we took our next and final camping trip. At the time, I was on the staff of the Division of American Missions which was having a Board/staff meeting at a retreat center at Asylmar, CA. With all the children except Mary out of the nest, Lorraine and I decided that we should incorporate the event into a vacation and take Mary with us. We had long since disposed of our camping gear but daughter Becky and her husband Tom (von Fischer) graciously offered to loan their popup tent trailer to us for the trip to California.

We made the trip west in good order and arrived some days later at the California state line. After a few miles, we were stopped by a State Patrolman who informed us that our side mirrors were not in compliance. We faithfully promised to correct the problem and he happily sent us on our way and we dutifully had the mirrors installed. Following the Board meeting, we headed down the Cost to visit the sites in the Los Angeles area. When we entered the freeway, we were soon greeted by flashing red lights again. This patrolman informed us that "Cars pulling trailers must use right lane." We explained our problem, "We are from Minneapolis and there our right lanes are exit lanes, so if we drive in them, it creates a problem." He was considerate and we promised to try to do better so we were on our way. The next day we were again greeted by red lights. This time we had missed the sign that said, "cars pulling trainers, use truck speeds." Once more he accepted our promise to do our best to comply and sent us on our way. From that point on, Lorraine was assigned the responsibility to watch the speed limits and Mary had the assignment of keeping me in the right lane.

With no more encounters, we finally turned east and began the journey home. On the way we spent a few days visiting our Indian mission at Rock Point. This mission was one of the responsibilities of my department and they were very grateful for our visit.

A thousand and some miles later we arrived home and were so pleased that we had complied completely with all the laws in every state along the way and in no other state did we see a sign saying, "Cars pulling trailers, use truck speed." Or "cars with trailers must use right lane." So ends the saga of our camping experiences. Well, not quite!

We still had to return the trailer to Tom and Becky who lived in Columbus, Ohio, at the time. I was scheduled to attend the World Conference on Leisure and Tourism in Germany, and Lorraine was going along, so we decided to drive to Columbus with the trailer and fly from there to Europe.

It was a beautiful day when we began our journey. Everything went well and as we entered the state of Illinois we dutifully stopped at the toll booth and paid the proper fee for the car and trailer. "Oh no, don't tell me!" Within minutes, the familiar red lights! This time the patrolman's voice was stern as he invited me to join him in his patrol car and his message for me was clear: "Cars pulling trailers, use truck speed! No excuses, no promises, here's your ticket, pay the fine." I got the message loud and clear but replied, "Sir, we're leaving on a trip and my wife has the Travelers Checks. I must go back to her in the car and get them." "Sorry," he said, "I can only accept cash. So if you don't have the cash, you will have to go with me to the police station twenty miles from here and pay your ticket there."

I sat beside the officer in the front seat of his squad car. I recall my mood but I don't recall any conversation between the two of us either coming or going those twenty miles. We did get the trailer safely back to Columbus and had a memorable trip to Europe. Our last words to Tom and Becky, as we boarded our plane, were, "Thanks for the trailer, but please, don't ever offer it to us again!

So ends the saga of our camping experiences and the tale of "Good Old Russell B."

Tom, Lorraine, Becky, Mary, and Tom von Fischer in front of the infamous pop-up camping trailer.

24

Just a Bit of This and That

The Helgesen story has been written but there are still a few things to share. Here they are; enjoy them.

A Crisis in the Ranks

The story of the skull fracture I sustained when I fell down the hay chute when I was five years old has already been told. We should remember that at that time I was not hospitalized and for the next 65 years I never was a patient. But in 1989 that changed. Shortly after moving to Mesa, I was stricken with viral pneumonia and after spending a week in the hospital, it took nearly a year to fully recover.

What follows are some reflections on my hospital stay which I wrote to my family shortly after my discharge. Though real and literal, they are philosophical, theological, and somewhat poetical. To appreciate my experience one must understand the rugged individualism and stoic nature of those of us of Nordic stock. My hope is that as you ponder this, you will see something of the real me and recognize a bit of the real you in return. This is really a statement of my faith. What follows is:

"A Saga of Three Tears"

It had to happen sooner or later! When one passes his 68th year, with nary a hospital stay, one must face the inevitable. It came on Monday,

January 9, 1989, but in such an uneventful way. No panic, no 911, no paramedics, no sirens, no flashing lights.

After three weeks, the doctor was still puzzled. The persistent fever and lethargy was never deemed to be life threatening, but finally the doctor felt the need for additional help from the hospital in getting to the bottom of the matter. So with Mom as chauffeur, we began our five mile trek to Valley Lutheran Hospital. During that short trip I tried to sort out some of my feelings.

Tear N° 1

Even though I was heading into uncharted waters there was no feeling of fear for I knew that "the Lord was my Shepherd." A strong emotion, however, welled up within me. I tried to suppress it but it brought a tear. Strange! As a child I had learned that "big boys don't cry." I had also learned to admire the poet who wrote, "I am the captain of my ship; I am the master of my fate!" But, suddenly the song came to mind, "A little bit of tear let me down, spoiled my act as a clown."

But this was no big deal; just tests; a few days of rest and added treatment and I'd be as good as new again. Then the truth suddenly came: I who was the leader, who could always manage the moment, the one that others depended on, was no longer in charge. I had to admit my inadequacy and turn things over to others. That was the trauma of the moment!

As I checked in at the hospital, I gave up everything: my clothing, my billfold (with money, identification, and credit cards) and as a final act of humiliation, they attached me to an IV machine (like a puppy on a leash.) Rock bottom? Not quite. "Two things they couldn't (or didn't) take from me: (1) My wedding ring. Even if they had taken that, it could not have altered the 45 years of love, loyalty, oneness, good times and tough times, joy, laughter, and pain and (2) My faith. Could this be the fulfillment of the promise that "My grace is sufficient for you, for *my* power is made perfect in weakness?" (II Cor. 12:9). So the tear went away!

Tear N° 2

The first night in the hospital went fine; the strange surroundings were friendly and supportive. "The next morning the sun was shining and I had come to grips with being that "puppy on a leash." Why should I feel that this was demeaning? After all, puppies love with unconditional love and with loving masters, the leash gives a real sense of security. With this new attitude, when Dr. Mom arrived, I announced with glee my first significant "puppy" accomplishment: without unleashing nor a nurse's help, I had mastered the art of reaching my private "fire hydrant!"

Following some levity, there came a sobering thought. Dr. Mom reported that she had informed all the family of my plight and behold, there was panic in the ranks! It was really no surprise. My thoughts had been running ahead. The "great leader" had fallen! No, he wasn't going to die but this shouldn't happen to him. If he's not in command, to whom do we turn? Everyone wants a strong father (and/or mother). That's the rock of our stability. We all need to turn to someone older and stronger. At the same time, we don't want to be called "kids." This is the object of our inner rebellion. For most of us, this struggle is never resolved until our parents are gone and we stand alone at the top as the "strong leader." At this point we are no longer "the kids" and it can be very lonely up there. That's why we need a strong (or even weak) faith in a strong, ever present and unchanging God.

My thoughts were suddenly interrupted. A nurse entered with a beautiful bouquet of flowers "FROM YOUR LOVING CHILDREN!" and with it tear(s) no. 2. We can't really define love and concern, but flowers do it so well. For me? Why? But I'm a man and men are strong and flowers are feminine and I've never had flowers before! With this symbol of love and caring concern came a strong message of faith. Flowers don't just happen. They're too perfect, too intricate, too planned. It must have taken God a lot of time to design them all; and in each one he invested a strong measure of love—love that we in turn pass on to others.

Tear N° 3

Suddenly my hospital room was transformed into a huge arena. When I saw the throng that filled this stadium to overflowing, there was a great flood of emotion and the tears flowed freely. No more games; no more pretending; no more trying to be the strong one. In the VIP box of this great arena were our children, spouses, grandchildren, brothers, sisters, fellow-workers, doctors, nurses, maids, friends! First quietly, then in resounding voices came the message, "we're thinking of you," "we're praying for you," "can we help you in any way?" "Get well soon!"

The words really didn't matter; the message was always the same. God's word puts it this way, "Likewise the Spirit helps us in our weakness; for we do not know how to pray as we ought, but the Spirit himself intercedes for us with sighs too deep for words." Romans 8:26 So we make no judgments; only God looks at the heart and then tells us that "If you have faith as a grain of mustard seed, you will say to this mountain, move hence to yonder place, and it will move; and nothing will be impossible for you." (Matt. 17:20)

With that the scene became clearer and more overwhelming. "Therefore, since we are surrounded by so great a cloud of witnesses, let us run with patience the race that is set before us, looking unto Jesus the pioneer and perfecter of our faith, who for the joy that was set before him, endured the cross, despising the shame and is seated at the right hand of the throne of God on high." (Hebrews 12:1–2)

So now, after seven days the experience is behind me. Some important lessons of life have become clear; the most important of which is that I no longer have to be strong! "Your strength is made perfect in weakness" has a new meaning now. What a poor match my strength is for the combined team of family, friends, doctors, nurses; all undergirded by the Spirit and power of God. Thanks, God, and thanks family and friends for walking with me down this unusual path and sharing an unforgettable experience.

High Mountains and Deep Valleys

Among my life's experiences, there is one day that stands out above most others. It was the day that Lorraine and I arrived in Acapulco,

Mexico, for a few days vacation. Lorraine's college education had been interrupted by a career of raising our five children. When Mary, our youngest, finished high school, Lorraine decided to go back to college and complete the work for her degree. As she neared the finish line, I promised her that when she graduated, I would take her on a trip to Acapulco. She graduated in 1973 and shortly after, we took off. But first there is more that you need to know to understand that there may be peaks and valleys of life such as we experienced, that can be blessings from the Lord.

Everywhere in America, the seventies were difficult times. While I was working in the national office of the Evangelical Lutheran Church, there was deep strife within the Church and I ended up as one of its casualties. At the time, the Church was restructuring and the department that I was heading up was eliminated. John Hauck, our director, evaluated the entire staff and gave all of us high grades and assured us that we would have positions within the new structure. Then one day "the roof fell in!" He informed me that I would no longer be

Lorraine's college education was put on hold while she raised five children. Her graduation in 1973 was a happy affair shared with grandson Jason Vennie, husband Russ, and children Jim, Tom, Jane and Mary.

needed and the only explanation given was that "the points just didn't add up!" Later I found that I had been a victim of politics.

One day while I was feeling sorry for myself, a young rancher from Montana, who was a member of my department's committee, came into my office. After unloading my feelings about the deep valley I was in, he asked how long I had worked for the national church. When I told him "14 years," he offered no sympathy but replied, "Man, after 14 years, it's time you move on." He was right and the move that I was about to experience changed and blessed my life.

With the termination final, I began to pick up the pieces. We put our house up for sale and I began interviewing for a new job. In the middle of the pain I was experiencing, I began planning a trip to Mexico. As director of Special Ministries, I had supervised the work of the Lutheran Church of Mexico. Before leaving the office, it was necessary for me to go to Mexico and meet with the officers of the church. This presented the opportunity to fulfill my promise to Lorraine of taking her on the trip to Acapulco. I arranged to include a few days vacation and Lorraine went along. As we prepared to leave, the dark and cloudy future hung heavy over me. No job and no prospect of selling our house.

BUT the day before we left for Mexico, the sun began to peep above the mountain tops. A letter from Bishop Edward Hansen informed me that the Board of the Southwestern Minnesota District had just voted to call me as his assistant, so now I knew that I would have a job and would be moving to Willmar. Our house, however was still not sold. Some days later when we arrived in Acapulco and checked in at our hotel, the desk clerk handed me a note which read, "Call your realtor." We called him immediately and agreed to accept the offer that he had for the sale of our house. Knowing that our house was now sold and a new job was waiting for me, there was a burst of sunshine as a great feeling of euphoria came over us as we came out of that deep valley and ascended one of the highest mountain peaks of our career.

Prologue

For all of us, life has its high mountains and deep valleys. In the life story of "Good Old Russell B." I have told about many of the peaks and valleys of my life. The Psalmist reminds us that "Weeping may linger for the night, but joy comes with the morning." (Ps. 30:5) and I have now come to the place in life where I have taken onto myself these words:

> "When peace like a river, attends my way;
> When sorrows, like sea billows, roll;
> Whatever my lot, thou hast taught me to say,
> It is well, it is well with my soul."

The title "Slow Poke" that was acquired during my childhood, still lingers in my memory but the injured relationship with my mother who gave me the name has since been resolved.

As I now approach the sunset of my life, I look forward to the time:

> "When the Lord will hasten the day
> When my faith shall be sight,
> And the clouds will be rolled back as a scroll,
> When the trumpet shall sound,
> And the Lord shall descend;
> Even so it is well with my soul."

Note: To understand the impact that the nickname "Slow Poke" had on me, one should re-read the first chapter of Book III.

Because I have always believed in my heart that Jesus is my Lord and Savior, I know that some day I will be standing at the Pearly Gates of heaven awaiting the better life. As I stand there, I will hear the angels as they blow their trumpets and as their music fades away, the gates will slowly open, and I will see that great throng, too large to be numbered, standing there to welcome me. At the head of that throng, I see the leader. As she comes closer to me, I am impressed by her youthful beauty that has been restored and as I listen closely, I recognize the voice and realize that I have heard it a thousand times before. That voice now rings out loud and clear and, as I listen more closely, I hear my name; yes, she the leader is calling my name! "Russ, Russell, listen to me, I have good news for you today; you are now no longer a child and no longer are you a Slow-Poke! That's all behind us now. But please, Russ, hurry up for the Lord is waiting for you!"

Russ and Lorraine Helgesen on their first trip back to Norway, the land of their ancestors, in 1974.

Personal Addendum

Beginning salary in each Call

Date	Call	Annual salary
2-15-1945	Lansing, Iowa	$1,800
9-18-1947	Uniondale, N.Y.	$2,600
4-24-1952	Massapequa, N.Y.	$4,500
12-11-1959	American Lutheran Church	$8,500
1-1-1974	Southwestern Minnesota District	$10,924
10-23-1978	Golden Valley Lutheran College	$22,000

Profit/loss on each home we owned

Purchase	Address	Cost	Sale	Profit
3-29-60	Edina, Minn.	$20,455	$26,500	$6,045
7-15-63	Burnsville, Minn.	$31,300	$41,876	$10,576
4-25-74	Willmar, Minn.	$53,767	$72,655	$19,889
12-1-78	Plymouth, Minn.	$74,257	$107,577	$33,320
3-1-89	Voyager Village, Wis.	$65,647	$75,651	$10,004
3-30-95	Quail Creek, Ariz.	$31,338	$39,500	$8,162
8-1-97	7500 York, Minn.	$28,269		

Edina

Burnsville

Willmar

Plymouth

Russ feeds his first grandchild, Jane's son Jason Michael Vennie, born February 13, 1971.

Book V

Genealogy

The descendents of Jon På Valebjørg 1370 A.D.

As you look carefully through the 14 generations from Jon På Valebjørg to Jon Høljesen Grovum you will see ancestors who show up multiple times. Jon Høljesen Grovum was related to Jon På Valebjørg, born 457 years before him, through both his father (as his eleventh-) and his mother (as his thirteenth-great-grandfater)!— not surprising given the rugged terrain and lack of mobility in Norway through those generations.

Note, also, the naming convention: A son took his father's first name and added "son" to it (or "sen"); a daughter took her father's first name and added "dotter" or "datter" to it. What we, in the U.S., would now consider a "last" name was taken from the farm on which they lived. If a husband moved onto his wife's farm, he took her farm name. We met relatives in 1993 who still follow that convention. Cousin Egil Tveit, in his genealogical work, refers to me as Russell Paulson Helgesen and one of my daughters as Mary Russellsdtr. Helgesen.

When Hølje Pålson Grovum and his son Jon moved to America in 1861, they were no longer tied to the age-old farms in Norway. Jon dropped the farm name, Americanized the spelling of his first name, and became John Helgesen.

14/16 Generations: Jon På Valebjørg, 1370 – Jon Høljesen Grovum (aka John Helgesen), 1827–1894

Jon På VALEBJORG (b.1370)
|
Helge Jonson VALEBJORG (b.1400)
|
Jon Helgeson VALEBJORG
|
Tellev Jonson VALEBJORG
|
Olav Tellevson VALEBJORG (b.1570)
sp. Jigrid TELLEIVSDTR.
|
Telleiv Olavson VALEBJORG (b.1546;d.1623)
sp. Gro BENDIKSDTR.
|
Tallak Telleivson (Grovum) VALEBJORG
|
Telleiv Tallakson GROVUM
|
Tallak Tellevison GROVUM (b.1618;d.1690)
sp. Gundjorg TORJUSDTR
|
Torjus Tallakson GROVUM (d.1700)
sp: Torbjoro OLAVSDTR
|
Aashild Torjusdtr. GROVUM (d.1755)
sp: Tarjei Tarjeison HATVEIT (b.1692;d.1730)
|
┌───┬──────────────────────────────────┐
Jon Tarjeison HATVEIT (b.1721;d.1761)   Pål Tarjeison GROVUM (b.1729;d.1792)
sp: Borjhild OLAVSDTR. (b.1726;d.1798) |
| Hølje Pålson GROVUM (b.1785;d.1863)
Torborg Jonsdtr. HATVEIT (b.1745;d.1812)   sp. Margit Sigurdsdtr. HEIMDEL
sp: Halvor TARJEISON (b.1739;d.1792)
|
Torbjorg HALVORSDTR. (b.1767)
sp: Sigurd Johnson HEIMDEL (b.1760;d.1826)
|
Margit Sigurdsdtr. HEIMDEL (b.1790;m.1818;d.1854)
sp. Hølje Pålson GROVUM
|
Jon Høljesen GROVUM (aka John Helgesen) (b.1827;d.1894)

Note: *Jon Høljesen Grovum (John Helgesen) was related to Jon På Valegjorg through both his father, Hølje Pålson Grovum, and his mother, Margit Sigurdsdatter: Hølje was the grandson of Tarjei Tarjeison Hatveit and Ashild Torusdatter; Margit was their great-great granddaughter.*

If you look closely at this list, you will see the pattern of a father's first name becoming the child's last name with either "son" or "datter" added. The name in ALL CAPS (mostly) represents the farm name where they lived: Presumably, this evolved from, "Oh, ja, you mean Jon, Hølje's son, over there on the Grovum farm."

Descendants of Jon Høljesen Grovum (aka John Helgesen), 1827–1894

John Helgesen had 14 children: four with his first wife, Jorand Gjermundsdatter Jorundland (b.1830; m.1854; d.1863); and ten (plus one that died following birth) with his second wife, Ingeborg Eriksdatter Docken (b.1847; m.1865; d.1901). What follows are the descendants of the eleven of those children who (as far as I know) had children themselves. If you are descended from John Helgesen, you should find yourself in these pages! The listing on page 261 is of John's children and their wives. Starting on page 262 are listed each of those children who had children, along with their known descendents.

1. John (AKA Jon Holjesen Grovum) HELGESEN (b.1827;d.1894)

sp: Jorand Gjermundsdtr JORUNDLAND (b.1830;m.1854;d.1863)

- 2. Marget HELGESON (b.1855)
- 2. Anne HELGESON (b.1857)
- 2. Halvor HELGESON (b.1859;d.1951)
  - sp: Aslaug BRATTLIE (b.1856;d.1919)
- 2. Johanna HELGESON (b.1863)

sp: Ingeborg Eriksdatter DOCKEN (b.1847;m.1865;d.1901)

- 2. Elias HELGESEN M. D. (b.1866;d.1937)
  - sp: Josephine Jane (Feen) WEISS (OR WISE) (b.1868;m.1886;d.1947)
  - sp: Kathryn WEISS
- 2. Peter Andrew HELGESEN M. D. (b.1868;d.1945)
  - sp: Anna S. DAKKEN (b.1873;m.1889;d.1911)
  - sp: Maude E. THOMAS (b.1878;m.1912;d.1962)
- 2. John HELGESEN M. D. (b.1871;d.1934)
  - sp: Teresa BAKKE (m.(Div))
  - sp: Margaret Burns
- 2. Thomas Olaus HELGESON (b.1873;d.1920)
  - sp: Mary
- 2. Henry Edward HELGESON (b.1876;d.1927)
  - sp: Hannah Catherine WILKINSON (b.1883;m.1901;d.1922)
  - sp: Anne AMUNDSON (b.1877;m.1897;d.1899)
- 2. Alfred HELGESON (b.1877;d.1877)
- 2. Mary J. HELGESON (b.1879;d.1960)
  - sp: John E. JOHNSON (b.1877;d.1948)
- 2. Sever HELGESEN (b.1882;d.1934)
  - sp: Mary Ann KUNDERT (b.1888;m.1905;d.1970)
- 2. Clara Mathilde HELGESON (b.1884;d.1949)
  - sp: Jacob Edmund STOLEN (b.1882;d.1953)
- 2. Albert Morris HELGESON (b.1887;d.1959)
  - sp: Alpha Theoline KITTLESON (b.1891;m.1912;d.1979)
  - sp: UNKNOWN
- 2. Paul Tenny HELGESEN (b.1890;d.1962)
  - sp: Helga Emelia KITTLESON (b.1892;m.1913;d.1984)

1. Halvor HELGESON (b.1859;d.1951)
sp: Aslaug BRATTLIE (b.1856;d.1919)
- 2. Julia HELGESON (b.1890;d.1959)
  - sp: Carl KAHL
  - 3. Beulah KAHL
    - sp: UNKNOWN MOEN
  - 3. Almira KAHL
    - sp: UNKNOWN SWENSON
- 2. Annie HELGESON (b.1893;d.1962)
  - sp: Carl IVERSON
  - 3. Carroll IVERSON
  - 3. Harold IVERSON
  - 3. Richard IVERSON
  - 3. DORIS IVERSON
    - sp: UNKNOWN JELLE
  - 3. Ann Marie IVERSON
    - sp: UNKNOWN SYFTESTAD
  - 3. Dean IVERSON
  - 3. Avis (d. age 9) IVERSON
- 2. Abner HELGESON (b.1896;d.1980)
  - sp: Hazel PAULSON (m.1936)
  - 3. Paul Abner HELGESON (b.1938)
    - sp: Karen JABS (m.1959)
    - 4. Roxanne HELGESON (b.1959)
    - 4. Suzanne Hillman HELGESON (b.1964)
    - 4. Alan HELGESON (b.1965)
  - 3. Janet Marie HELGESON (b.1941)
    - sp: Alan "Pete" KIEL (m.1965)
    - 4. Kristin KIEL (b.1966)
    - 4. Daniel KIEL (b.1970)
    - 4. Peter KIEL (b.1971)

3. James Edward HELGESON (b.1944)
     sp: Susan HARRIS (m.1965)
        4. Kim HELGESON (b.1966)
        4. Shawn HELGESON (b.1969)
        4. Konni HELGESON (b.1971)
2. Ida Amelia HELGESON (b.1898;d.1978)
   sp: Amos STEENSLAND (m.1934)

1. Elias HELGESEN M. D. (b.1866;d.1937)
   sp: Josephine Jane (Feen) WEISS (OR WISE) (b.1868;m.1886;d.1947)
   2. John Selmer (AKA Sam) HELGESEN
      sp: Irene B. SCHMID (m.1936)
      3. Marvin HELGESEN
         sp: June ANDERSON (m.1936)
         4. Susan HELGESEN
            sp: David JOHNSON
            5. Phillip JOHNSON
      3. Verna M. HELGESEN
         sp: Raymond E. BRIGGS (m.1937)
         4. Raymond E. BRIGGS
            sp: Donna HOLMES
            5. Johnny BRIGGS
               sp: Susan SCHAFFER
               6. Alyssa BRIGGS
               6. Angela BRIGGS
            5. Lawrence BRIGGS
               sp: Gabriel CHRISTENSON
               6. April BRIGGS
            5. Barbara BRIGGS
               sp: Marty CLIFT
               6. Matthew CLIFT
               6. Adam CLIFT
               6. Brandon CLIFT
               6. Andrea CLIFT
            5. Brian BRIGGS
               sp: Margaret
            5. Scott BRIGGS
      3. Harlan E. HELGESEN (d.1942)
   2. James Walter Erwin HELGESEN (b.1891;d.1967)
      sp: Ida Clara OLSON (b.1893;d.1965)

2. James Walter Erwin HELGESEN (b.1891;d.1967)
   sp: Ida Clara OLSON (b.1893;d.1965)
      3. Walter Burnell HELGESEN
         sp: Unknowan
            4. Stephan HELGESEN
      3. Lavine Pearl HELGESEN
2. Reuben L. HELGESEN (b.1893;d.1937)
   sp: Mabel HANSON (m.1918)
      3. LaVerne B. HELGESEN (b.1919)
         sp: Jean E. HANSON (m.1946)
2. William J. HELGESEN (b.1895;d.1962)
   sp: Grace JACOBS (m.(Div))
      3. Genieve K. HELGESEN (b.1916)
         sp: Edward KOSANKE (m.1940)
   sp: Hazel MAHNEY (m.1931)
sp: Kathryn WEISS
   2. Lillian Marion WEISS (b.1895;d.1971)
      sp: Jacob VOEGELI (b.1892;m.1918;d.1978)
         3. Frances L. VOEGELI (b.1919)
            sp: John B. HOSKINS (m.1942;d.1980)
               4. Douglas HOSKINS (b.1947)
                  sp: Dianne SOLZEMAN (m.1970)
                     5. Corinne Arlene HOSKINS (b.1973)
                     5. Jessica Leigh HOSKINS (b.1976)
               4. Jean Ann HOSKINS (b.1949)
                  sp: Tom HEFTY (m.1968(Div))
                     5. Sarah Ann HEFTY (b.1973)
                     5. Ann Kathryn HEFTY (b.1976)
         3. Virginia VOEGELI (b.1922)
            sp: Charles SCHNETZLER (m.(Div))
               4. Janet SCHNETZLER
                  sp: KERR (m.(Div))

3. Royal J. VOEGELI (b.1926)
   sp: Harriet TYEAS (m.(Div))
   4. Mark VOEGELI
   4. Anne VOEGELI
3. Howard F. VOEGELI (b.1930)
   sp: Alice LIEN
   4. Rhonda Kay VOEGELI
      sp: Curtis INNE
         5. Rhonda Kay INNE
         5. Brittany INNE
   4. Jacalyn Olivia VOEGELI
      sp: Rick OLIVA
   4. Bryan VOEGELI
      sp: Beth CARSON
         5. Brienna VOEGELI
   4. James Jacob VOEGELI

1. Peter Andrew HELGESEN M. D. (b.1868;d.1945)

sp: Anna S. DAKKEN (b.1873;m.1889;d.1911)
- 2. Walter Andrew HELGESEN (b.1891)
    sp: UNKNOWN
    - 3. UNKNOWN HELGESEN
- 2. Lillian E. HELGESEN (b.1893;d.1896)
- 2. Russell John HELGESEN (b.1898;d.1982)
    sp: Fern Erica FLATLAND (b.1901;d.1941)
    - 3. Gloria Jeanne HELGESEN (b.1925;d.1986)
        sp: Dale Erwin SCHOENEMAN
        - 4. Mark Charles SCHOENEMAN (b.1950)
            sp: Sandra Jean BOLES (b.1953;m.1972)
            - 5. Heather Ann SCHOENEMAN (b.1974)
            - 5. Adam Charles SCHOENEMAN (b.1978)
    - 3. Marilyn Faye HELGESEN (b.1931)
        sp: Mitchell P. BARAN (b.1927;m.1949(Div))
        - 4. Mary Candace BARAN (b.1950)
        - 4. Stanley Mitchell BARAN (b.1952;d.1969)
        - 4. Mitchell Thomas BARAN (b.1953)
        - 4. April Ann BARAN (b.1956)
        sp: Gary Walter WILCOX (b.1936;m.(Div))
    sp: Hilda WALKUP (d.1992)
    - 3. John (son of Hilda) WALKUP (b.1943)
        sp: Sondra LIEBERMAN (b.1944)
    - 3. Susan Mary HELGESEN (b.1946;d.1995)
        sp: OLSON Steve (m.1961(Div))
        - 4. Eva ROSE (b.1961)
            sp: Randy NELSON (friend) (b.1960)
            - 5. Cager ROSE (b.1980)
        - 4. Paul NELSON (adopted) (b.1964;d.2003)
- 2. Lillian J. HELGESEN (b.1897;d.1897)

sp: Maude E. THOMAS (b.1878;m.1912;d.1962)

2. Harold I. HELGESEN (b.1914;d.1979)
   sp: Evelyn ARNESON (b.1915;m.1940;d.2001)
   3. John HELGESEN Adopted
      sp: UNKNOWN
         4. Ann Elizabeth HELGESEN
         4. Alicia HELGESEN
            sp: UNKNOWN
   3. Mary HELGESEN Adopted
      sp: Mark BREKKE
         4. Jennifer Renae BREKKE
         4. Sarah Nicole BREKKE

1. John HELGESEN M. D. (b.1871;d.1934)

sp: Teresa BAKKE (m.(Div))
- 2. Earl Adrian HELGESON (b.1897;d.1979)
  - sp: Marguerite DUTCHER (b.1903;m.1924;d.1997)
    - 3. Richard Charles HELGESON (b.1928)
      - sp: Frances Rosamund KIKER (m.1951)
        - 4. Richard C. HELGESON Jr.
        - 4. Steven HELGESON
        - 4. David HELGESON
        - 4. Edward HELGESON
        - 4. Peter HELGESON
    - 3. Earl Adrian HELGESON JR (b.1931;d.1997)
      - sp: Janet HIPPSLEY (b.1931;m.1955)
        - 4. Ann HELGESON (b.1958)
          - sp: Gage Randolph JOHNSON (m.1987)
        - 4. Eric John HELGESON (b.1958)
        - 4. Judith HELGESON (b.1962)
    - 3. John Paul HELGESON (b.1935)
      - sp: Sarah (AKA Sally) SLATER (b.1935;m.1957)
        - 4. Daniel Wood HELGESON (b.1961)
          - sp: Anne JACOBS (m.1995)
        - 4. Susan Courtenay HELGESON (b.1962)
          - sp: Thomas LOEPFE (m.1988)
            - 5. Jennifer N. LOEPFE (b.1991)
            - 5. Sarah LOEPFE (b.1995)
        - 4. James Seymour HELGESON (b.1966)

sp: Margaret Burns
- 2. John Martin HELGESEN (b.1907;d.1977)
  - sp: Evelyn BRONSON (b.1916;m.1945;d.2000)
    - 3. Gregg Stuart B.F.: Erickson HELGESEN Adopted (b.1939)
      - sp: Marne GEORGE (b.1939)
        - 4. Jeffrey Michael HELGESEN (b.1963)
          - sp: Debbie SHELDEN

- 4. Catherine Elizabeth HELGESEN Cassy (b.1965)
  - sp: Gene MC CABLE
    - 5. Maggie Jean MC CABLE
    - 5. Andrew Patrick MC CABLE
- 4. Anne Marie HELGESEN (b.1970)
  - sp: Steven Nelson PANKEY
    - 5. Ryan McKenzie PANKEY
- 4. Mary George HELGESEN Molly (b.1975)
- 3. Lisa HELGESEN (b.1960)
  - sp: UNKNOWN

- 2. FRANCIS Xavier Or Marion HELGESEN (b.1909;d.1983)
  - sp: Cecilia Stella KOWALEWSKA (b.1903;m.1933;d.2002)
    - 3. Barbara Lynn HELGESEN (b.1938)
      - sp: Jerry SCHLIEP (b.1936;m.1961)
        - 4. Kristin SCHLIEP (b.1962)
        - 4. Monica SCHLIEP (b.1964)
        - 4. Karen SCHLIEP (b.1966)
    - 3. Stephanie Margaret HELGESEN (b.1943)
      - sp: (father) Dan Erwin LOWE
        - 4. Cecily Elizabeth HELGESEN (b.1967)
    - 3. Timothy John HELGESEN (b.1946)
      - sp: Christine EVENSEN (m.(Div))
      - sp: Jeannie PETERS (m.1972)
        - 4. FRANCIS Xavier HELGESEN (b.1979)
        - 4. Mathew HELGESEN (b.1984)
        - 4. Eric HELGESEN (b.1988)
- 2. Paul Arnold HELGESEN (b.1914;d.1989)
  - sp: Hermoine AKA Teddy KOLSTAD (b.1923;m.1943)
    - 3. Michael Paul HELGESEN (b.1944)
      - sp: Betty CONRAD (m.1964(Div))
        - 4. Laura Renee HELGESEN (b.1964)
        - 4. UNKNOWN HELGESEN

sp: Ernestine (m.1972)
- 4. Kunu HELGESEN (b.1970)
- 4. Hinu HELGESEN (b.1972)
- 4. Wehau HELGESEN (b.1976)

3. John Thomas HELGESEN (b.1945)

sp: Dollie HALL (m.1967(Div))
- 4. Tricia Faye HELGESEN (b.1970)
- 4. Cory James HELGESEN (b.1976)

sp: Marilyn WHITE (m.1977)
- 4. Rhonda White HELGESEN (Adpt) (b.1965)

3. Mary Margaret HELGESEN (b.1946)

sp: Rodney DRAYER (m.1968(Div))
- 4. Christian John Paul DRAYER (b.1970)

2. Charles Richard HELGESEN (b.1919;d.1997)

sp: Anne Marie LAFOLLETTE (b.1926;m.1947;d.1976)

3. Sarah James (Sally) HELGESEN (b.1948)

sp: Bart GULLEY (m.2001)

3. Rebecca Ann HELGESEN (b.1951)

sp: David COMPE (m.1988)

3. Martha Burns HELGESEN (b.1955)

sp: David A. MARTIN (m.1978)
- 4. Louis Donovan MARTIN (b.1985)
- 4. Peter Charles MARTIN (b.1988)

sp: Toni FINELLI (m.1985)
- 4. Arianna Terese HELGESEN (b.1992)

3. Christine Margaret (CeCe) HELGESEN (b.1961)

sp: Michele SANTANASTASIO (m.1993)
- 4. Shane Helgesen SANTANASTASIO (b.1997)
- 4. Dario Helgesen SANTANASTASIO (b.2000)

sp: Luanne MOREY (m.1983)

2. Mona Mae HELGESEN (b.1923)

sp: William ELSHAM (m.1945(Div))

3. Nancy ELSHAM (b.1946)
  sp: James JARDINE
    4. Christopher JARDINE (b.1977)
    4. Benjamin JARDINE (b.1981)
    4. Daniel JARDINE (b.1985)
3. Susan ELSHAM (b.1949)
  sp: Thomas GRANDE
    4. Andrew GRANDE (b.1975)
    4. Elizabeth GRANDE (b.1977)
    4. Katherine GRANDE (b.1981)
3. William ELSHAM JR (b.1951)
3. Robert Burns ELSHAM (b.1953)
sp: Dr. Richard ZAHRLING

1. Thomas Olaus HELGESON (b.1873;d.1920)
sp: Mary
　2. Benjamin J. HELGESEN (b.1910;d.1963)

1. Henry Edward HELGESON (b.1876;d.1927)

sp: Hannah Catherine WILKINSON (b.1883;m.1901;d.1922)

- 2. Beulah T. HELGESON (b.1904;d.1927)

  sp: John GLADEM (m.1924)

  - 3. Harlan Dean GLADEM (b.1925;d.1987)

- 2. Lemon Vivian HELGESON (b.1906;d.1906)

- 2. Leon Vivian HELGESON (b.1908;d.1976)

  sp: Mildred HOOK (b.1914;m.1933;d.1982)

  - 3. Stanley HELGESON
  - 3. Janet HELGESON
  - 3. Audrey HELGESON
  - 3. Twila HELGESON
  - 3. Lyle HELGESON

- 2. Irvin Stanley HELGESON (b.1910;d.1972)

  sp: Helen Louise OLSON (b.1911;m.1957;d.1981)

  - 3. Jean HELGESON
  - 3. Howard HELGESON
  - 3. Nola HELGESON
  - 3. Beth HELGESON

- 2. GLEN Joyce HELGESON (b.1912;d.1989)

  sp: Burless Viola ANDERSON (b.1913;m.1935;d.1957)

  - 3. Dean HELGESON
  - 3. Elaine HELGESON

  sp: Burless Viola ANDERSON (m.1935)

  - 3. Dean HELGESON
  - 3. HELGESON
  - 3. Elaine HELGESON

- 2. Lela Maxine (Twin) HELGESON (b.1915;d.1988)

  sp: Victor William POLLOW (b.1912;m.1934;d.1949)

  - 3. Lavonne POLLOW
  - 3. Geraldine POLLOW
  - 3. James POLLOW
  - 3. Vernon POLLOW

  sp: Peter BURNO (m.1956)

- 2. Lynette Eldred (Twin) HELGESON (b.1915)
  - sp: Martel Lavern ENGLAND (b.1916;m.1933(Div))
    - 3. Carol ENGLAND
    - 3. Merlyn ENGLAND
    - 3. Wayne ENGLAND
    - 3. Euneva ENGLAND
    - 3. Sharon ENGLAND
    - 3. Marlys ENGLAND
    - 3. Dallas ENGLAND
  - sp: Guy HOOD (m.(Div))
  - sp: Edward RICE
- 2. Hazel Colletta HELGESON (b.1917;d.1921)
  - sp: UNKNOWN
- 2. Mabel Twila HELGESON (b.1918)
  - sp: Johannas TVIET (b.1914;m.1938;d.1977)
    - 3. Judith TVIET
    - 3. Verna TVIET
      - sp: John TVIET
    - 3. John TVIET
    - 3. Dawn TVIET
    - 3. Debra TVIET
- 2. Violet Thelma HELGESON (b.1921;d.1921)
- 2. Delbert HELGESON (b.1922;d.1985)
  - sp: Marjorie J. CLIFF (m.1942(Div))
    - 3. ROSE Ann HELGESON (b.1943)
      - sp: Gary Norman WOOLEVER (b.1961;m.1961(Div))
        - 4. Stephanie Ann WOOLEVER
        - 4. Steven Allen WOOLEVER
        - 4. Michael Todd WOOLEVER
      - sp: Richard A. PHELPS (m.1972)
        - 4. Kenneth J. PHELPS
          - sp: Amy UNKNOWN
  - sp: Ada Mae ROOD (b.1921;m.1947;d.1988)
    - 3. Thomas HALE Step son

      sp: Marie Julie HALE (m.(Div))
- 4. Robbie HALE
- 4. Vicky HALE
- 4. Nancy HALE (Deceased)

3. Annette Lucille HALE Step daughter
    sp: Freeman Trice SMITH
- 4. Donna SMITH
    sp: George LINDSEY
    - 5. Jody SMITH
    - 5. Richard LINDSEY
    - 5. Scott SMITH
- 4. Diann SMITH
    sp: Raymond LA CONSAY
    - 5. Justin LA CONSAY
    - 5. Heather LA CONSAY
- 4. Denise SMITH
    sp: Tim POWELL
    - 5. Mandi POWELL
    - 5. Tiffany POWELL

3. Della HELGESON (b.1959)
    sp: Gary GILBERTO
- 4. Connie GILBERTO Step or adopted (b.1973)
    sp: Aaron SCHNIEDER
- 4. David GILBERTO (b.1976)
- 4. Jesse GILBERTO (adopt by Gary) (b.1978)
- 4. Gary Jr. GILBERTO (b.1983)
- 4. Angelica MONETTE (adopted) (b.1974)
    sp: Chris TUMA
    - 5. Dylan TUMA (step son)

3. Suzan HELGESON (b.1962)
    sp: Chris TALBOT (m.(Div))
- 4. Christopher TALBOT
- 4. Erica TALBOT

sp: Anne AMUNDSON (b.1877;m.1897;d.1899)

1. Mary J. HELGESON (b.1879;d.1960)
sp: John E. JOHNSON (b.1877;d.1948)
- 2. Earl JOHNSON (b.1902;d.1987)
    sp: Margaret KULP (b.1911;m.1937)
- 2. Irene JOHNSON (b.1903;d.1972)
    sp: Silas FJELSTAD (b.1903;m.1922;d.1971)
- 2. James M. JOHNSON (b.1905;d.1962)
    sp: Florence E. KILEY (b.1907;m.1925;d.1993)
- 2. Aldro JOHNSON (b.1907;d.1970)
    sp: Ruby BARSNESS (b.1912;m.1930;d.1981)
- 2. Hazel JOHNSON (b.1909)
    sp: Ralph BARSNESS (b.1906;m.1930;d.1985)
    - 3. Betty BARSNESS
        sp: UNKNOWN RUE
        - 4. Patti RUE
- 2. Alvin JOHNSON (b.1912;d.1983)
    sp: Avilda VALSTAD (b.1917;m.1938)
- 2. Milford JOHNSON (b.1914;d.1982)
    sp: Olivia BOLLENBACK (b.1916;m.1950)
- 2. Marvin JOHNSON (b.1917;d.1979)
    sp: Helen KUYKENDALL (b.1920;m.1940)
- 2. Russell JOHNSON (b.1920;d.1989)
    sp: Carol Jean YOST (b.1925)
- 2. Janice Charleen JOHNSON (b.1922;d.1922)

1. Sever HELGESEN (b.1882;d.1934)
　sp: Mary Ann KUNDERT (b.1888;m.1905;d.1970)
　　2. Edna Alvina HELGESEN (b.1906;d.2000)
　　　sp: Carl H. BEYER (b.1899;m.1926;d.1997)
　　　　3. William Robert BEYER D.C. (b.1929)
　　　　　sp: Carol WILEMAN (b.1955;m.1955)
　　　　　　4. Holly BEYER (b.1957)
　　　　　　　sp: Bruce BODE (m.1982)
　　　　　　　　5. Lauren Lee BODE (b.1982)
　　　　　　　　5. Ashley Alma BODE (b.1984)
　　　　　　　　5. Austin CARLSON BODE (b.1991)
　　　　　　4. Robert BEYER (b.1959)
　　　　　　　sp: Debra Kultgen (m.1989)
　　　　　　　　5. Kyle Kultgen BEYER (b.1991)
　　　　　　4. Bradley BEYER (b.1961)
　　　　　　4. Chris BEYER D.C. (b.1964)
　　　　3. Elizabeth D. BEYER (b.1931)
　　　　　sp: Richard W. CONWAY D. C. (m.1955)
　　　　　　4. Steven Robert CONWAY D.C. (b.1957)
　　　　　　　sp: Cynthia STOLLE D.C. (m.1983)
　　　　　　4. Peter Carl CONWAY (b.1959)
　　　　　　4. William Warren CONWAY (b.1963)
　　　　　　　sp: Mika HAYAMA (m.1992)
　　　　　　4. Susan Elizabeth CONWAY (b.1965)
　　2. Marvin Fredlein HELGESEN (b.1910;d.1995)
　　　sp: Eleanor Fern (Isaac) ISAAC (b.1915;m.1934(Div);d.1994)
　　　　3. Barbara Ann HELGESEN (b.1935)
　　2. Hilda HELGESEN (b.1908)
　　　sp: Leo F. NITZ (b.1907;m.1937)
　　　　3. Larry L. NITZ (b.1942)
　　　　　sp: Karla (b.1946;m.1975)
　　　　　　4. Samuel Leo NITZ (b.1981)
　　　　3. Dan L. NITZ (b.1946)

sp: Linda RHODES (b.1946;m.1967)
- 4. Marnie Marie NITZ (b.1971)
- 4. Mandy Jane NITZ (b.1975)
- 4. Samuel Leo NITZ (b.1981)
- 3. Ronald L. NITZ (b.1949)
  sp: Linda MARHAM (b.1949;m.1985)
- 2. Lillian HELGESEN
  sp: UNKNOWN
- 2. Elmer HELGESEN
  sp: UNKNOWN
- 2. Lester A. HELGESEN (b.1917;d.1992)
  sp: Phyllis Morgan (b.1921;m.1939)
  - 3. Leigh Lynn HELGESEN (b.1941)
    sp: David MOLLENHOFF (b.1939;m.1964)
    - 4. Kristin Kathryn MOLLENHOFF (b.1967)
    - 4. Peter David MOLLENHOFF (b.1969)
  - 3. Steven Morgan HELGESEN (b.1942)
    sp: Harriet Jean DAHL (b.1939;m.1965)
    - 4. Andrew Steven HELGESEN (b.1966)
    - 4. Elizabeth Virginia HELGESEN (b.1969)
  - 3. Kathryn Louise HELGESEN (b.1943)
    sp: Paul Canary (b.1939;m.1967)
  - 3. Alix Marie HELGESEN (b.1949)
    sp: Edward Allan BARTOLOMEI (b.1945;m.1970)
    - 4. Jason Edward BARTOLOMEI (b.1974)
    - 4. Harper Watts BARTOLOMEI (b.1978)
    - 4. Edward Allan II BARTOLOMEI (b.1982)
  - 3. Debra Kay HELGESEN (b.1952)
    sp: Michael DUFFEY
- 2. Merwood HELGESEN (b.1919)
  sp: Mertibelle REIMER (b.1922;m.1945)
  - 3. James M. HELGESEN (b.1947)
    sp: Esther FONG (m.1970)

         4. Joshua James HELGESEN (b.1978)
         4. Melani Ann HELGESEN (b.1981)
      3. Sallie Leigh HELGESEN (b.1952)
         sp: David WALLACE (m.1975)
            4. Todd David WALLACE (b.1980)
            4. Michelle Mary WALLACE (b.1983)
      3. Pamela Sue HELGESEN (b.1957)
         sp: Michael FITZGEARD (m.1981)
            4. Ryan Michael FITZGEARD (b.1983)
            4. Jaimie Ty FITZGEARD (b.1987)
   2. Alvin HELGESEN (b.1924)
      sp: Dorothy BRANDT (b.1926;m.1947)
         3. Susan Lee HELGESEN (b.1948)
            sp: Richard PAAPE (m.1976)
               4. Brent Richard PAAPE (b.1978)
         3. Nancy Jane HELGESEN (b.1949)
            sp: Larry NEUENSCHWANDER (m.1969(Div))
               4. Jenna Sue NEUENSCHWANDER (b.1975)
               4. Amy Marie NEUENSCHWANDER (b.1977)
            sp: Eric NELSON (m.1985)
               4. Eric Charles, Jr. NELSON (b.1986)
         3. Gregory BRANDT HELGESEN (b.1953)
            sp: Robin TEMPLETON (m.1975)
               4. Jason Gregory HELGESEN (b.1976)
               4. Jeremy BRANDT HELGESEN (b.1977)
         3. Constance Ann HELGESEN (b.1959)
            sp: Thomas OLSON (m.1989)
               4. Tyler Thomas OLSON (b.1990)
   2. Robert HELGESEN
      sp: UNKNOWN
   2. Donald HELGESEN (b.1928)
      sp: Mary Anne PETERSON (b.1932;m.1950)

- 3. Jeffy Wayne HELGESEN (b.1951)
  - sp: Linda (m.1976)
- 3. Lisa Marie HELGESEN (b.1953)
- 3. Gina Anne HELGESEN (b.1955)
  - sp: Jeffery BROOM (m.1991)
- 2. Richard HELGESEN
  - sp: UNKNOWN

1. Clara Mathilde HELGESON (b.1884;d.1949)

sp: Jacob Edmund STOLEN (b.1882;d.1953)

- 2. Roy Marvin STOLEN (b.1904;d.1980)

  sp: Margaret PLACHETA

- 2. Ida Elmira STOLEN (b.1906;d.1971)

  sp: Lyle GRINDE

- 2. Torris Jerome STOLEN (b.1909;d.1992)

  sp: Viola May KLUSENDORF (m.1926)

  - 3. Joyce STOLEN
  - 3. Fredrick STOLEN
  - 3. Vernon STOLEN
  - 3. Roger STOLEN

- 2. Cora Marie (AKA Betty) STOLEN (b.1912)

  sp: Michael Thomas WHALEN (b.1910;m.1930;d.1973)

  - 3. James Kenneth WHALEN (b.1930;d.1991)

    sp: Helen HELMLE

  - 3. Thomas Raphael WHALEN (b.1932;d.1932)

  - 3. Patricia Anne WHALEN (b.1934;d.1985)

    sp: Gary Clarence GOTH Elect. Engineer (b.1933;m.1953(Div))

    - 4. Dianne Patrice GOTH (b.1953)

      sp: Michael FRANCIS

    sp: David Norman JOHNSON

  - 3. Arlene Mae WHALEN (b.1936)

    sp: Harlan Donald MC GEE

  - 3. Joanne Kathryn WHALEN (b.1939)

    sp: Patrick RYAN (m.1966)

  - 3. Thomas Michael WHALEN (b.1941)

    sp: Nancy UNKNOWN (m.(Div))

    sp: Jolynn UNKNOWN (m.1979)

1. Albert Morris HELGESON (b.1887;d.1959)

sp: Alpha Theoline KITTLESON (b.1891;m.1912;d.1979)

  2. Kennell Jordon HELGESON (b.1912;d.1998)

    sp: Alma Janette ROEN (b.1916;m.1938;d.1974)

    sp: Edna Marie PAULSON KELLESVIG (b.1917;m.1976)

  2. Agnes Ione HELGESON (b.1915)

    sp: Joseph SLOTTEN (b.1912;m.1934;d.1957)

      3. Wayne SLOTTEN (b.1937)

        sp: Connie PETERSON (m.1963)

        4. Paul SLOTTEN (b.1963)

        4. David SLOTTEN (b.1967)

        4. Mark SLOTTEN (b.1971)

      3. Nancy SLOTTEN (b.1938)

        sp: Albert HEFTY (m.1957)

        4. Bruce HEFTY (b.1958)

          sp: Gail RILEY (m.1985)

          5. Brandon HEFTY (b.1986)

          5. Amanda HEFTY (b.1988)

        4. Jeanne HEFTY (b.1960)

          sp: Jeff MEYER (m.1980)

          5. Nickolus MEYER (b.1987)

        4. Julie HEFTY (b.1966)

          sp: David MOLITOR (m.1986)

        4. Kristien HEFTY (b.1972)

        4. Brian HEFTY (b.1973)

      3. Kay Louise SLOTTEN (b.1949;d.1949)

      3. Beth Ann SLOTTEN (b.1951;d.1986)

        sp: Dale HUSTAD (m.1969)

        4. Becky HUSTAD (b.1969)

        4. Cory HUSTAD (b.1973)

        4. Gretchen HUSTAD (b.1979)

    sp: Ivan RHYNER (b.1921;m.1963)

2. Crystal June HELGESON (b.1924)
   sp: Edward BASTIEN (b.1914;m.1949)
      3. James Edward BASTIEN
         sp: Brenda PRESTON (m.1971(Div))
            4. Desirae Em BASTIEN (b.1975)
            sp: Terry KOPP (m.1984)
            4. Taylor James BASTIEN (b.1985)
      3. Jon Michael BASTIEN
         sp: Janet WONN (m.1975(Div))
         sp: Kathryn NORRIS (m.1985)
            4. Kelly Kathryn BASTIEN (b.1986)
            4. Edward BASTIEN (b.1989)
      3. Cheri Ann BASTIEN (b.1956;d.1956)
      3. Barbara Ellen BASTIEN (b.1958)
         sp: James WEDEL (m.1990)
            4. Paul Edward WEDEL (b.1991)
      3. Jean Ann BASTIEN (b.1962)
         sp: UNKNOWN
   sp: UNKNOWN

1. Paul Tenny HELGESEN (b.1890;d.1962)

sp: Helga Emelia KITTLESON (b.1892;m.1913;d.1984)

  2. Kenneth Joel HELGESEN Pastor (b.1915;d.2009)

    sp: Esther Luella HENDRICKSON (b.1916;m.1941;d.2000)

      3. Ingrid Paula HELGESEN (b.1945)

        sp: David WAGGONER (b.1943;m.1966)

          4. Brian David WAGGONER (b.1970)

            sp: Heidi Ann HUFFMAN (b.1973;m.1998)

              5. Nicholas Brian WAGGONER (b.2001)

              5. Kenneth Michael WAGGONER (b.2003)

          4. Eric Eugene WAGGONER (Twin) (b.1973)

            sp: Katherine Elizabeth PYLE (b.1975;m.2000)

              5. Payton David WAGGONER (b.2003)

              5. Gavin James WAGGONER (b.2006)

              5. Lauren Alexis WAGGONER (b.2008)

          4. Joel Charles WAGGONER (Twin) (b.1973)

            sp: Shelly Ann VANLANDINGHAM (b.1975;m.1997)

              5. Luke David WAGGONER (b.2002)

              5. Allison Christine WAGGONER (b.2005)

          4. Aaron Daniel WAGGONER (b.1975)

            sp: Julie Anne STAUFFER (b.1977;m.2000)

              5. Zachariah Aaron WAGGONER (b.2004)

              5. Joshua Victor WAGGONER (b.2005)

              5. Blake Noah WAGGONER (b.2007)

      3. John Kenneth HELGESEN (b.1948)

        sp: Vicki Ann ARNDT (b.1949;m.1970)

          4. Daniel Shin HELGESEN (Adopted) (b.1975)

            sp: Jeannie Un Hye KWON (b.1976;m.2007)

              5. William Kwon HELGESEN (b.2010)

          4. Peter Arndt HELGESEN (b.1976)

            sp: Melissa Emma Lee FIENE (b.1978;m.2002)

              5. Charles Peter HELGESEN (b.2009)

- 3. Kristine Marie HELGESEN (b.1950)
  - sp: Larry Gene PAULSEN (b.1948;m.1971)
    - 4. Jill Marie PAULSEN (b.1976)
    - 4. Anne Kristine PAULSEN (b.1979)
      - sp: Donald Alexander COLE (b.1980;m.2005)
- 3. Marc Erbeck HELGESEN (b.1954)
  - sp: Masumi Konta (b.1960;m.1984)
    - 4. Kent Konta HELGESEN (Japanese name Kento) (b.1987)
- 2. Gilford Sylvan HELGESEN Pastor (b.1918)
  - sp: Virginia Mae GANTHER (b.1919;m.1943;d.2009)
    - 3. Sonja Jean HELGESEN (b.1945)
      - sp: Eugene THOMPSON (b.1945;m.1967(Div))
        - 4. Sheri Lynn THOMPSON (b.1969)
          - sp: Matt MILLER (m.2001)
        - 4. Kristi Jean THOMPSON (b.1972)
          - sp: Robert ZANETT (m.1998)
        - 4. Steven Eugene THOMPSON (b.1978)
        - 4. David Harmon THOMPSON (b.1980)
          - sp: Alissa Ann MURPHY (m.2007)
    - 3. Anita Marie HELGESEN (b.1947)
      - sp: F. Joseph EIDEM (m.1965(Div))
        - 4. Joseph Dean EIDEM (b.1966)
          - sp: Sharon Lee BURNHAM (m.2000)
        - 4. David Paul EIDEM (b.1968)
        - 4. Paul Gilford EIDEM (b.1969)
          - sp: Andrea GRIFFITH (b.1962;m.1998)
    - 3. Paul Douglas HELGESEN (b.1950)
      - sp: Mary DUDLEY (m.1972(Div))
        - 4. Anthony Obadiah HELGESEN (b.1975)
      - sp: Patti RAY (m.1983)
        - 4. Charles RAY (Adopted) (b.1979)
        - 4. Jordan RAY HELGESEN (b.1986)
          - sp: Tashia Nicole HESMEISTER (m.2005)
        - 4. Taylor RAY HELGESEN (b.1989)

- 3. Ruth Virginia HELGESEN (b.1952)
  - sp: Robert MC CARTY (m.1970(Div))
  - sp: Merle GARDENER (m.1975(Div))
  - sp: Glen SUESS (b.1941;m.1992)
- 3. Rachael Ann HELGESEN (b.1955)
  - sp: George HERMAN (m.1976(Div))
  - sp: Michael WALSH (m.1980;d.1980)
  - sp: T. Joseph LUTTER (m.1981(Div))
    - 4. Lia LUTTER (Step child) (b.1970)
    - 4. Vicki LUTTER (Step child) (b.1973)
  - sp: Charles Mark MAHDFFY (b.1943;m.2000)
2. Russell Burnell HELGESEN Pastor (b.1920)
  - sp: Lorraine Theona SAMPSON (b.1919;m.1944)
    - 3. Rebecca Lynn HELGESEN Pastor (b.1945)
      - sp: Thomas von FISCHER Pastor (b.1943;m.1968)
        - 4. Kristen Joy von FISCHER (Adopt) (b.1971)
          - sp: Yemane GABRE-MICHAEL (m.1999(Div))
          - sp: Kenny JOHNSON (b.1970;m.2005)
            - 5. Rayah JOHNSON (b.2006)
            - 5. Dominick JOHNSON (b.2009)
        - 4. Benjamin William von FISCHER (b.1974)
          - sp: Norah J. GUEGUIERRE (m.2000)
            - 5. Nyah von FISCHER (b.2007)
    - 3. Jane Marie HELGESEN (b.1946)
      - sp: De Wayne VENNIE (m.1966(Div))
        - 4. Jason Michael VENNIE (b.1971)
          - sp: Dani KEIPER (m.2001)
            - 5. Bennett VENNIE (b.2007)
        - 4. Erika Lynne VENNIE (b.1974)
          - sp: Anthony CURELLA (b.1967;m.2001)
            - 5. Rocco Anthony CURELLA (b.2003)
            - 5. Ava CURELLA (b.2006)

    4. Britt Elise VENNIE (b.1979)

        sp: Matthew STANTON (b.1978;m.2002)

            5. Blaise STANTON (b.2007)

    sp: Floyd MC MILLON (m.1982(Div))

    4. Shawna Marie MC MILLON (b.1983)

    sp: Robert LOWE (b.1946;m.1991(Div))

3. Thomas Russell HELGESEN (b.1947)

    sp: Rebecca April FILLER (b.1948;m.1986)

        4. Nathan Phillip HELGESEN (b.1988)

        4. Leah Jeanette (AKA Ligua) HELGESEN (b.1991)

3. James Philip HELGESEN (b.1951)

    sp: Julia Anne BOSCHEE (b.1949;m.1989)

        4. Dixie Lee BOSCHEE (Step child) (b.1969)

            sp: Brian SMITH (b.1958;m.2004)

        4. Sarah Jean BOSCHEE (Step child) (b.1974)

            sp: James SANG (b.1976;m.2006)

                5. Lily SANG (b.2008)

                5. Ava Jean SANG (b.2010)

3. Mary Lorraine HELGESEN (b.1953)

    sp: Medard Anthony GABEL (b.1946;m.1994)

        4. Medard Tobias GABEL (adopted) (b.1996)

        4. Zoe Allegra GABEL (adopted) (b.1998)

2. Ila Arlene HELGESEN (b.1922;d.1999)

    sp: Philip FRANCIS WEIGAND (b.1922;m.1944(Div);d.1996)

        3. Jaclyn Dianne WEIGAND (b.1945)

            sp: Gerald SMITH (b.1940;m.1973)

                4. Sara Maureen MORIARTY (adopted) (b.1966)

                    sp: James DOYLE (b.1967;m.1992(Div))

                    sp: Gregory RIES (m.2000)

                        5. Emily Moriarty RIES (b.1998)

                        5. Maxwell W. RIES (b.2001)

- 3. Richard Philip WEIGAND (b.1946)
  - sp: Judy CONLON (b.1941;m.1970)
    - 4. Christopher Blues WEIGAND (b.1971)
- sp: Donald WOLLUM (b.1919;m.1979;d.1995)
2. Paul Phillip HELGESEN Supt. (b.1926)
  - sp: JoAnn Marquis JOHNSON (b.1928;m.1945)
    - 3. David Lynn HELGESEN (b.1945;d.1994)
      - sp: Darlene HORNE (m.1973(Div))
      - sp: Patricia LEASE (m.1980(Div))
    - 3. Lou Ann Kay HELGESEN (b.1946)
      - sp: Richard ANDERSON (m.1965)
        - 4. Julie Jo ANDERSON (b.1968)
          - sp: Douglas BIRSCHBACH (m.1988)
            - 5. Brittney Jo BIRSCHBACH (b.1991)
            - 5. Briana Jo BIRSCHBACH (b.1994)
            - 5. Joshua Douglas BIRSCHBACH (b.1994;d.1996)
        - 4. Laura Lynn ANDERSON (b.1972)
          - sp: Mitch KAHL (m.1996)
    - 3. Cynthia Jean HELGESEN (b.1952)
      - sp: Gregory JUDD D.C. (m.1970)
        - 4. Troy Gregory JUDD (b.1972)
          - sp: Anne (m.1994)
            - 5. Taylor Gregory JUDD (b.1996)
        - 4. Tamara Rae JUDD (b.1976)
          - sp: Vernon Michael CARLSON (m.1998)
        - 4. Kimberly Jo JUDD (Twin) (b.1980)
        - 4. Heather Lynne JUDD (Twin) (b.1980)
    - 3. Steven Phillip HELGESEN (b.1957)
      - sp: Karen KENNELLY (m.1981)
        - 4. Kelly ERIN (Step child) (b.1977)
          - sp: UNKNOWN
        - 4. Kathryn JoAnn HELGESEN (b.1983)
        - 4. Emily Kay HELGESEN (b.1985)

2. Dolores Marie HELGESEN (b.1930)
   sp: Donald Paul PAULSON (b.1929;m.1953)
     3. Jeffery Donald PAULSON (b.1955)
       sp: Paula KRUEGER (b.1957;m.1977)
         4. Jake Daniel PAULSON (b.1980)
           sp: Kathryn Shurkrieh AWADALLAH (b.1983;m.2009)
         4. Megan Christina PAULSON (b.1984)
           sp: Charles PRELLWITZ (b.1983;m.2006)
         4. Ben Donald PAULSON (b.1991)
     3. Steven Dennis PAULSON (b.1957)
       sp: Crystal LOKKEN (m.1987)
     3. Barbara Ellen PAULSON (b.1959)
       sp: Thomas FRYKMAN (b.1957;m.1982(Div))
         4. James William FRYKMAN (b.1984)
         4. Marissa Anne FRYKMAN (b.1989)
       sp: Kevin Mitchell MCANNANY (b.1955;m.1997)
         4. Kaitlin Sue MCANNANY Stepchild (b.1983)

Please send corrections, additions, and modifications to:
    Russell B. Helgesen
    7500 York Ave. S. — Apt. 208
    Edina, MN 55435

       email: rhelgesen@msn.com
       phone: 952.835.5578

       www.thehelgesenstory.com